Computer
Visualization

GRAPHICS TECHNIQUES
FOR SCIENTIFIC
AND ENGINEERING
ANALYSIS

Computer Visualization

GRAPHICS TECHNIQUES FOR SCIENTIFIC AND ENGINEERING ANALYSIS

EDITED BY

Richard S. Gallagher

Swanson Analysis Systems

CRC Press

Boca Raton   Ann Arbor   London   Tokyo

A Solomon Press Book

Library of Congress Cataloging-in-Publication Data

Computer visualization: graphics techniques for scientific and
   engineering analysis / edited by Richard S. Gallagher.
      p.   cm.
   Includes bibliographical references and index.
   ISBN 0-8493-9050-8
   1. Computer graphics. 2. Visualization. I. Gallagher, Richard S.
   T385.C5935 1994
   501′.1336—dc20
   DNLM/DLC
   for Library of Congress   93-35637
                                                           CIP

Contents

Contents

Section II. SCIENTIFIC VISUALIZATION TECHNIQUES

Contents

Preface

Technology, at its most basic level, seeks to understand how the world behaves. Over the past three decades, computer graphics methods have fueled a growing understanding of physical phenomena, which in turn have helped scientists and engineers substantially improve the quality of life.

The growth of these graphics techniques for scientific behavior developed in spurts over the past twenty years—some might say in fits and starts, as the field has grown rapidly from an area of academic research to a commercial field, accounting for sales of hundreds of millions of US dollars per year in the early 1990s. The first spurt came in the 1960s, when digital numerical simulation techniques became popular, and the need to graphically display their output on at least a pen plotter became immediately apparent.

The next spurt came in the 1970s, when techniques were developed for the display of states of behavior using methods such as color-coding, contour displays, and vector symbols. Most of these techniques shared a common purpose of representing behavior on the outside visible surfaces of a model. In the late 1980s these same techniques remained the norm for displays of behavior.

Today the relatively new field of 3-D scientific visualization has made a major impact on the display of behavior. Originally developed to address large-scale visualization needs such as medical imaging, real-time data reduction, and satellite imagery, the techniques of scientific visualization are now being applied to numerical analysis and simulation to understand complex volumetric, multidimensional or time-dependent behavior.

More important, numerical methods such as finite element analysis and computational fluid dynamics have begun over the last few years to make a substantial impact in the development of algorithmic visualization techniques. This harks back to the situation in the early days of computer graphics, when graphics techniques for design and analysis applications made a central impact on the computer graphics field as a whole.

In applying this new and developing area of technology, the student or practitioner of 3-D visualization techniques has frequently needed to refer to such source materials as computer graphics journals or published collections of papers. A reference work to summarize developments in this field for those who wish to understand and apply them is clearly required.

Computer Visualization represents a single, unified collection of computer graphics techniques for the scientific visualization of behavior. It is a reference work for professionals who use computing techniques to visualize data, and for the academic and software communities who support them. The book combines a basic overview of the fundamentals of computer graphics with a practitioner-oriented review of the latest 3-D graphics display and visualization techniques, as they are applied to science and engineering. All of its chapters are written by key researchers or experts in their specialties.

Section One reviews how computer graphics visualization techniques have evolved to work with digital numerical analysis methods. Its introductory chapter examines the growth of computer visualization from the perspective of my own profession of computer-aided engineering. This section also introduces the fundamentals of computer graphics which apply to the visualization of analysis data.

The chapters of Section Two contain a detailed review of the algorithms and techniques used to visualize behavior in 3-D, as static, interactive or animated imagery. This section begins with a discussion of the mathematics of engineering data for visualization, and then covers the current methods used for the display of scalar, vector and tensor fields. Another chapter examines the more general issues of visualizing a continuum volume field, and the section ends with a chapter on animating the dimensions of time and motion in a state of behavior.

The final section is particularly useful for those implementing production visualization capabilities, including the practical computational aspects of visualization such as user interfaces, database architecture and interaction with a model. The concluding chapters outline successful practical applications of visualization, and future trends in scientific visualization.

To produce things better, faster, and less expensively than before, visualization tools have evolved to help scientists and engineers understand more about how things behave. In the process we have gained an insight into a whole new realm of information which has heretofore been hidden from us.

Richard S. Gallagher
July 1994

Acknowledgments

The most important acknowledgment in a project such as this goes to its contributing authors. It is a privilege for editor and reader alike to have some of the well-known researchers in computer graphics and numerical methods join forces to explain the field of scientific visualization to a wider audience.

A great many other people contributed their time in providing technical advice and detailed reviews of the chapters. Particular credit is due to Gordon Ferguson of Visual Kinematics, Dr. Yu-Hua Ting of Swanson Analysis Systems, Prof. Robert Haber of the University of Illinois, William Lorensen of General Electric Company, and Prof. David Johnson of Penn State–Behrend College, as well as many of the contributors themselves.

This book would not have been possible without the efforts and encouragement of Dr. David Dietrich, or the support of Dr. John Swanson and Swanson Analysis Systems. Jackie Williamson and Charmaine Grunick provided needed support for correspondence and artwork at SASI.

Sidney Solomon and Raymond Solomon of The Solomon Press saw a complex project through with unfailing courtesy, good humor, and professional know-how. Kip Shaw of Pageworks provided the excellent typesetting, and Lawrence Werbel was a most perceptive copyeditor. Joel Claypool, of CRC Press, provided skilled publishing expertise and enthusiastic support to the project.

I acknowledge three people who served as mentors to many others, including me, in this young field: Professor Donald P. Greenberg, Humberto Sachs, and Lou Crain. Another important mentor is my own father, Dr. Richard H. Gallagher. As one of the pioneers of the finite element method, Dr. Gallagher's enthusiasm for his work inspired many engineering careers, including those of his five children.

Finally, my wife Colleen deserves equal credit in spirit for any contributions of mine.

SECTION I

Introduction

C H A P T E R

Scientific Visualization: An Engineering Perspective

RICHARD S. GALLAGHER

COMPUTER GRAPHICS VISUALIZATION of behavior is a young field which has grown to have a major impact on the practice of engineering design and analysis. This chapter outlines the historical development of engineering visualization, and examines some of its major areas of impact in the engineering field.

1.1
INTRODUCTION

Visualization is defined in the dictionary as "a mental image." In the fields of computer graphics and engineering design the term has a much more specific meaning: The technical specialty of visualization concerns itself with the display of behavior, and, particularly, with making complex states of behavior comprehensible to the human eye.

Its parent field of computer graphics was once described as "a solution in search of a problem," in the early days of its development. One of the earliest problems it addressed was engineering analysis, and the two fields have contributed substantially to each other's development in the years since. In the process, the two discliplines have become merged within the field of Computer Aided Engineering (CAE), which has grown from an academic concept to become a standard part of engineering today.

This chapter examines the relationship between visualization and engineering in the CAE field, as a microcosm of the impact of visualization on technology as a whole. The development of this profession has an analogy in the growth of computer graphics visualization techniques for science, medicine, and other fields sharing numerical data in common.

As in actual analysis work, the effects of visualizing engineering behavior are best shown through pictures. In the example shown in Figure 1.1, a structure subjected to a point load is analyzed by using the finite element method. The results

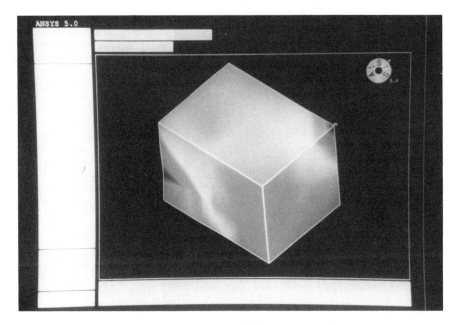

(a)

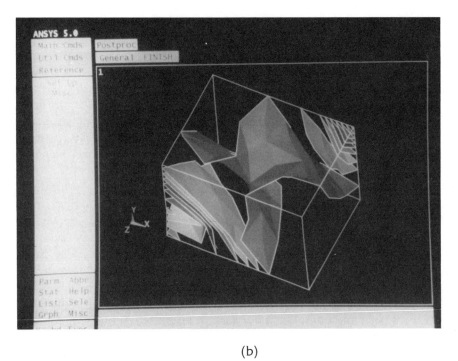

(b)

displayed include contour and isosurface displays of the maximum equivalent stress in the structure, and a particle distribution showing the gradient or rate of change of this stress in space.

All these images share a common procedure: i.e., taking numerical data computed at vertices of this model's "elements," performing computation of geometric and color data from this data on an element-by-element basis, and displaying the derived data on computer graphics output.

Figure 1.2 is an example from another discipline, computational fluid dynamics. This flow model is a streamline representing the flow of air through a room from a point location. The color, thickness and cross-section of this streamline vary with additional independent variables within the volume field.

This image represents a specific case of a larger issue, that of using visualization to comprehend a state of behavior involving multiple dimensions. Human perception is naturally geared towards the three dimensions of physical space, and can easily adapt to a fourth dimension such as color variation. Techniques such as this seek to combine these natural capabilities to help understand more complex phenomena, such as the nature of this figure's 3-D vector field.

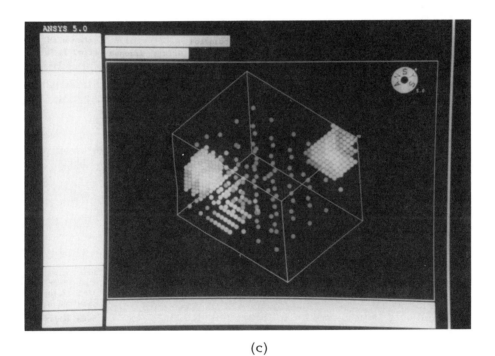

(c)

Figure 1.1(a, b, c). Contour, isosurface and particle gradient displays of the equivalent stress from a structural analysis. (Courtesy Swanson Analysis Systems, Inc.) (See plate 1.1 in color section)

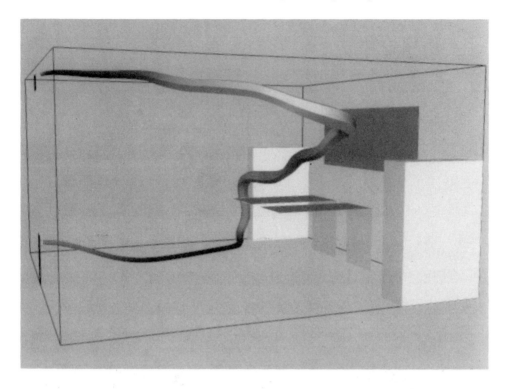

Figure 1.2. A stream polygon describing the air flow through a room. The streamline itself represents the path of an air particle, with color and thickness used to represent other solution variables. (From Schroeder et al., reference 10, copyright 1991 IEEE.) (See plate 1.2 in color section)

This issue represents one of the major problems in scientific visualization, and has produced much useful research in recent years. Chapter 5, for example, summarizes recent work in techniques to visualize a tensor field as part of a general framework for the visualization of flow problems. Even simple tensor fields such as strain can represent a 3×3 matrix of values at each point, yet paring the physical properties of such tensor distributions in space with visual cues such as streamline properties or symbols can yield a deeper understanding of the underlying behavior.

Finally, Figure 1.3 shows images from one aspect of visualization that is not well captured in print—the variation of behavior over time, and in motion. Hardware and software techniques for capturing animated sequences of behavior are becoming more common, and are getting more use in engineering practice. In much the same manner in which pictures resolve the perceptional bottleneck of numerical results, animated images resolve a similar bottleneck of interpreting changing behavior through static images.

All of these cases share the common practice of taking abstract, physical information and rendering it in a form that can be seen. Over time, trends in the field of visualization have moved towards the display of more complicated behavior, both in the sense of introducing more variables, and in the interaction of these variables over time and location. This, in turn, facilitates a greater level of detail and complexity within analysis work itself.

1.2
A LOOK AT COMPUTER AIDED ENGINEERING

Computer graphics visualization techniques have formed a natural marriage with computer simulations of behavior in understanding the physical phenomena of engineering problems.

1.3
A BRIEF HISTORY OF COMPUTER AIDED ENGINEERING

While the formal study of engineering design and analysis automation is a relatively recent phenomena, its technical fundamentals have a long history in engineering research. At the same time, the growth of computing hardware has spurred much current work in the field, particularly as it became cost-effective for a wide range of applications. The engineering analysis and visualization aspects of computer aided engineering have developed along separate yet interrelated paths, particularly over the past three decades.

1.3.1 Computational Methods For Analysis

Many fundamental aspects of understanding engineering behavior date back well into the previous century, including the basic theories of elasticity and the Navier-Stokes relationships for fluid flow. Computational methods for engineering analysis combine principles such as these with approximate analysis techniques suited to digital computation. Interest in so-called "matrix" methods of approximate analysis dates back to publications in the 1940s by Courant [4] and others.

These matrix methods—based on the concept that a model or structure can be approximated by a network of small, connected elements contributing to the terms of a matrix equation—began to stimulate serious interest in the 1950s and 1960s. Researchers such as Argyris [1], Gallagher(Sr.) [5] and Zienkiewicz [13] developed the fundamentals of the finite element method, which forms the basis for much of today's analysis work in solid mechanics, fluid mechanics, and many other related areas. Finite element analysis generally involves performing the matrix solution of a defined set of elements, measuring the solution error using techniques such as energy methods, and refining this mesh of elements until the solution converges. A more recent approach, known as the p (polynomial) method, can solve certain classes of problems by increasing the polynomial order of the elements themselves until convergence occurs.

Other technical areas in approximate analysis include the boundary element method, which describes surface or volume behavior through integral equations

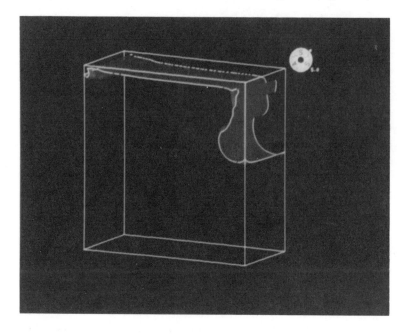

(a)

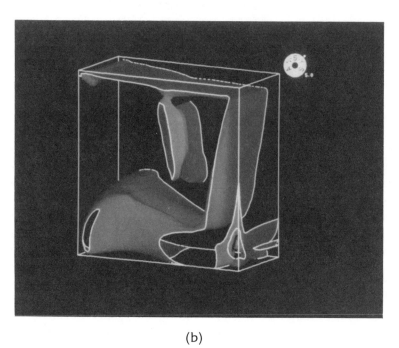

(b)

(c)

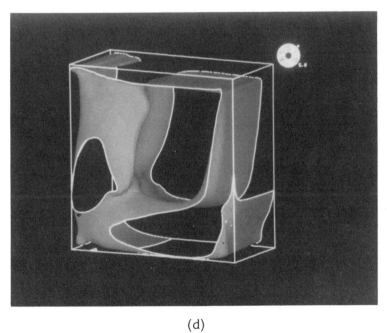

(d)

Figure 1.3 (a, b, c, d). Animated sequence of isosurfaces describing the behavior of a fluid, as a frictional surface is dragged across the top of the fluid volume. (Courtesy Swanson Analysis Systems, Inc.) (See plate in color section)

solved at elements along the boundary, and the finite difference method, which replaces elements with points in the domain described by relationships such as a Taylor series expansion. The finite difference method merits particular notice in its early application to the field of computational fluid dynamics (CFD)—a growing area where finite element methods are also increasingly used.

Much of the first commercial software for numerical analysis began to appear in the mid-1960s, first in early finite element applications, and quickly expanded to include other disciplines such as CFD, magnetics, and kinematic analysis. The field has matured considerably in the last three decades, and its present capabilities range from basic linear force and displacement analysis to the simulation of complex multi-state, multi-mode behavior over time.

Digital numerical analysis techniques generally shared the common feature of producing numerical results at points in space, representable by polygonal, polyhedral or higher-order geometry. The need to see and understand this data, combined with its readily accessible geometric form, made numerical methods an ideal early application for the emerging field of computer graphics.

1.3.2 Computer Graphics And Visualization

The idea of using a computer to display data in a graphical format dates back to the earliest days of computing itself. The first implementations of this concept into practice evolved as quickly as the pace of hardware development itself permitted. By the early 1960s, many of the basic concepts in the early computer graphics field were outlined in a 1962 PhD thesis by Ivan Sutherland [12], describing a system entitled Sketchpad. Beyond its technical specifics, this publication is widely regarded as the first to establish computer graphics as a technical discipline. Following the early work of Sutherland and many others, the 1960s witnessed the development of such major advancements as color raster display, hidden surface removal, and light source shading.

By the early 1970s, Hank Christiansen's MOVIE.BYU, made at Brigham Young University [3], developed one of the first major applications of computer graphics to the display of behavior using irregular grids such as finite element models. Around the same time, a *Scientific American* article by Cornell University's Professor Donald Greenberg [7], whose animated film "Cornell in Perspective" used a geometric database to explore possible sites for Cornell's stunning Johnson Art Museum, began to popularize the concept of computer graphics among the general public.

The expense of early computer graphics equipment was such that many of its early users were heavy industries, who could leverage productivity benefits against equipment which easily cost millions of US dollars per computing installation. Some of these early projects include General Motors' DAC-1 project in 1964, and the Man-Computer Systems project in the same year led by Sylvan Chasen at Lockheed Corporation.

Originally, computer graphics was a largely unified discipline revolving around the display of geometry. As time passed and the field gained rapid commercial acceptance, a number of subspecialties developed including rendering techniques, simulation of natural phenomena, and radiosity. With this growth came an increasing interest in the study of techniques for the display of behavior. The term "visualization" was eventually coined to describe this subspecialty, perhaps first made popular in a 1987 National Science Foundation initiative on scientific visualization [9]. Thereafter, early visualization applications generally involved large-scale interpretation of visual data, such as medical tomography, satellite imagery, and scientific data reduction.

More recently, newer 3-D visualization techniques allowing the display of volumetric, multivariate and time-dependent behavior have joined earlier display techniques in numerical analysis applications. In addition to the visualization algorithms themselves, this trend has been driven by increasing computing capabilities, which allow for more complex analyses. Today, the move towards further real-time 3-D graphics display capabilities is helping visualization become part of a more interactive approach to analysis.

1.4
THE PROCESS OF ANALYSIS AND VISUALIZATION

Many engineering design and analysis applications share common components of modeling, analysis, and the visualization of results. The first and last of these are often described in engineering practice as "pre-processing" and "post-processing," respectively, as functions which take place before and after analysis. These terms describe a process which is as shown in Figure 1.4—a sequential cycle of building a model, analyzing it, reviewing its behavior, and then changing the model and repeating the cycle until a satisfactory result is obtained.

There has been an increasing trend towards combining these functions within an interactive analysis "laboratory," outlined in Figure 1.5. In such an environment, the analysis itself may govern geometric changes, and the results can be visualized as the analysis proceeds. Within this framework, one can still describe the individual components of this analysis cycle as modeling, analysis or visualization activities.

Steps involved in modeling include operations such as:

Geometric Modeling. An analysis project often begins with construction of a geometric model describing the problem. Examples of such models include a structural component, a model of the air mass surrounding an aircraft wing for

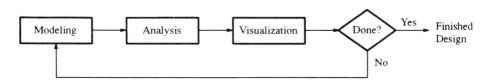

Figure 1.4. The traditional sequential design process. (Courtesy Swanson Analysis Systems, Inc.)

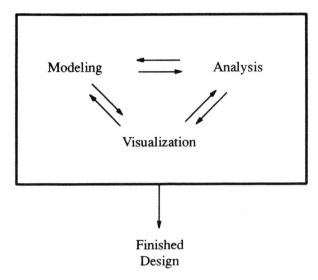

Figure 1.5. The more current trend towards an integrated design, analysis and visualization environment. (Courtesy Swanson Analysis Systems Inc.)

flow analysis, or an idealization of an integrated circuit chip for heat transfer analysis. This model can be constructed specifically for analysis purposes, using interactive, graphics-based operations on geometric data, or imported from existing geometric data such as computer aided design (CAD) systems.

Analysis Modeling. This geometric model is used to create the data needed to perform an analysis. This often involves selecting the appropriate types of elements used to represent the behavior of the model, the creation of a *mesh* of these elements approximating the geometric model, and definition of the material and/or physical properties of the elements.

Generation of Initial Conditions. The same analysis model can conceivably be used to solve for a number of states of behavior: different loads, initial states, or boundary conditions, for example. There has been a clear trend over time towards interactive, graphically oriented methods for specifying this transient analysis data, and towards modifying this data directly within the analysis process itself.

Once a model has been created and its conditions specified, an analysis can be performed. Upon completion of this analysis, or increasingly at intermediate stages of analysis, results are available to be visualized in the *post-processing* step.

While the specific kinds of visualization techniques used in post-processing vary as widely as analysis applications themselves, some of its more common operations include the following:

Result Rendering. Techniques such as contour displays, isosurfaces, tensor field streamlines and many others are employed to create images representing the behavior of a scalar, vector, tensor or multivariate state of behavior.

Model Transformation. The more complex the models, the more important it becomes to be able to interactively modify the view of the model, as well as other display attributes such as perspective, distance, and the position of the observer. Depending on the software and hardware environment, these capabilities can range from modifying static image settings to real-time 3-D transformation of the result data.

Animation. A great deal of actual behavior involves motion, or variations over time. In result visualization, animation involves two principal issues: the display of behavior over time; and navigating or "walking through" a model in 3-D space. Animation is a relatively young and hardware-dependent visualization tool, requiring techniques for either the rapid redraw or storage and playback of individual "frames" of visual information.

Result Field Manipulation. Beyond the animation of a fixed, known result quantity, newer user interface and display techniques make it possible to interactively explore the nature of a result field. Such techniques include probing 3-D locations within a model to display field data at a given point, interactive display of isovalues and result value levels, volume clipping and slicing, and the rapid comparison of multiple states of behavior.

Modeling, analysis and visualization form an analogy to the physical process of engineering design. Its early development closely followed the existing practice of product design, modeling, testing, and changing. With greater interactive computing resources, it is now becoming easier to go beyond the conceptual limitations of physical design, and simultaneously design, test, and modify objects by computing simulation.

1.5
THE IMPACT OF VISUALIZATION
IN ENGINEERING DESIGN

The rapid growth of visualization applications in the engineering field results due in large part from its tangible benefits within the design process. A better understanding of behavior has a clear impact on the cost, productivity, and accuracy of engineering design and analysis work.

Some of the ways visualization techniques have affected engineering practice today include:

Decreased Physical Testing. Analysis and visualization generally provide a simulation of something in real life. This testing on the computer translates to much less physical testing, often at substantial cost savings. Moreover, computer simulations allow an engineer to observe phenomena which may be difficult, dangerous or impossible to reproduce physically.

Greater Integration of Design and Analysis. The better one can visualize analysis results, the easier it is to modify a design to correct flaws shown by the analysis. Moreover, as computing and display speeds allow quicker analysis and visualization, there has been a gradual evolution in engineering practice towards doing "what if" studies at an earlier stage of the design process.

Increased Analysis Complexity and Sophistication. Digital numerical analysis has always been limited by the ability to visualize its results. In the early days of the field when numerical output or wireframe pen plots were the norm, models were generally restricted to small or two-dimensional idealizations. Color graphics displays have had a direct impact on problem size and complexity, and newer 3-D visualization techniques in particular have made it possible to examine complex phenomena which are not readily seen on the exterior visible surfaces of an analysis model.

Design Optimization. By using analysis results to change parametric attributes of a model, such as length or shape values, analysis can be used to automatically guide design changes. This has helped analysis evolve from a tool for evaluating static designs to a means of optimizing the design itself. Visualization tools play a key role in this process, allowing engineers to evaluate automated design changes and analysis results.

Productivity and Accuracy. Improved visualization tools help relieve a perceptional bottleneck in the man-time spent in the analysis cycle, allowing a faster and more thorough design process. In addition, more accurate control of the result data seen by the engineer can lead to better design decisions. Beyond the technical advantages produced by computer graphics visualization techniques, there is a clear economic benefit in design productivity.

A better visual understanding of physical phenomena opens up as many new questions about engineering behavior as it answers. We are not only seeing more accurate simulations of engineering problems, but a move towards examining the interrelationship between multiple design variables. There is, in this sense, a growing releationship between visualization and the increasing base of knowledge in engineering design principles.

1.6
TRENDS IN VISUALIZATION ENVIRONMENTS FOR ANALYSIS

Computer aided engineering tools first began to appear as individual components in areas such as analysis, modeling and graphics display. Early commercial analysis software in particular tended to function as a black box, taking input for a single analysis solution, and outputting numerical results. Around these programs, other products such as geometric modeling, analysis pre- and post-processing, and data visualization tool grew.

Early adopters of numerical analysis tools were faced with the problem of interfacing these products across a wide variety of proprietary interfaces. By the late 1970s and early 1980s, *translators* became a common mechanism for converting, say, the output file of one analysis program to the input format of a post-processing program.

While interfacing of proprietary tools continues to the present, there is an increasing degree of integration between modeling, analysis and visualization tools. Over time, the trend in commercial software design has been towards fully functioned packages; for example, many major analysis systems now offer integrated modeling and visualization tools, and firms which once specialized in pre- and post-processing generally offer some level of analysis capabilities.

This increasing level of integration has been accompanied by the growth of standards for data interchange between software. The IGES (Initial Graphics Exchange Specification) standard has become a common mechanism for transfer of geometric models and finite element information, and the more recent PDES/STEP proposal is one attempt to establish data standards for the global engineering design and manufacturing process. In addition, proprietary *de facto* standards, such as CAD system output specifications, and visualization system data formats, are making it easier for end users to integrate visualization tools specific to their needs.

Engineers can choose between specific visualization tools, such as those offered with analysis software, and more general-purpose visualization enviroments used to examine a wide variety of numerical data over time and in space. These latter tools often interface with analysis software, while offering more of a general set of tools for the display of this data. In this area as well, there is an increasing degree of integration among commercial software packages—analysis tools are become more visualization-oriented, and vice-versa.

All these issues are part of a move towards what has been referred to as an adaptive environment for analysis, where the result of analysis creates direct feedback into design decisions, often in an increasingly automated fashion. At the same time, analysis and visualization environments still exist to facilitate, rather than replace, the judgement of the human engineer.

1.7
SUMMARY

Computer graphics visualization techniques for analysis have quickly become an active area of research and development. Beyond its most obvious aspects of the display of behavior, engineering analysis visualization involves issues such as interaction with a 3-D model, operations on result data and optimization of design variables.

Overall, visualization techniques have become part of a larger trend in the engineering design field, leading towards a computing environment where design is an interactive process which encourages the exploration of design alternatives. These capabilities have helped the engineer use the computer as a flexible test bed where a model can be subjected to conditions, and then observed and improved more quickly, cheaply and safely than would be possible in the actual physical world.

1.8
REFERENCES

[1]. Argyris, J. and S. Kelsey, *Energy Theorums And Structural Analysis,* Butterworth Scientific Publications, London, 1960.
[2]. Chasen, S.H., "Historical Highlights of Interactive Computer Graphics," *Mechanical Engineering,* No. 103, ASME, November 1981.

[3]. Christiansen, H.N., "Applications of Continuous Tone Computer-Generated Images in Structural Mechanics," in *Structural Mechanics Computer Programs,* W. Pilkey, K. Saczalski and H. Schaeffer eds., University of Virginia Press, Charlottesville, VA, 1974.

[4]. Courant, R., "Variational Methods for the Solution of Problems of Equilibrium and Vibration," *Bulletin of the American Mathematical Society,* No. 49, pp. 1–43, 1943.

[5]. Gallagher, R.H., *Finite Element Analysis Fundamentals,* Prentice Hall, 1975.

[6]. Gallagher, R.S. et al, "Applying 3-D Visualization Techniques to Finite Element Analysis," panel summary in *Proceedings of Visualization '91,* IEEE Computer Society Press, October 1991.

[7]. Greenberg, D.P., "Computer Graphics in Architecture," *Scientific American,* Vol. 230, May 1974, pp. 98–106.

[8]. Kaufmann, A. ed., *Volume Visualization,* IEEE Computer Society Press, 1990.

[9]. McCormick, B.H, DeFanti, T.A. and Brown, M., "Visualization In Scientific Computing," Report of the *NSF Advisory Panel on Graphics, Image Processing and Workstations,* 1987.

[10]. Schroeder, W. J., Volpe, C. R., and Lorensen, W. E., "The Stream Polygon: A Technique for 3-D Vector Field Visualization," *Proceedings of IEEE Visualization '91,* IEEE Computer Society Press, October 1991 pp 126–132.

[11]. Shriver, B. and G. Nielson, eds., Visualization in Scientific Computing, IEEE Computer Society Press, 1990.

[12]. Sutherland, I.E., "Sketchpad: A Man-Machine Graphical Communication System," Proc. Spring Joint Computer Conference, No. 23, AFIPS Press, Montvale, NJ, 1963, pp. 329–346.

[13]. Zienkiewicz, O.C., Finite Element Fundamentals, Fourth Edition, McGraw Hill, 1989.

CHAPTER

An Overview of Computer Graphics for Visualization

ALAIN FOURNIER AND JOHN BUCHANAN

COMPUTER GRAPHICS FORMS the basis for much of scientific visualization. This chapter provides an overview of history and fundamentals of computer graphics for visualization. Topics covered include modeling, transformations, shading, pixel and volume display techniques, and graphics display architecture.

2.1
WHAT IS COMPUTER GRAPHICS?

As in every discipline, it is always interesting, if not necessarily fruitful, to ask what defines its content, and what makes it different from other close disciplines. In our case the question is "What Is Computer Graphics?" Another question immediately following is "Why Computer Graphics?"

The first question used to have a simple answer: *Computer Graphics* is making pictures with computers. This definition has become too comprehensive to be really useful. There is hardly any aspect of picture making as practiced these days which does not involve computers. Television shows, photos in the morning paper, illustrations in textbooks, magazine ads: probably all have been generated, manipulated, transmitted or touched up using computers.

Another approach is to define computer graphics as a scientific discipline, and the fact that many universities have computer graphics groups in their midst, mostly, of course, in computer science departments, and that PhD and other degrees are granted for work in computer graphics is a *de facto* existence proof. In fact, we could use the aggregate content of theses, papers, communications in journals and conferences to define the area. This will help, but, as with any definition, there will be "grey" areas, with work at the boundary between computer graphics and computer vision, image processing, human factors, various engineering disciplines especially electrical engineering), and even mathematics.

When all is carefully considered, we come back to the original simple definition, both extended and restricted: Computer graphics is the science and practice of producing images by mechanical means. In a brief history, we will see that this definition has the advantage of linking the present to many pre-computer developments.

2.2
WHY COMPUTER GRAPHICS?

It is endless to list all the areas of application of computer graphics, as indicated above, but if we make a short list of applications where computer graphics plays an important role, it could read as follows.

Data Plotting
Cartography
Mechanical CAD
Electronic CAD
Architectural CAD
Business Graphics
Flight and Driving Simulation
Film Animation (2-D and 3-D)
Video Animation (2-D and 3-D)
Document Generation
Video Games
Display of Mathematical Objects
Process Control
Office Information Systems
Free Hand Drawing and Painting

The reader is encouraged to examine this list, and try to decide why computer graphics has value in these applications. Reasons found or generally given include the following.

Pictures could not be made otherwise
Pictures can be made faster
Pictures can be made cheaper by computer
Pictures look different by computer
Pictures look better by computer
I have this hardware to sell you.
I have this software to sell you.

This book contains many elaborations of these basic reasons (excepting the last two, which are nevertheless very powerful). At the outset it is important to note that the most "obvious" reason—pictures can be made faster by computer—is often the least true in practice. It is only recently that producing 2-D and 3-D diagrams and figures actually became easier and faster with computers, and still now many CAD and modelling tasks take longer with a computer (especially if quality is taken into account). The real power of computer graphics is in the ability to repeat at little human cost, and the ability to manipulate and reuse.

2.3
TRADITIONAL PICTURE MAKING

It will prove instructive to consider some pictures from non-computer media, and to analyze the processes which created them. Let us consider a classical drawing, a photograph (Figure 2.1), a television frame, or a technical drawing. What they have in common, beyond the variety of intent, talent and media, can be summed in four characteristics:

an intent to communicate through images
a model, either real or imaginary, to provide the form underlying the image
a medium to output the picture
a process to go from the model to the output medium.

Figure 2.1. A photograph

This can directly involve highly human skills, as in a woodcut, be totally mechanical as in the television frame, or can involve elaborate transformations, as with a photograph, which is imaged on a negative, possibly framed, cropped, enlarged and/or contrast-enhanced before it is printed. All of this is shared with images produced with computer graphics. The intent remains the same, the model has to be storable and manipulable in the machine, the output medium must be controllable by computer, and the progression from the model to the image, often called *rendering* in computer graphics, is the core of the discipline.

2.4
THE GRAPHICS PROCESS

Using this analysis of the graphics process (a more thorough analysis is necessary to validate our conclusions, but these are essentially correct), we can now put into a diagram the basic components of the graphics system (Figure 2.2).

This diagram is clearly connected to traditional picture making, containing a model, an imaging process and an output medium, as well as to the computer graphics process, although different people within computer graphics will have a different view of the same components. To programmers, each module is a piece of software, to be written or acquired; to system designers, each is software or hardware to be selected and matched; to users they will be functional blocks, seen for their uses, but not for their specific implementations. In fact, the middle module, which is the most important for the programmers and designers of the graphics system will be the least "visible" for the users, since they will take it for

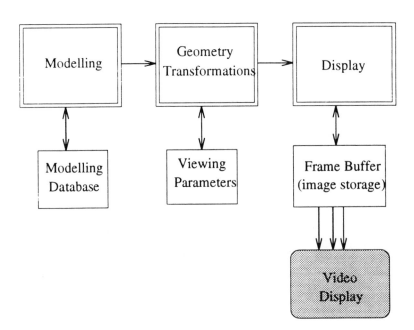

Figure 2.2. The graphics system

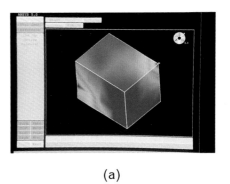

Plate 1.1 (a, b, c). Contour, isosurface and particle gradient displays of the equivalent stress from a structural analysis. (Courtesy Swanson Analysis Systems, Inc.)

(a)

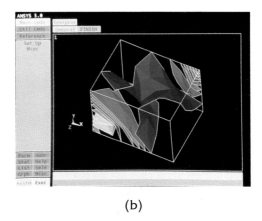

(b)

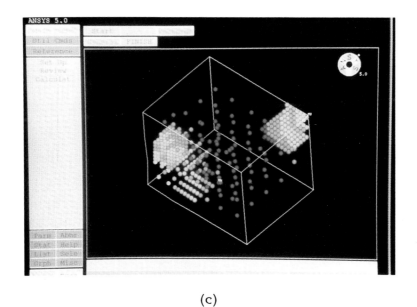

(c)

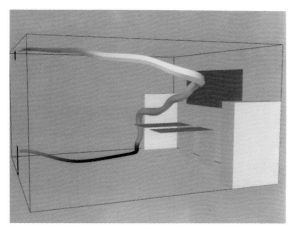

Plate 1.2. A stream polygon describing the air flow through a room. The streamline itself represents the path of an air particle, with color and thickness used to represent other solution variables. (From Schroeder et al., reference 10, copyright 1991 IEEE.)

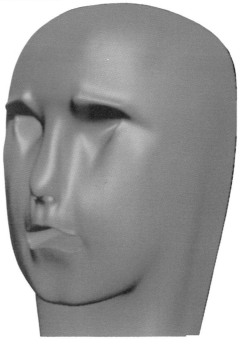

Plate 2.6. Face modeled with patches. (Courtesy David Forsey, University of British Columbia.)

Plate 2.13. Ray-traced scene.

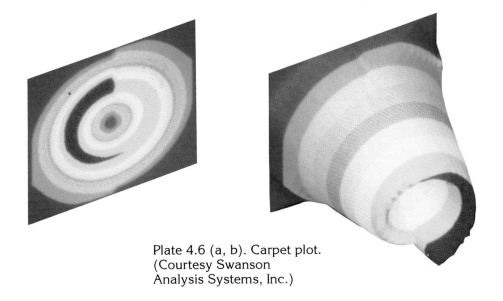

Plate 4.6 (a, b). Carpet plot.
(Courtesy Swanson
Analysis Systems, Inc.)

Plate 4.15. Isosurfaces of stress within a comprehensive
seal. (Courtesy Dedo Sistemi–Italcae SRL, Italy.)

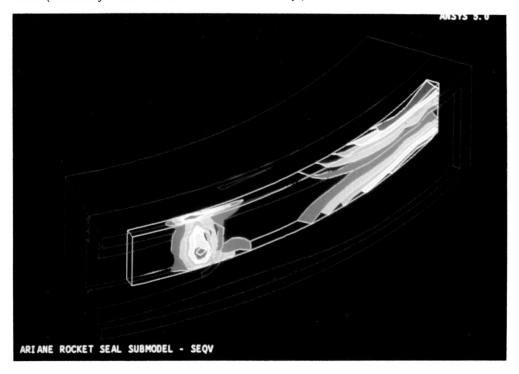

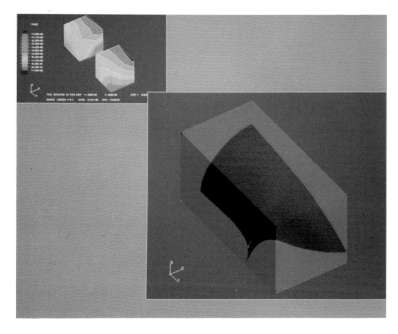

Plate 4.22. Isosurface smoothing—two element test case. (Copyright 1989, Association for Computing Machinery, Inc. Reprinted by permission.)

Plate 4.24. Translucent isosurfaces. (From Gallagher & Nagtegaal, reference 5, copyright 1989, Association for Computing Machinery, Inc. Reprinted by permission.)

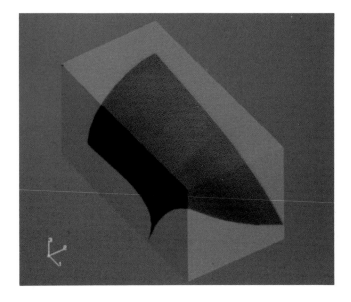

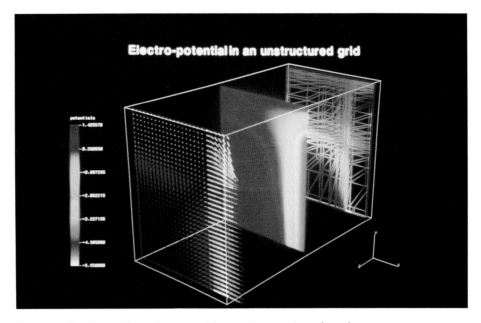

Plate 4.28. Sampling planes, with continuous tonal and particle results displayed across the slice planes. (Courtesy Wavefront Technologies—Data Visualizer.)

Plate 4.29. Isosurface used as a clipping and capping surface. (Courtesy Visual Kinematics, Inc.)

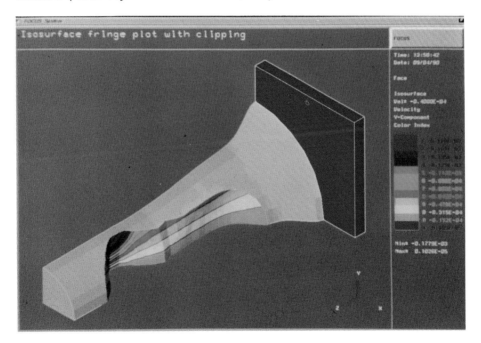

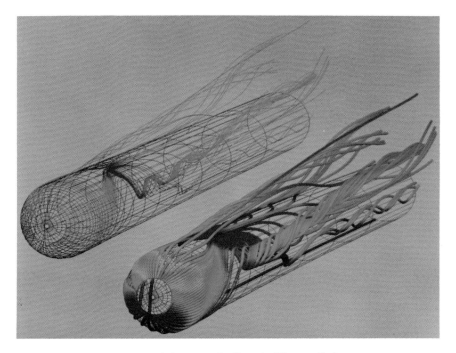

Plate 5.5. Streamlines of the steady flow in Figure 5.4.
Color maps kinetic energy density according to the scale
in Plate 5.21.

Plate 5.6. Anisotropic
texture representing the 2-D
flow tangent to the cylinder
in Figure 5.4. The cylinder
surface is shown unfolded.
Blue, green, yellow, and red
correspond to increasing
velocity magnitude.

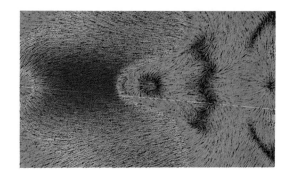

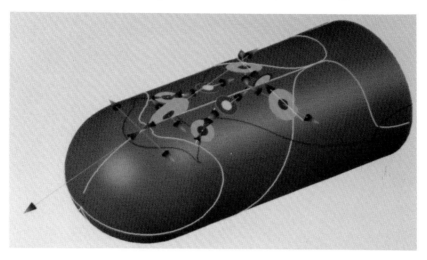

Plate 5.11. Local characterization of the velocity field in Figure 5.4. (From Hellman & Hesselink, reference 48, copyright 1991 IEEE.)

Plate 5.15. Topological surfaces depicting the time evolution of the 2-D flow past a circular cylinder. Time increases from back to front. (From Hellman & Hesselink, reference 48, copyright 1991 IEEE.)

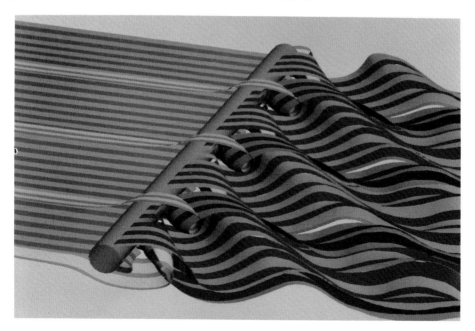

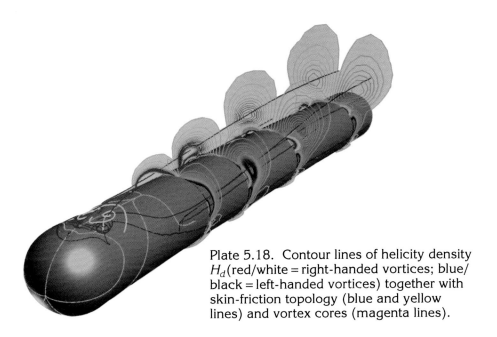

Plate 5.18. Contour lines of helicity density H_d(red/white = right-handed vortices; blue/black = left-handed vortices) together with skin-friction topology (blue and yellow lines) and vortex cores (magenta lines).

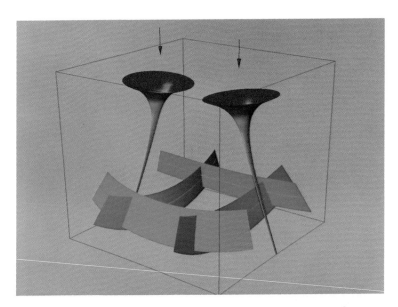

Plate 5.20. Stress tensor induced by two compressive forces. Minor tubes, medium and major helices. Color scale is shown in Plate 5.21. (From Delmarcelle and Hesselink, reference 9, copyright 1993 IEEE.)

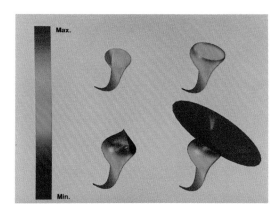

Plate 5.21. Four different stages of a minor tube in an elastic stress tensor field. (From Delmarcelle & Hesselink, reference 9, copyright 1993 IEEE.)

Plate 5.22. Reversible momentum flux density tensor in the flow past a hemisphere cylinder. Color scale is shown in Plate 5.21.(From Delmarcelle & Hesselink, reference 9, copyright 1993 IEEE.)

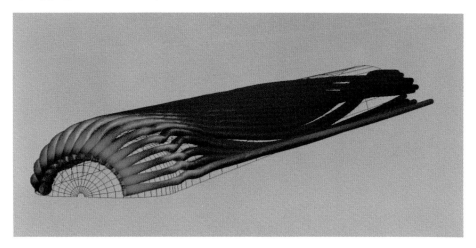

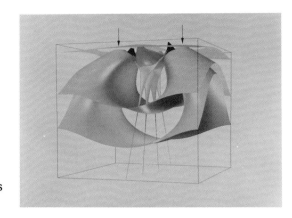

Plate 5.23. Global icon of
the stress tensor of Figures
5.19 and 5.20.

Plate 5.24. Stress tensor *(top)* and viscous stress tensor
(bottom) in the flow past a hemisphere cylinder. Color
scale is shown in Plate 5.21.

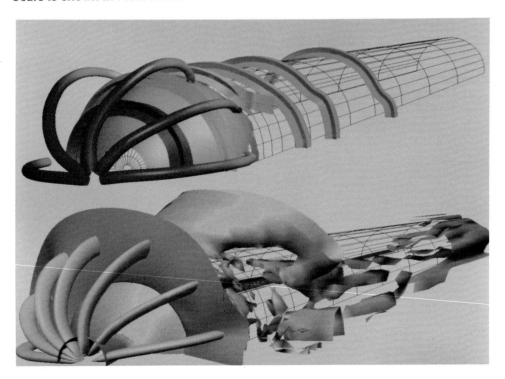

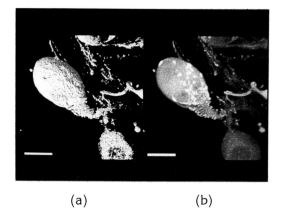

(a)   (b)

Plate 6.12. (a) A surface
projection of a nerve cell.
(b) A maximum projection
of a nerve cell.

Plate 6.18. (a) VolVis polyhedral representation of a
complex scene. (b) VolVis PARC rendering of the scene.

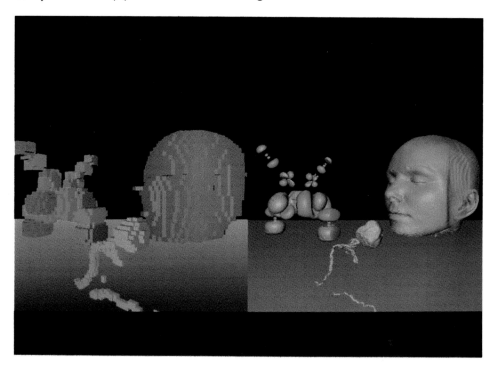

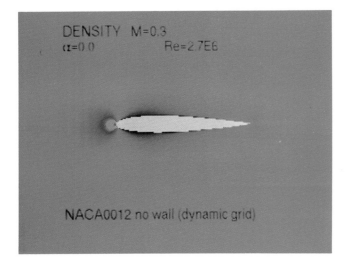

(a)

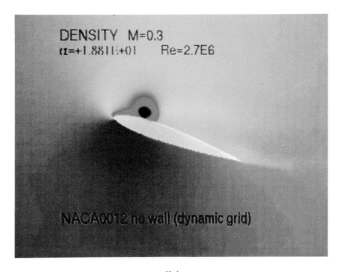

(b)

Plate 7.4. Data over an animated deformed grid. The same grid shown in Figure 7.3 is used to display density from a CFD calculation by Taekyu Reu and Susan Ying.

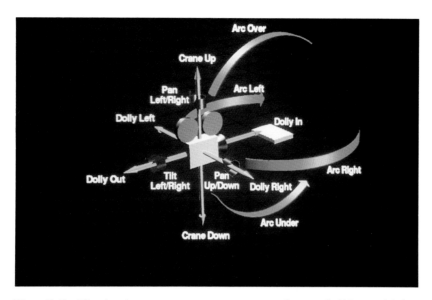

Plate 7.5. The basic camera moves are panning and tilting, which are rotations of the camera about its axis, dollying and craning, which are linear motions of the camera in space, and arcing, which is motion of the camera in an arc around a subject of interest. Zooming is not a camera move but is rather a change to the camera lens.

Plate 7.8. An NTSC test pattern. Columns show background colors from left to right ordered black, red, green, yellow, blue, magenta, cyan, and white. Rows show foreground colors from bottom to top in the same order. Note the artifacts produced in some horizontal color transitions.

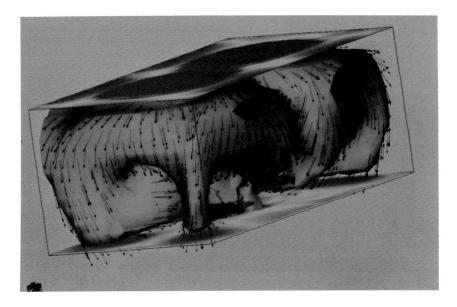

Plate 8.9. Air flow patterns in a multiphysics simulation of a room air conditioner can be studied through visualizations showing temperature isosurfaces, airflow velocities, and temperature contours.

Plate 8.10. The sloshing behavior of a fluid with a free surface in a fuel tank and its complex interaction with a flexible baffle and tank roof can be simulated and characterized through visualization of mesh deformation and hydrostatic pressure contours.

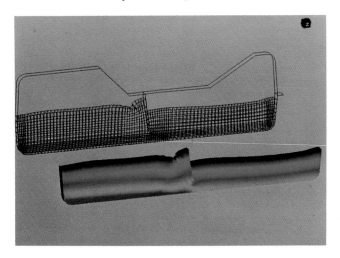

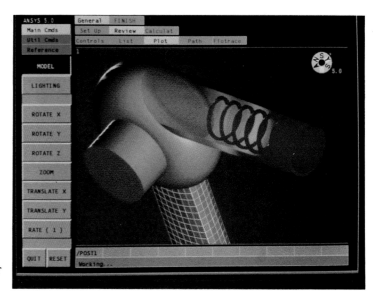

Plate 9.6. Interior thermal distribution for a hair dryer model.

Plate 10.3. The Spaceball, a 3D tracking and positioning device for use with interactive computer systems.

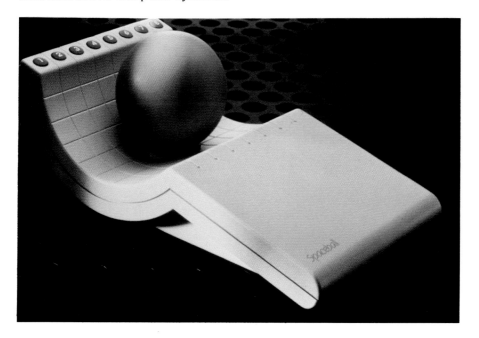

Plate 10.4 University of Illinois researcher Bob Wilhelmson takes part in a live teleconference and visualization session between a supercomputing center in Illinois and a remote workstation. (from Haber et al., reference 6. Reprinted from *The International Journal of Supercomputer Applications* by permission of MIT Press, Cambridge, MA, copyright 1990 Massachusetts Institute of Technology.)

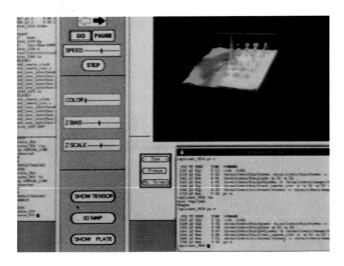

Plate 10.5. Interactive visualization imagery, displayed by satellite video imagery from Illinois under the control of the remote workstation.

granted if it works well. Still it is important for user to understand what it includes and how it works, so that one can know what to expect and what to demand. In this book the interest and attention shifts from modelling to display or the reverse, but one must realize that the two can be decoupled.

2.5
HISTORICAL CONNECTIONS

Our definition of "computer" graphics encompasses more than just computers as we know them. As a matter of fact, the beginning of the history of computer graphics can be dated to 2150 BC, the date of the oldest extant plan for a building. It falls within our definition because it is the result of a recipe to mechanically project a model (the building) onto a display (the trace of an orthographic projection on the tablet).

In modelling, all of early geometry is concerned with the description of shape and spatial properties. Primitives such as line segments, polygons, spheres, etc. are still the basic modelling primitives of computer graphics. Splines used today are the direct descendents of the mechanical splines used to design ship hulls, and architects from classical Greece to Le Corbusier have tried to design buildings from standard primitive elements.

Most of geometry and mathematics was developed in some sense to provide tools for transformation. We will not retrace here the development of perspective, for example (except to note that it was known and practiced substantially before the Renaissance). Non-linear transformations were also practiced, for example with *anamorphic* art.

Display has also a long history, even with *raster* display. After all, mosaic, carpets and woven material all are raster displays—an image from a 19th century weaving can be seen as a 3000×3000 black and white raster display. Gray-scale was achieved by dithering, and since it was produced on a *Jacquard* loom it was displayed by a machine controlled by punched-card. It has therefore all the characteristics of a "computer picture."

2.6
THE MODERN ERA

When computers appeared, recorders were almost immediately adapted to draw graphs and figures under machine control, and, from the 50s on, such plotters have been the main apparatus for permanent output, also known as *hard-copy*.

The mechanical system needed to effectively move the pen in a plotter is complex, bulky and slow. It is easier and faster to move something like an electron beam. Oscilloscopes, where an electron beam inside a *cathode-ray tube* is made visible by striking a fluorescent screen, were developed even before 1900. Turning them into computer displays required only computer control of the deflection of the beam. CRT displays were associated with some of the earliest computers, such as the WHIRLWIND computer at MIT in 1950, and, in the mid-

1950s, the computers of the SAGE Air Defense System were equipped with inter-active CRTs with *light-pens*. Since the phosphor light decayed rapidly, the necessity to constantly refresh the image on the CRT was a burden on both the hardware and software, and made graphics specialized and expensive. The development of the *Direct View Storage Tube* (DVST) by Tektronix in the late 60s permitted afford-able computer displays that were easily connected with their host computer.

As soon as computer printers appeared, people realized that pictures could be displayed with them. The first printers, with fixed line positions, and fixed char-acter positions on the line, constituted coarse *raster* displays, and, for many, were the first raster displays available. The next logical step was to control the inten-sity of the beam of the television set's CRT according to an array of values stored in the computer or computed on the fly. This was an improvement over previous methods of making possible true gray levels and color. The first such computer driven raster displays appeared around 1966. The limited size and the high cost of memory was long the main obstacle to the development of raster displays. By 1970, there were about half a dozen companies in North America selling raster display devices. By 1980, memory had become faster, larger and cheaper, and there were about 20 companies selling raster systems. Today they are so prevalent that for most people they "are" computer displays.

Personal computers, from their beginnings in the early 1970s, had some graph-ics capabilities, and their resolution increased rapidly from a feeble 200×64 image elements to 500×500 image elements and more. It is now very hard to imagine a computer system without decent graphics display, including, of course, color.

2.7
MODELS

In the study of our world a popular approach has been the development of rep-resentations or models of the world. These models will depict the particular aspect of our environment being studied. In many cases, the study and analysis of these models has provided us with results which help us to better understand our world. This generation of models is also a proven way to study computer graphics, but before we explain these models, a word about models and their purposes is necessary.

Newtonian physics provided a model that served to unlock many of the uni-verse's secrets. This model still explains most of the physical occurrences which we encounter from day to day. Einstein's relativity theory provided a more sophis-ticated model that allows us to explain other physical occurrences.Unfortunately, or fortunately, depending on your mindset, most of the effects which this model explain are not part of our everyday reality. Does the development of this model mean that the model proposed by Newton is no longer valid? By no means; it simply teaches us that we must live with a variety of models, each of which serves us in a different way.

Computer graphics models do not unlock secrets of the universe. For the most part, these models are designed to allow us to approximate the visual world which we encounter from day to day. We are far from the point where we can claim to have developed a comprehensive set of models for the world. In fact, most of the models that computer graphics has used to date are rather simple. Fortunately our vision system is rather good so that by skillfully combining these models and displaying them we can generate images of considerable complexity. In particular, when these graphical models or primitives are tied to some model from another discipline, insights into data derived from that model may be displayed so that the process being modelled can be visualized.

To model objects for the purposes of computer graphics we must first understand the space in which these objects live. Given an object and a reference position we need three numbers to describe the position of the object relative to this reference point. For example, we could say that the object is 3 meters north, 2 meters west, and 1 meter up from the reference point. Given these numbers or coordinates we have uniquely identified the position of the object relative to the reference point. In this example we have chosen the coordinate directions to be orthogonal to each other which makes this a Euclidian coordinate system. Another possible coordinate system is the polar one. In this system two angles and a direction are used to describe the position of the object relative to a reference point. This system is a "natural" system for astronomy where the angles are typically called azimuth and elevation.

As three-dimensional creatures we have no problem finding and manipulating objects of three dimensions or less. Unfortunately, we find it hard to precisely represent objects of higher dimensions even though we can imagine them. We can get a good idea of the properties of these objects by viewing their projections into three dimensional space. This task has been made considerably easier by computer graphics.

Points are objects of zero dimensions and are the simplest objects we know, but, in their zero dimensional space, they are of little interest to us. However, when we represent them in two- or three-dimensional space these points are of interest to us. The representation or model of points is simply the coordinate of their location. Given any two points we can define a set of paths between these two points. Each of these paths is what we call a line or curve. To represent these lines we must generate models for them. These are what we commonly know as line or curve equations.

Using lines and points we now have a simple but rich set of modelling primitives. By computing a set of vertices and edges (points and lines) we can begin to approximate those objects we wish to model. In Figure 2.3 we see such a model of a human face. Even though most of us will have little trouble identifying this object as a human face we can make two observations. The faces we are used to seeing are not transparent, and nor are they made up of flat components. If, instead of simply generating a model which is comprised of vertices and edges, we use polygons, we can begin to address the transparency problem. The problem of flat-looking objects can be addressed by using a more complex set of lines or curves.

If we consider three points, and the lines which join them pairwise, we notice that they define a two-dimensional triangle or polygon. We can use collections of

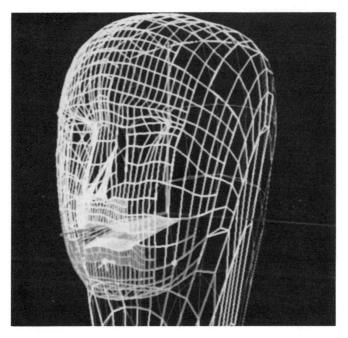

Figure 2.3. Face modelled with lines (Courtesy David Forsey, University of British Columbia)

Figure 2.4. Face modelled with triangular polygons (Courtesy David Forsey, University of British Columbia)

these triangles to model a surface. When we display a polygon we usually assume that it represents the surface of some solid object and thus display it as if it were a solid. This solid display of the polygon allows us to better display our model of the head since now we are not seeing those regions of the head we would normally not see. The term polygon mesh is typically used when a large number of polygons are used to model an object, as is the case in Figure 2.4.

A straight line or edges between two points are defined by

$$l(P_{0,P_1}) = P_0 + t(P_1 - P_0) \qquad\qquad [2.1]$$

We can model more complex lines or curves by using more points and a higher order polynomial for t. In particular let us consider 4 points P_0, P_1, P_2, P_3 and the polynomials known as the Bernstein cubic polynomials. $B_{0(t)}$, $B_{1(t)}$, $B_{2(t)}$, $B_{3(t)}$. If we use the 4 points (control points) as coefficients for the polynomials we have a curve defined by

$$C(t) = \sum_{i=0}^{3} P_i B_i(t) \qquad\qquad [2.2]$$

Such a curve is illustrated in Figure 2.5.

Depending on the choice of polynomials $B_{i(t)}$, a variety of curves with different properties can be generated. One application of cubic curves is the design of font types.

If the tensor product of two cubic curves is taken, a two-dimensional patch is produced. This is a parametrically defined surface which is controlled by the position of 16 control points. In Figure 2.6 we observe the use of patches for the

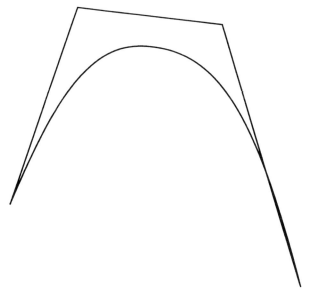

Figure 2.5. Bezier curve and control points

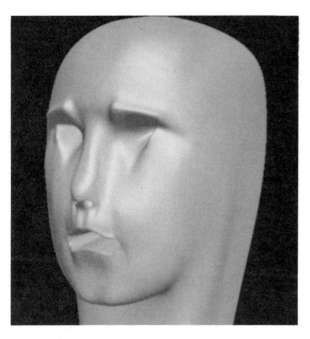

Figure 2.6. Face modelled with patches
(see color section plate 2.6) (Courtesy David
Forsey, University of British Columbia)

modelling of our head. We see the use of patches for the modeling of our head
example.

$$P(u,v) = \sum_{i=0}^{3} \sum_{j=0}^{3} P_{ij} B_i(u) B_j(v) \qquad [2.3]$$

All of the objects which we have described can be classed as explicit models.
That is we have a definition of the "exact" location of the object, be it a point,
line, or surface element. It is possible to define a surface in an implicit way. If we
consider for a moment the classical definition of the unit sphere

$$1 = x^2 + y^2 + z^2 \qquad [2.4]$$

We see that in fact there is no explicit definition of the surface but rather the
surface is the set of points in 3-D space which satisfy the condition that their distance from the origin is exactly one. For a variety of applications this model
proves to be useful, in particular if we consider volumes as models.

Even though one of the purposes of computer graphics is to allow us to model
what we see, it is equally useful for helping us to "see" what we cannot see. A case
in point is the study of volumetric data derived from internal scans of our bodies.
By using computer graphics we can generate stylized images of the inside of the
head as in Figure 2.7.

One way in which these data sets can be displayed is by modelling the inter-

Figure 2.7. Human head as volumetric data. Volume rendered from bridge of nose to collarbone.

nal surfaces of the object in question. By far the most popular way of generating models of these surfaces is to apply an implicit surface model to the data. A particular example of these implicit surface models applied to the data is the case where we are trying to display the bone structure. If we define the surface of the bone as the set of all points in the data near which there is a transition from high density d_1 to low density d_2 we have provided an implicit model of the surface of the bone. By varying the values of d_1 and d_2 we can generate representations for a wide variety of the internal structures of the head.

As we said before it is important to determine which properties of the object we wish to model. The choice of properties which we must model is significantly reduced when we think of the modelling required for computer graphics. For the most part models which allow us to simulate the visual behavior of the objects will suffice. It will often be the case that there are properties of the object which we do not see but which do influence the way in which we see the object behave. In this case, we must extend our model to accommodate this property so that the correct behavior is modelled. An example of such a property is mass. For a large percentage of the modelling required by computer graphics applications, mass is a property of objects that does not need to be a part of any of the models. However, if we are attempting to develop an animated model of the way in which we see objects interact, we must consider mass.

Thus, for static image generation it is often the case that simple geometric models of the surfaces of the object are sufficient. These models may be made up of a combination of points, lines, surfaces, and volumes. If these models are to be animated then we must incorporate other properties into them.

2.8
TRANSFORMATIONS

A *transformation,* in our context, is an operation on a model which results in another model, differing from the original only by geometric parameters. It is traditional, and indeed useful, to distinguish three categories of transformations: *modelling transformations,* which take a master object (often called a *canonical* object) and create a specific *instance* of that object; *instance transformations,* which are mostly to position the instance in the *world coordinate system* (the coordinate system in which the objects are created); and the *viewing transformations,* which put the objects into the camera (or "eye") coordinate system for display purposes.

For example, using a unit sphere centered at the origin as the master object, a modelling transformation could transform it into an ellipsoid with a major axis along X of length 5 and a minor axis along Y of length 3; an instance transformation might take that ellipsoid, rotate it by 20 degrees around the Z axis and translate it so that its center is at (20, 10, –5), and the viewing transformation will transform it so that it is viewed from a point of coordinates (100, 200, 50) looking at a point (0, 10, 10) (the latter transformation is not completely specified; as an exercise for the reader, what is left to specify?).

In most systems the range of transformations that can be used for the first two types is limited to *affine* transformations. Two definitions of affine will help show why this is a useful class: affine transformations leave parallel straight lines straight and parallel, and they can be expressed in N dimensions as $N \times N$ matrices of constants. The first property means that all parallelograms can be transformed into squares by an affine transformation, or inversely, that an affine transformation cannot do "worse" on a square than to transform it into a parallelogram, and the second means that any combination of affine transformations can be expressed as a single matrix. That is very important for both conceptual and practical reasons: one can build complex affine transformations from simple ones, easy to write, and one can build hardware applying related affine transformations to thousands or millions of points.

The basic transformations that can be used to build up to any affine transformation are *scaling, rotation* and *shearing*. While the first two are familiar, the last might not be. In shearing, a coordinate is scaled proportionally to another (see Figure 2.8). It is interesting to note that this is not a "minimal" list: shearings can be expressed as scalings and rotations, and rotations can be expressed as scalings and shearings. Note also that rotations are the transformations that can be applied in the real world to rigid objects, since all distances are conserved in a pure rotation. The matrices expressing the basic transformations are as follows in 2-D. For scaling (around the origin):

$$S = \begin{bmatrix} S_x & 0 \\ 0 & S_y \end{bmatrix} \qquad [2.5]$$

For rotation (around the origin):

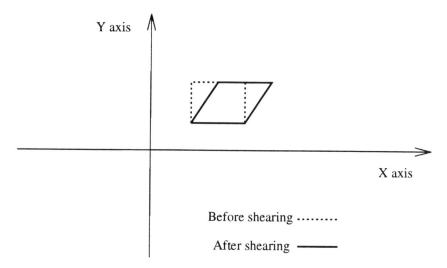

Figure 2.8. Shearing in X

$$\mathbf{R} = \begin{bmatrix} \cos\alpha & \sin\alpha \\ -\sin\alpha & \cos\alpha \end{bmatrix} \qquad [2.6]$$

For shearing:

$$\mathbf{Sh} = \begin{bmatrix} 1 & Sh_x \\ Sh_y & 1 \end{bmatrix} \qquad [2.7]$$

In 3-D, the matrices are as follows.
  For scaling (around the origin):

$$\mathbf{S} = \begin{bmatrix} S_x & 0 & 0 \\ 0 & S_y & 0 \\ 0 & 0 & S_z \end{bmatrix} \qquad [2.8]$$

For rotation (for instance around the X axis):

$$\mathbf{R} = \begin{bmatrix} 1 & 0 & 0 \\ 0 & \cos\alpha & \sin\alpha \\ 0 & -\sin\alpha & \cos\alpha \end{bmatrix} \qquad [2.9]$$

For shearing (in X):

$$\mathbf{Sh} = \begin{bmatrix} 1 & 0 & 0 \\ Sh_y & 1 & 0 \\ Sh_z & 0 & 1 \end{bmatrix} \qquad [2.10]$$

45

The alert reader will have noted that *translation* did not appear in our list, because the classic theory of transformations considers only vectors, and vectors are not translated (that does not mean, of course, that the origin of a vector cannot be translated, rather that it is still the same vector). Since the ability to express the transformations as matrices is critical to compose them and apply them in hardware/firmware/software, a means to include translation in the transformation matrices has been found. It is through the use of *homogeneous coordinates* and their associated transformation matrices. In brief, the trick was to add an extra coordinate (x, y, w) in 2-D, (x, y, z, w) in 3-D), that is to be multiplied by the translation factors, so that the resulting expression always makes each term a product of a coordinate by a scalar (hence the term "homogeneous"). In effect, this achieves a translation by shearing in a higher dimension. The small cost is that we have to use 3×3 transformation matrices in 2-D, and 4×4 in 3-D.

Using homogeneous coordinates, the matrix for translation is, in two dimensions,

$$T = \begin{bmatrix} 1 & 0 & 0 \\ 0 & 1 & 0 \\ \Delta x & \Delta y & 1 \end{bmatrix}$$

[2.11]

and in three dimensions,

$$T = \begin{bmatrix} 1 & 0 & 0 & 0 \\ 0 & 1 & 0 & 0 \\ 0 & 0 & 1 & 0 \\ \Delta x & \Delta y & \Delta z & 1 \end{bmatrix}$$

[2.12]

The reader can verify that when multiplying a vector ($x, y, 1$) in 2-D or ($x, y, z, 1$) in 3-D the matrices given do indeed effect a translation by Δx, Δy and Δz.

Viewing transformations can include a non-affine transformation, namely the *perspective projection*. The result of perspective is a *foreshortening* of objects proportional to their distance from the eye. As Figure 2.9 shows, the formula to express it is extremely simple, and correspond to a division of two coordinates by a third, once put on the camera coordinate system.

Perhaps surprisingly, one can use the homogeneous transformation matrices to include the perspective transform as well. This does not come for free, however, as each coordinate has to be divided by the resulting extra coordinate w at the end of the transform.

2.9
DISPLAY

The output of the transformations just discussed is made of points whose coordinates have been transformed into screen coordinates. In fact, there is still a simple change of coordinates to do. The view from the camera is limited by a

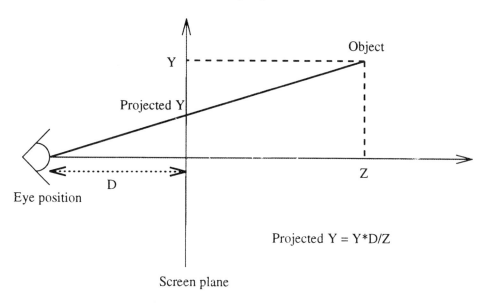

Figure 2.9. The geometry of the perspective transformation

window, usually a rectangular opening into the world. The section of the screen to which this window will map is called a *viewport,* and is also usually rectangular, with sides parallel to the screen coordinate axis.[1]

The next issue is *clipping,* that is figuring out what is within the window, without, or partially in. Note that the problem could be posed in terms of the viewport, and indeed clipping can be done in world coordinates (with respect to the window) or in screen coordinates (with respect to the viewport). At this stage we have to worry about the meaning of our objects. Transforming the end-points of a line segment or transforming the vertices of a polygon is the same operation, but line segments do not clip like polygons (see Figure 2.10).

Since every object has to be tested for clipping, speed is essential, and a slow clipper can defeat the best transformation hardware. In both the line segment and the polygon cases clever algorithms have been developed to speed up the process.

The fact that line segments and polygons behave differently under clipping shows that it is important to consider *display primitives* as different from modelling primitives. This is especially important when it comes to convert them into pixels, which is the final output from the digital side of the image. One can call the process *rasterization,* but it is generally known as *scan-conversion,* because most algorithms proceed one scanline at a time. The goal is to write with the right color (either uniform value or shaded according to a specific shading model) each pixel covered by the object. The basic scan-conversion algorithm is easily illustrated with a convex polygon, as shown in Figure 2.11(a).

1. This is the standard terminology in computer graphics. Unfortunately, in recent years screen managers and user interfaces have developed under the name *window managers,* when they should have been called *viewport manager* according to this terminology.

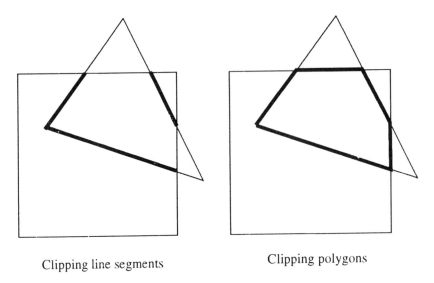

Clipping line segments   Clipping polygons

Figure 2.10. Clipping line segments

The method is based on the fact that for each scanline the intersection of the scanline and the polygon is a single segment (usually called a span) and exploits the *coherence* of the object, and the fact that the intersection of the polygon with the next scanline is not very different from the intersection with the current scanline. The X coordinates on the left and right edge are each incremented by a constant depending on the slopes of the edges, and this increment is updated when a vertex is crossed; this is easy to determine, since the left vertices and the right vertices are both linearly ordered by Y coordinates without any sorting necessary.

In the case of non-convex polygons, one has to sort the vertices first, and the fact that the scanline intersects the polygon in a variable number of spans (see Figure 2.11(b)) means that a more complex data structure is necessary to insert and delete spans efficiently. This explains why most hardware/firmware supported systems only support convex polygons.

The scan conversion process is only a special case of the problem of *filling* an area defined either by its boundary or by its interior (this is a basic operation of *paintsystems*). Even though the filling operation can be described very simply, algorithms to do so efficiently can be rather involved, and can be relatively slow (much slower than scan conversion for a polygon).

2.9.1 Shading

Shading generally means computing a color for the pixels based on properties of the surface and some specification of the lighting. In its full generality it is a very difficult and costly computation, but fortunately in most applications what is needed is not absolute physical verisimilitude, but enough visual cues to communicate the three-dimensional shapes, positions and relationships of the objects in the scene. For this purpose most display systems in computer graphics used a conventional set of light specifications, *illumination models* and *shading methods*. The lights are either *directional,* that is modelled as parallel rays, such that intensity and direction in space are the only parameters, or *point,* where a three-dimensional position and an intensity are given. *Intensity* is a rather vague word, but it is enough in our context to think of it as a power by unit area for directional light sources (for instance watt$/m^2$) or a power per solid angle for a point light source (watt/steradian). Of course we are interested in light only because it is what makes things visible, and its effect on the human visual system is what is really relevant. The same power (watts) has different effects on our eyes depending on the wavelength. *Photometric* quantities have been defined to take this into account, as opposed to *radiometric* quantities, which are in terms of physical energy.

Even more complex is the issue of *color*; for now all we will say is that color is not a physical quantity, but a perceptual one, and that *wavelength* of light and perceived color are strongly related but not identical. In most display systems color is handled as a *triple* of values (generally called *red, green* and *blue*), and while it accurately reflects the fact the the human color vision system perceives three dimensions of color, it is not sufficient, strictly speaking, to fully model the interaction of light and materials.

When materials receive light, they can transmit it, reflect it or absorb it (it is then transformed into non-visible forms of energy). The basic illumination model distinguishes (arbitrarily) three "modes" of reflected light: *ambient, diffuse* and *specular.* The ambient term is a constant term, used both to make sure objects do not appear too dark, and to approximate the effect of indirect illumination. The diffuse term emulates the diffuse reflection typical of matte objects, such as chalk, cotton, etc. In this case the reflected intensity is independent of the direction of view, and only dependent on the light received. The last term is introduced to simulate the behavior of glossy materials, such as polished metals and plastics, and it is computed as a function which has a maximum in the direction of pure mirror reflection, and then falls off rapidly as a function of the angle away from that direction.

These simple parameters and rules, together with the geometric information about the surface (position of point to be shaded and direction of normal) are enough to make an effective and believable display of a three-dimensional scene.

Shading computations can be quite costly, and several methods have been devised to speed up the process. They are based on computing the shade only at the vertices of a polygon and interpolating the values in the interior. This is done in parallel with the scan-conversion described above. If the color is interpolated, it is known as *Gouraud shading,* but if the normals are interpolated, then the shading computed from these is known as *Phong shading.* The initial motivation for these techniques was more to hide the fact that the polygons are generally an approximation to a continuously curved surface (as when a sphere is approximated as a icosahedron). In this case Gouraud or Phong shading will hide the discontinuities along the edges of the polygons (see Figure 2.12).

2.9.2 Texture Mapping

When computing the shade at a pixel, one can use a color retrieved from an auxiliary image instead of a constant color. To do this one must define a map from the pixel to the surface of the object to the image, where this image plays the role

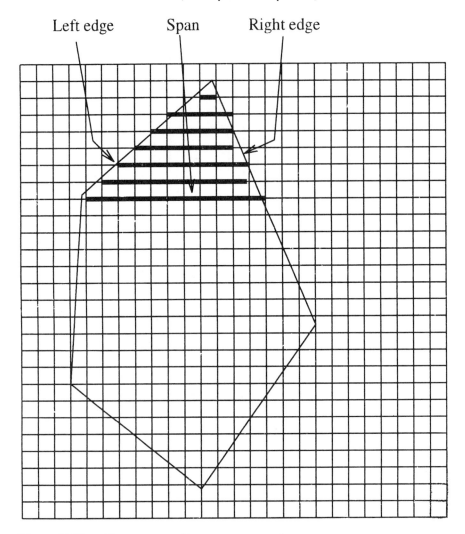

Figure 2.11a. Scan-converting a convex polygon

of a texture on the surface. This technique is then called *texture mapping*. It is a powerful way to improve the visual richness of an object, since the texture can be arbitrarily detailed. Textures are generated from real images scanned, from simple algorithms (for instance for a checkerboard or a stripe pattern) or by more elaborate methods based on stochastic processes. The method can also be applied to other properties of the surface besides color, such as its surface normal (known as *bump mapping*), transparency or reflectivity.

2.10
VISIBILITY

In the preceding section we have implicitly assumed that only one object covers a given pixel, but, of course, in any reasonable scene this is not the case.

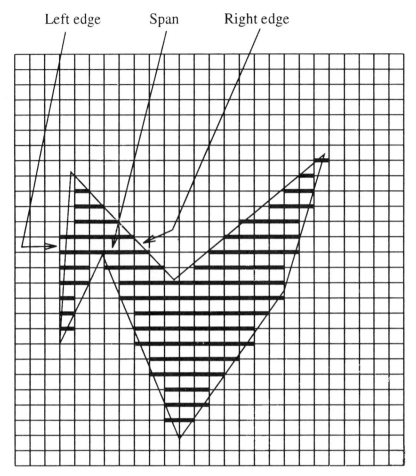

Figure 2.11b. Scan-converting a non-convex polygon

Methods have to be developed to decide what ought to be seen when this happens. It used to be called *hidden line* or *hidden surface* removal, but is better called *visibility* determination. The easiest solution is the so-called *painter* algorithm, where each object overwrites whatever has been written before. This will give the correct answer only if there is a unique ordering of the visible object (not always true in real scenes) and if the objects are "painted" in that order. Various clever schemes have been developed to determine that order efficiently, and they range from simple priority ordering to structures based on *binary space partitioning trees*.

The most popular method, very easily implemented in hardware is based on a *depth-buffer* also known as *Z-buffer*. In the eye coordinate system after the perspective transformation the Z coordinate of a point is equal to its distance from the eye (its *depth*). If two objects cover the same pixel, the visible one (ignoring transparency) will be the one with the smallest Z coordinate. So if one stores the Z value of the currently visible object (initialized to a large background value) for each pixel, then one can write a new object only if its Z is smaller than the current

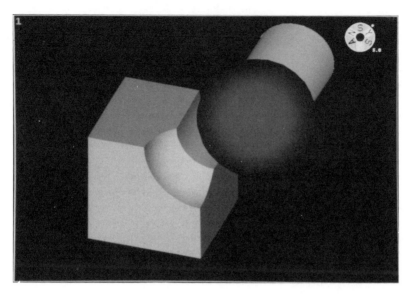

Figure 2.12. Gouraud shaded image (Courtesy Swanson Analysis Systems)

one at that pixel. In the scan conversion of a polygon the Z value is computed along with the X value along each span, and does not add much to the cost of the computation. This simple algorithm was made practical when video memories became cheap enough to afford the storage space. The Z value has to be stored with at least 16 bits to ensure accurate depth comparisons between objects (24 to 32 bits is more common) which means that the Z-buffer can be as big as or bigger than the image buffer.

2.11
PIXEL DRIVEN RENDERING

2.11.1 Ray-Tracing

The rendering method that might occur first to somebody presented with the problem is to "send" rays from the eye to the screen (in practice to the pixels) and compute what they intersect first in the scene. This approach, simple in concept, actually requires extreme cleverness to be implemented in a reasonable way. It is now known as *ray-tracing,* and has been considerably developed and popularized in the 1980s, in particular under the influence of Turner Whitted. The advantages of the approach are that it is conceptually simple and very general as long as one knows how to intersect a primitive with a ray (which is a straight line) inherently modular (each primitive can be dealt with separately), and it is easy to incorporate secondary but important illumination effects such as shadows (by sending a ray towards the light source), reflections and refractions. This has produced many unique and visually appealing pictures. Its drawbacks are significant as well. Each intersection can be costly, and the naive approach requires one to test the intersection of each ray with each object in the scene. One cannot easily use the *object coherence* that is basic to a scan-conversion approach: in general, rays do not benefit from the "knowledge" acquired by the other rays. Many improvements have been devised to address these problems; today, with a standard graphics workstation, one can ray-trace thousands of objects in minutes. For instance Figure 2.13 shows a scene containing 50,000 primitives that has been ray-traced in 5mn on a 50 MIPS workstation. This is even more impressive when one considers that there is no built-in hardware assistance for ray-tracing as there is for scan-conversion. There are many current efforts to remedy this, but there is still no workstation in use that can ray-trace a usable scene in real time.

2.11.2 Voxel-Based Rendering

Another context where the two different approaches to rendering, from the objects to the screen or from the screen to the objects, are easily contrasted is with *volume rendering,* which is itself a part of *volume visualization* (see Chapter 6 for more details). In this case the object "primitives" are *voxels,* or volume elements. What voxels are is actually quite ambiguous because they can be seen as point samples from a continuous three-dimensional function, filtered samples of the same, where the filter can be a box filter the size of the voxel or some more sophisticated overlapping filters. As in similar situation with signals, these samples can be variously used, in turn, to reconstruct the original signal with the help of reconstruction filters (these always exist whether or not the implementor or the user is explicitly aware of them.

The methods used to render volumes, and the meaning of the results, are critically dependents on the answer to the previous questions. Some methods use some criterion (usually a threshold value) to define a surface, and the surface is then ren-

Figure 2.13. Ray-traced scene (See color section plate 2.13)

dered by standard methods. A different approach, however, is to render the voxels directly. If the model for the interaction between "rays" and voxel is absorption, then the result is the line integral along the ray through the volume. This is a rather costly operation, especially since the values along the rays have to be interpolated. The result will have the look of tradional 2-D X-ray images, which can be hard to interpret. In this case the direction of integration is not important. One can "bias" the rendering to speed up the process. These categories of methods can be usefully divided into *front-to-back* and *back-to-front* approaches. Proceeding front-to-back has the advantage of allowing one to stop when the *opacity* along the ray has reached a preset value, and therefore one does not have to process all the voxels. This can lead to sampling problems, however. Proceeding back to front, usually by voxels, allows various operators to *composite* the overlapping voxels, and avoids most sampling problems, but has the disadvantage of having to process all the visible voxels.

Many methods have been proposed to speed up the processing, mostly based on hierarchical pre-processing of the volumetric data, but we are still some way off from being able to display useful volumetric data (that is bigger than about $128 \times 128 \times 128$) in real time.

2.12
ARCHITECTURE OF DISPLAY SYSTEMS

It is clear from the preceding discussion that a typical display system will include a processor to define and manipulate the models, enough storage for the models, a processor to effect the geometric transformations, a processor to do the scan conversion, a frame buffer to store the pixel values and the depth values, and a *video chain* to read the pixels at video rates and drive the display (usually the electron guns of a *cathode ray tube* (CRT)), and thus correspond functionally to the diagram of Figure 2.14.

Of course in real systems all these elements are not necessarily physically distinct. There could be only one processor, and even the frame buffer can be part of general purpose memory. In fact, in personal computers such as the Apple Macintosh, which first appeared as a black and white bit-mapped display, the architecture is characterized by the fact that the image is in main memory, and there is basically no hardware assist for any drawing function (see Figure 2.15).

More typical of many personal computers enhanced with a graphics *card* is the diagram in Figure 2.16 which shows a separate memory for the frame buffer linked to the CPU by a fast internal data bus. They are typically at or close to commercial video resolution (around 480 by 640 pixels) and from 8 bits of color per pixel to 24 bits.

Current high-end graphics workstations take specialization of function a few steps further, and the display *back-end* can be quite elaborate, as shown in the diagram of Figure 2.17.

Typical of these is a 1280 by 1024 pixel display, and 24 bits per pixel or more (especially when Z-buffer is included). They are capable of drawing several hundred thousand 3-D triangles per second.

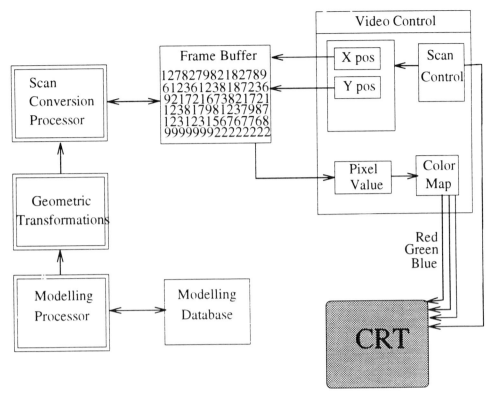

Figure 2.14. Generic raster display system

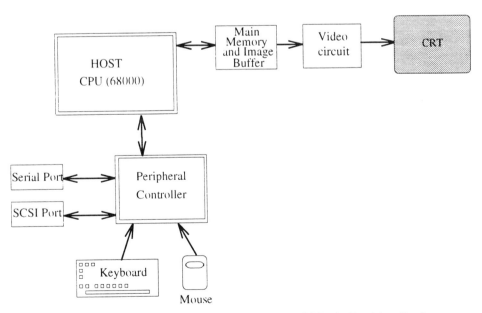

Figure 2.15. Personal computer with bit-mapped black & white display

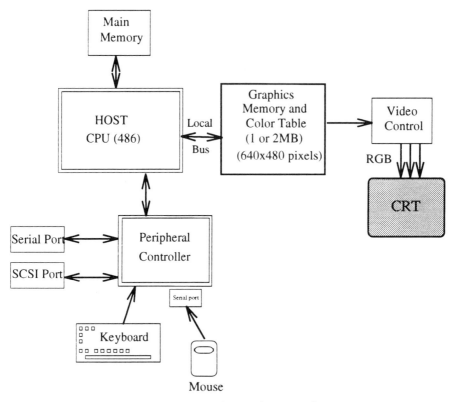

Figure 2.16. Personal computer with graphics card

There are two trends in graphics architectures (of course closely related to corresponding marketing trends). One is the meeting of the high end of personal computers and the low end of workstations, both in performance and price. This will be essentially achieved when PCs adopt RISC chips for their main CPU. The last and biggest difference, likely to remain for some time, is in the operating systems. Most workstations use some variant of Unix. This means the users belong to a different "culture," with different software tools and development "style."

The other trend is towards *multimedia* workstations, where in addition to powerful graphics capabilities there is real-time video input and output, image and animation compression hardware/software built-in, sound input and sound synthesis, and easy access to media such as CD-ROM. Figure 2.18 diagrams the architecture of such a workstation.

It is useful at this point to speculate about what the "next" graphics workstation will be like, if the horizon is about ten years away. Quite obviously CPU power will continue to rise (putting on PCs what is now on workstations costing around $100,000), and memory cost will continue to fall. As far as graphics is concerned, the bggest change will be the influence of *High Definition Television* (HDTV). While the broadcast standards are still being discussed, it is certain that the resolution will be about 2000 by 1000 pixels with an aspect ratio of 16/9, better than current workstations, and will make available, at consumer prices, the nec-

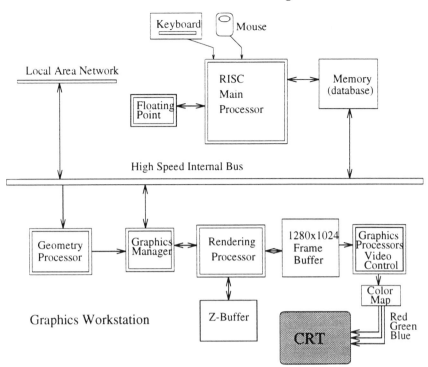

Figure 2.17. Graphics workstation

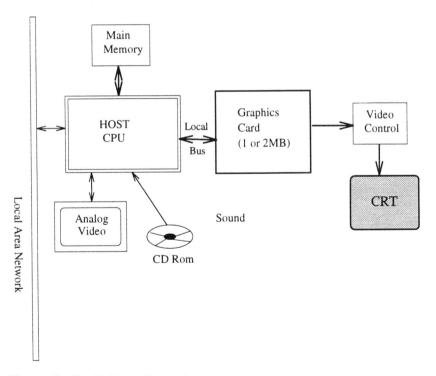

Figure 2.18. Multimedia workstation

essary elements of frame-buffer, video control and monitor for a graphics system. The only drawback is that HDTV will almost surely be interlaced video, which is not desirable for workstation use. HDTV will create the nucleus of the multimedia system, and the workstation itself is likely to be an add-on, with the extra computing power and memory necessary to achieve high-rate image generation. This will provide the ability to model, display and animate scenes with from 100,000 to 1 million shaded polygons in real time. This might seem high, but remember that a human body shown at a level of detail so that hands, for instance, would look moderately realistic should require more than a million polygons.

At the same time the media will be more integrated, with, for example, the ability to display real images in real time merged with computer-generated images, with common point of view, visibility and illumination.

2.13
FURTHER READING

The interested reader can find more information about computer graphics fundamentals in some of the following publications:

Foley, J.D., Van Dam, A., Feiner, S.K. and Huges, J.F., *Computer Graphics Principles and Practices,* Second Edition, Addison-Wesley, Reading, MA, 1990

Newman, W. and Sproull, R., *Principles of Interactive Computer Graphics,* Second Edition, McGraw-Hill, 1979

Conrac Corporation, *Raster Graphic Handbook,* Second Edition, Van Nostrand Reinhold, New York 1985

In addition, the annual proceedings of the ACM SIGGRAPH (Special Interest Group on GRAPHics) conference and the IEEE VISUALIZATION conferences provide a good review of current research in the field. The latter conference, in particular, publishes current research in computer graphic applications for scientific visualization.

SECTION II

Scientific Visualization Techniques

CHAPTER

Analysis Data for Visualization

MARK S. SHEPHARD AND
WILLIAM J. SCHROEDER

MODERN ANALYSIS AND design is based upon complex numerical modeling techniques. These techniques typically decompose a problem into many smaller pieces, and then solve the simpler but much larger problem on a computer. The results of such analysis, however, generate such large data size as to be nearly incomprehensible. To address this problem, engineers and scientists have turned to visualization. In this chapter we present an overview of engineering analysis techniques, and describe the forms of data that might be expected from such analysis.

3.1
INTRODUCTION

The goal of visualizing engineering analysis is an improved understanding of the results of the information generated in that analysis process. It is not difficult to imagine the potential advantages of using advanced visualization methodologies to convert masses of discrete numbers, often measured in gigabits, produced by a numerical analysis procedure into physically meaningful images. What is more difficult is the actual construction of the visualization techniques, which can provide a faithful depiction of those results in a manner appropriate for the engineer or scientist who performed the analysis. The development of successful visualization techniques for engineering analysis results requires a knowledge of, (i) the basic analysis procedures used, (ii) the information input and output from the analysis procedure, and (iii) the goals of the analyst applying the visualization procedures.

This chapter provides a very brief introduction into the ways commonly used numerical analysis techniques operate, as well as the forms and methods used to construct the discrete models they require. Consideration is then given to the form of the output information produced by these procedures. This analysis input and output information provides the raw data to be used for producing meaningful visualizations. The chapter concludes with an examination of how that information can be visualized.

3.2
NUMERICAL ANALYSIS TECHNIQUES

Engineering analysis is the process of taking given "input" information defining the physical situation at hand and, through an appropriate set of manipulations, converting that input into a different form of information, the "output," which provides the answer to some questions of interest. The goal of visualization techniques, when used in conjunction with engineering analysis, is to provide the most meaningful means for engineers to view both the "input" and "output."

Although there are several classes of analysis problems, this chapter focuses on one class which typically provides the greatest challenges to the visualization of the output. In this class of problem the input consists of some physical domains for which there are known boundary conditions, initial conditions and loads. The goal of the analysis is to determine one or more response variables over that domain. The common method to develop and perform an analysis is to select, or derive, a mathematical model appropriate for the physical problem that can accept as input the material properties, initial conditions, boundary conditions and loads, and produce as output the desired response variables. The mathematical models produced by this process are typically sets of partial differential equations. In some simple cases, the exact continuous solution to these equations can be determined. However, in most cases such exact continuous solutions are not available.

For these classes of problems, where exact solutions are not available, the introduction of the digital computer has had a profound impact on the way in which engineering analysis is performed, and on its role in the engineering design process. Today, most engineering analyses associated with the solution of partial differential equations over general domains are performed using generalized numerical analysis procedures which approximate the continuous problem in terms of a discrete system. This yields large sets of algebraic equations which can be quickly solved by the computer. Software to perform these analyses is readily available in the engineering community. Therefore, these numerical analyses are now performed on a routine basis during engineering design.

A major problem confronted by users of these techniques is that the volume and form of the discrete information produced does not lend itself to simple interpretation, particularly when an understanding of the behavior of the parameters of interest over the domain of the analysis is desired. Properly constructed visualization techniques represent the key technology needed to extract the desired information from the volumes of discrete data produced by the analysis procedure.

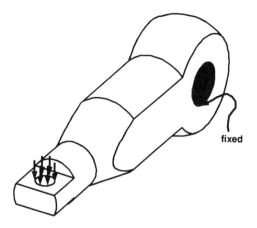

Figure 3.1. Solid model of a mechanical part
showing loads and boundary conditions

As a simple example of the power of the numerical analysis techniques available today, consider the geometric model of a mechanical part shown in Figure 3.1 defined in a commercial solid modeling system. We wish to determine the deflections and stresses for this model subjected to the loads and boundary conditions also shown in Figure 3.1. For this example an automated adaptive analysis was performed in which the engineer simply specified the level of accuracy desired. Given the desired accuracy, the geometric model and analysis attributes of loads, material properties and boundary conditions, finite element procedures automatically generated the mesh, analyzed it, and adaptively improved it until the specified accuracy was obtained. The final mesh for this example is shown in Figure 3.2. At that point the engineer is faced with the problem of interpreting the results of the analysis which for even this simple example constitute many megabytes of data. The visualization techniques discussed in this book are key to supporting that results interpretation process.

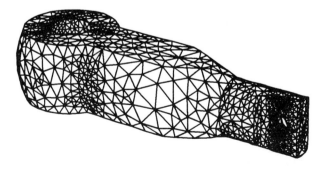

Figure 3.2. Automatically generated and adaptively
refined finite element model of a mechanical part

3.3
BRIEF OVERVIEW OF ELEMENT BASED DISCRETIZATION TECHNIQUES

The majority of current numerical analysis procedures for solving partial differential equations employ cell-based discretizations of the domain of interest. The commonly applied cell-based discretization techniques are finite element, finite difference, boundary element and finite volume.

In finite difference methods the continuous differential operators are replaced by difference equations, using the value of the dependent variables at discrete locations. With all differential operators replaced by difference equations, the solution by finite differences consists of covering the domain with a set of evaluation points to be used in the difference equations. The values of the dependent variables at these locations are only known at specific locations dictated by the boundary and initial conditions. In a properly formulated problem, the substitution of these known values and the differenced load yields a solvable system algebraic equation in terms of the values of the dependent variables at the difference locations.

A different set of steps is employed in the application of finite element, boundary element, and finite volume techniques. In these techniques a two-step process is performed. The first step is to convert the governing partial differential equations, the strong form, into an equivalent integral form, the weak form. The weak form is then discretized by approximating the appropriate terms in the weak form by given distributions written in terms of unknown multipliers. The mathematical manipulations performed in the construction of the weak form differentiate the basic methods and dictate the requirements placed on the distributions which can be validly used. The details of the specific method are further dictated by the methods used to construct the distributions. The commonly applied methods employ piecewise distributions which are non-zero only over individual cells, typically called elements, written in terms of values on their boundary. By the proper matching of the boundary values on neighboring elements, the valid distribution over the entire domain is constructed. Appendix 3.9 outlines the basic mathematical steps in the finite element method. Interested readers should consult basic finite element references for additional information [13, 26, 30].

3.3.1 Commonly Used Element Geometry and Shape Functions

As indicated in the Appendix to this chapter, a key ingredient in the construction of the finite element equations is the selection of element shape functions and the integration of the operators, equations (3.13–3.15) over the domain of the elements. The selection of the element shape functions must satisfy specific requirements so that the elemental integrations and their summation are meaningful. Considering the generic second order partial differential equation (Equation 3.9) which can represent many of the physical problem types of interest, the minimum requirement is that the dependent variable and first partial derivatives are continuous within the element, C^1, and the dependent variable be

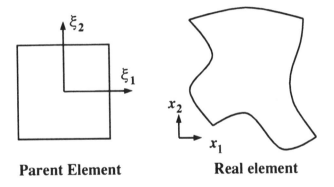

Parent Element   **Real element**

Figure 3.3. Parametric coordinate system for element description

continuous between elements C^0. Considering the use of topologically simple finite elements, for example three- and four-sided in 2-D, these requirements are easily met by selecting the value of the dependent variable at locations on the boundary of the element and using polynomial shape functions. For example, it is easily shown that the C^1 intra-element and C^0 inter-element continuity requirements are easily met by selecting linear element shape functions written in terms of the values at the triangle's vertices. Considering a simple scalar field, the element shape functions for the linear triangular element can be written as

$$u^h = \sum_{a=1}^{3} N_a d_a^e \qquad [3.1]$$

where d_a^e are the values of u^h evaluated at the node a of element e, and N_a are linear shape functions having a value one at node a and zero at the other nodes.

If all finite elements were constructed using linear shape functions acting over simplex[1] elements, the process of visualizing finite element results would be simplified. This is not, however, the case. It is common in finite element analysis to employ higher order functions to represent both the variation of the dependent variable over the element as well as its shape. To support the process of forming the elemental integrals needed these higher order elements typically employ a parametric coordinate system. Figure 3.3 depicts a parent element in the parametric coordinate system and the real element in a global coordinate system for a 2-D quadrilateral. The 3-D parametric coordinate system for a brick adds a ξ_3 coordinate to that shown in 2-D. Area and volume coordinates are typically used for triangular and tetrahedral elements [8].

Using parametric coordinate systems the variation of the dependent variables and element shape are written as

$$u^h = \sum_{a=1}^{n_{en}} N_a(\xi) d_a \qquad [3.2]$$

1. Triangles in 2-D and tetrahedra in 3-D

65

and

$$\underline{x} = \sum_{a=1}^{n_{sh}} N_a^s(\xi)\tilde{\underline{x}}_a \qquad\qquad [3.3]$$

where $\underline{x}$ represents the shape of the element, $N_a(\xi)$ are the dependent variable shape functions written in terms of the parametric coordinate system, $N_a^s(\xi)$ are element geometry shape functions written in terms of the parametric coordinate system, and $\tilde{\underline{x}}_a$ represents the discrete shape parameters, such as the global coordinates of points on the boundary of the element.

The most commonly used finite element shape functions are defined in terms of linear, quadratic or cubic Lagrange polynomials interpolated through nodes on the closure of the element [8, 13, 30]. In 2- and 3-D the individual shape functions are combinations of products of 1-D Lagrange polynomials. The use of nodal interpolation and parametric coordinates make it easy to construct these shape functions to satisfy the C^0 inter-element continuity requirements, since the values along a boundary are uniquely defined in terms of nodal values on that boundary, and nodal values are common to neighboring elements sharing boundaries. It is also common in the use of these shape functions to employ the same shape functions for the dependent variables and element geometry. Such elements are referred to as isoparametric elements. Figure 3.4 shows the common forms of these elements, from linear to cubic shape functions over four sided 2-D elements.

Over the past several years finite element developers have expanded the classes of geometric functions used in the construction of finite elements. One of the main drivers of these developments is the desire to employ *p-version* finite element techniques. Unlike fixed polynomial order finite element methods where the solution accuracy is increased by increasing the number of finite elements (the so called *h-version*), the *p-version* maintains a fixed mesh and increases the solution accuracy

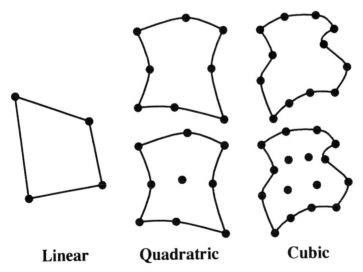

Linear   **Quadratric**   **Cubic**

Figure 3.4. Common isoparametric element forms

by increasing the polynomial order of the finite elements. It is also possible to combine the two technologies yielding the *hp-version* of the finite element method which has been shown to provide the greatest increases in solution accuracy for a fixed computational effort [26].

In the *p-version* the polynomial order of elements in the mesh can become quite high in which case the Lagrangian type shape functions commonly used in the *h-version* are not acceptable. Therefore, Lagendre polynomials are commonly used for the dependent variable shape functions in *p-version* elements because they are numerically well conditioned, allow the hierarchic construction of element matrices, and can be easily used to construct meshes where the polynomial order varies over the mesh. One minor drawback is that the individual degrees of freedom (**dof**) terms are no longer just the value of the dependent variable at a node point. Instead, they are often various higher order derivatives evaluated at element mid-edges, mid-faces and at the centroid of the element. These **dof** are selected and shared between elements such that maintaining the required C^0 interelement continuity is not difficult.

The finite elements employed in p-version meshes are typically quite large, and cover sizeable portions of the boundary of the domain being analyzed. Therefore, it is critical that the geometry shape functions used for these elements introduce very little approximation error. For example, it is common to have only four element edges around a circular hole. Clearly, a piecewise linear geometry approximation which would yield a square would introduce substantial errors into the analysis results. One approach that has been applied to construct geometric shape functions is to employ transfinite mapping techniques using implicit geometric functions for the geometric boundary of the elements of a high order geometric approximation [10, 11].

3.3.2 Element Integration

With the shape functions selected for the dependent variables and geometry of the elements the next task is to perform integrals over the elements to form the element stiffness matrices and load vectors. Consider a term in the stiffness matrix

$$k_{pq}^e = a\big(N_a, N_b\big) = \int_{\Omega_e} \mathcal{H}^1(N_a)\big(\mathcal{G}^1(N_b)\big)d\Omega \qquad\qquad [3.4]$$

where, for sake of discussion, we examine a 2-D element and a particular typical integral as

$$k_{pq}^e = \int_{\Omega_e} \lambda N_{a,x_1} N_{b,x_2} dx_1\, dx_2 \qquad\qquad [3.5]$$

where N_{a,x_i} in the x_i first partial derivative of N_a. Since the element shape functions are written in the parametric coordinate system ξ, the relationship between the coordinate systems must be established. Consideration of Equation 3.3 shows it is easy to form N_{a,ξ_i}, therefore the N_{a,x_i} are found by first applying the chain rule of differentiation for N_{a,ξ_i} which in 2-D can be written

$$\left\{\begin{matrix} \dfrac{\partial}{\partial \xi_1} \\[2mm] \dfrac{\partial}{\partial \xi_2} \end{matrix}\right\} \tag{3.6}$$

and then inverting that expression to yield

$$\left\{\begin{matrix} \dfrac{\partial}{\partial x_1} \\[2mm] \dfrac{\partial}{\partial x_2} \end{matrix}\right\} = \dfrac{1}{|J|} \begin{bmatrix} \dfrac{\partial x_2}{\partial \xi_2} & -\dfrac{\partial x_2}{\partial \xi_1} \\[2mm] -\dfrac{\partial x_1}{\partial \xi_2} & \dfrac{\partial x_1}{\partial \xi_1} \end{bmatrix} \left\{\begin{matrix} \dfrac{\partial}{\partial \xi_1} \\[2mm] \dfrac{\partial}{\partial \xi_2} \end{matrix}\right\} \tag{3.7}$$

where $[J]$ is referred to as the Jacobian matrix and $|J|$ is its determinate. Note that the terms in Equation 3.7 are easily constructed by the use of Equation 3.3 and the element geometry shape functions. The final substitution required in Equation 3.5 is the proper coordinate change to integrate in the local coordinates. This is accomplished by the use of $dx_1 dx_2 = |J|\, d\xi_1\xi_2$. Substituting these into the specific case of Equation 3.5 yields

$$k_{pq}^e = \int_{\Omega_e} \left(\lambda(\xi)\right)\left(N_{a,x_1}(\xi)\right)\left(N_{b,x_2}(\xi)\right)|J|d\xi_1 d\xi_2 \tag{3.8}$$

$$= \int_{\Omega_e} \lambda \left\{ \dfrac{1}{|J|}\left(\dfrac{\partial x_2}{\partial \xi_2}\dfrac{\partial N_a}{\partial \xi_1} - \dfrac{\partial x_2}{\partial \xi_1}\dfrac{\partial N_a}{\partial \xi_2}\right)\right\}$$

$$\left\{\dfrac{1}{|J|}\left(-\dfrac{\partial x_1}{\partial \xi_2}\dfrac{\partial N_b}{\partial \xi_1} + \dfrac{\partial x_1}{\partial \xi_1}\dfrac{\partial N_b}{\partial \xi_2}\right)\right\}|J|d\xi_1 d\xi_2$$

Since the final form of the element stiffness integrals are in terms of rational polynomials, they are not easily integrated in closed form. Therefore, numerical integration techniques are employed [13, 26, 30]. Since the integrals are over fixed domains in the parametric coordinate system, optimal techniques such as Gauss quadrature are typically applied.

3.4
METHODS TO CONSTRUCT AND CONTROL ELEMENT MESHES

A key aspect of the finite element method is the construction of the finite element mesh used to represent the domain over which the analysis technique will be applied. Consideration of the type and distribution of finite elements in the mesh is key because:

• The accuracy and computational efficiency of the finite element method is dictated by type and distribution of finite elements.

• The generation of the finite element mode dominates the cost of application of the finite element method. Its construction typically represents 70–80% of the total cost.

• The finite element mesh is the approximate representation of the domain to which solution results will be tied. It represents a basic component of the information used for visualization processes.

The next subsection indicates the methods used to generate finite element meshes. The following subsection mentions the area of adaptive techniques to control the mesh to provide the desired level of accuracy.

3.4.1 Mesh Generation

In the early application of the finite element method there was no computerized representation of the domain, and few tools were available to generate the finite element mesh. Therefore, the finite element meshes were manually drawn and converted into the computer by creating input "decks" defining each and every finite element entity. As computing hardware began to mature, and interactive graphics techniques became cost effective, interactive finite element preprocessors became available. These programs provided users with tools to interactively define the boundaries of mesh patches, which could then be filled with finite elements using appropriate mapping procedures. These programs had a major impact on the finite element model generation process. However, they still represented a bottom-up approach to the generation of the domain to be analyzed in terms of finite element mesh entities.

Over the years these finite element preprocessors have been extended to allow simple links with computer-aided geometric modeling systems. These links allow users to import basic boundary entities from the geometric modeling system, which can then be manipulated and used in the construction of the finite element entities which bound mesh patches. Today the majority of finite element meshes are generated using these interactive graphics tools based on these techniques.

Recently, fully automatic mesh generators, capable of operating directly with the CAD representation to produce meshes of domains without user interaction, have been introduced [9, 22]. An automatic mesh generator can be defined as an algorithmic procedure which can create a mesh, under program control and without user input or intervention. All automatic mesh generation approaches must address the same basic issues of

• Determining a distribution of mesh vertices to provide the form of mesh gradation requested.

• Constructing the higher order finite element entities of mesh edges, faces and regions using the node points, and

• Ensuring the resulting triangulation represents a valid finite element mesh.

The primary differences in the approaches developed are the manner in which they perform the steps above. At one end of the spectrum are techniques which

(i) place all the mesh vertices throughout the domain to be meshed, (ii) apply a criterion to connect the points to create a set of elements, and (iii) apply an assurance algorithm to convert the initial triangulation into a geometric triangulation. At the other end of the spectrum is a technique that works directly off the geometric model, carefully removing elements one at a time, creating individual mesh vertices on an as needed basis, and ensuring that at each step in the process the requirements of a geometric triangulation are satisfied.

Currently four algorithmic approaches receiving considerable attention are Delaunay [2, 5, 20], advancing front [3, 15], medial axis [12, 27], and octree techniques [4, 14, 20, 24].

An example of an automatic mesh generator is the Finite Octree procedure in which the mesh is generated as a two-step meshing process [24]. In the first step the geometric domain is discretized into a set of discrete cells that are stored in a regular tree structure, referred to as the Finite Octree. In the second step the individual cells within the Finite Octree are discretized into finite elements, with specific care to ensure the proper matching to the elements in the neighboring cells. All of the individual operations performed during the mesh generation process are performed in such a manner to ensure the result is a geometric triangulation of the original domain [21, 25].

The construction of the Finite Octree can be easily visualized by first placing the domain to be meshed into a parallelopiped cell, typically a cube, which encloses it. This original cell, which represents the root of the Finite Octree, is subdivided into its eight octants, which represent the eight cells at the first level of the tree. Each of these cells can be recursively subdivided into its eight octants producing the next level in the tree for that cell. Since the finite elements to be generated in the second step are of the size of the individual cells, element size and gradation are controlled by those cells that are subdivided, and how many times they are subdivided. The regular tree structure of the Finite Octree supports efficient procedures to generate the resulting mesh.

An important difference between the Finite Octree representation, and a basic octree decomposition of a domain, is that during the generation of the Finite Octree a cell level discrete representation of the portion of the domain within the cell is constructed. This construction is simple for the cells entirely inside or outside the object being meshed. It is those cells that contain portions of the boundary of the domain for which carefully structured geometric interrogation processes are required to ensure that the discrete cell level representation is topologically equivalent and geometrically similar to the portion of the geometric domain in that cell. The discrete geometric information generated during this process is stored in a non-manifold topological data structure, a compact form of which is also used to store the final mesh [29]. Figure 3.5 shows a Finite Octree decomposition of the model shown in Figure 3.2.

The finite element mesh is generated on a cell-by-cell basis using a set of element removal operators. The cell level element removal procedures employ the pointwise geometric interrogations to ensure that the resulting mesh is topologically compatible and geometrically similar to the geometric domain. When a cell is meshed, the information in the Finite Octree, and a non-manifold topological

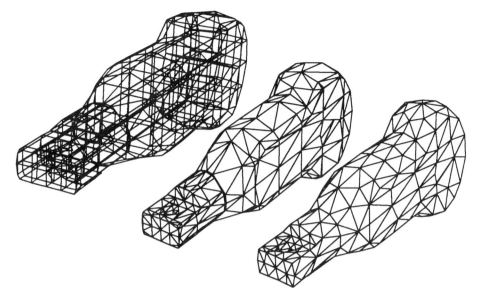

Figure 3.5 Finite Octree decomposition of domain (left), element mesh after element removal (center), and after mesh finalization (right) for the example problem.

data structure, is used to ensure that it will properly match the mesh in any neighboring cells that have already been meshed. After the mesh has been generated a specific set of finalization procedures are applied to eliminate poorly shaped elements and to reposition the node points to improve the shapes of those that are maintained. Figure 3.5 shows the mesh for the example problem after the application of the element removal procedures and after the finalization procedures are applied.

For a more complete technical explanation of the Finite Octree mesh generation procedure the interested reader is referred to Reference [24].

3.4.2 Adaptive Finite Element Mesh Control

Since the accuracy of the solution obtained is a function of the finite element mesh, it is critical that the type and distribution of finite elements within the domain be controlled. Broadly speaking the methods to control the finite element discretization can be grouped as *a priori* and *a posteriori*. In *a priori* methods, the individual generating the mesh exercises explicit control on the type and distribution of finite elements, based on their knowledge of the physical problem being solved. Since the individual analyzing the problem does not have perfect knowledge of the problem (if they had that knowledge, they would not need a finite element analysis), the *a priori* methods can provide a computationally efficient mesh, but the actual accuracy of the analysis is not known. The goal of *a posteriori* mesh control is to employ the results of the previous analysis to estimate the mesh discretization errors and then improve, in an optimal manner, the mesh until the desired degree of accuracy is obtained. Such *a posteriori* mesh control capabilities, referred to as *adaptive methods,* are capable of generating efficient meshes for a wide variety of problems as well as providing explicit error values [1, 7, 16, 17, 18].

The combination of an automatic mesh generator and adaptive analysis techniques allows the reliable automation of finite element analysis. The main components of such an automated adaptive finite element procedure are:

- An automatic mesh generator that can create valid graded meshes in arbitrarily complex domains
- A finite element analysis procedure capable of solving the given physical problem
- An *a posteriori* error estimation procedure to predict the mesh discretization errors, and to indicate where it must be improved
- A mesh enrichment procedure to update the mesh discretization

Clearly, the *a posteriori* error estimation procedures are central to the ability of an adaptive procedure to reliably control the mesh discretization errors. The approaches that have been developed to estimate the errors range from simple indicators that indicate where the solution variables are changing rapidly, to procedures that convert the residuals of the approximate solution to bounded estimates of the errors in norms, e.g., measures, of interest.

There are also a number of possible methods to enrich the finite element discretization based on the results of the error estimation and correction process. They include (i) moving nodes in a fixed mesh topology (r-refinement), (ii) subdividing selected elements in the mesh into smaller elements (h-refinement), (iii) increasing the order of polynomials (p-refinement), and (iv) superimposing selective enriched mesh overlays (s-refinement). Each of these methods has relative advantages and disadvantages. Often, a combination of methods provides the most effective strategy. For example, the optimal combination of h- and p-refinement has been shown, both theoretically and numerically, to provide greatly improved computational efficiency over the application of a single method.

Figure 3.6 shows a comparison of *a priori* and adaptive *a posteriori* mesh control. The mesh on the left was defined using *a priori* mesh control, where the user specified a finer mesh at the common areas of stress concentration around the holes. This mesh was then used as an initial mesh in an adaptive analysis procedure, aiming for less than the 5% error, that produces the mesh on the right. A comparison of the two meshes indicates that the initial mesh was not fine enough around two holes and at specific reentrant corners, while it was finer than required around the third hole.

3.5
VISUALIZATION GOALS

Since the fundamental goal of visualization is effective communication, it is imperative to understand both the audience of the communication as well as the information that needs to be communicated. In the following section we describe

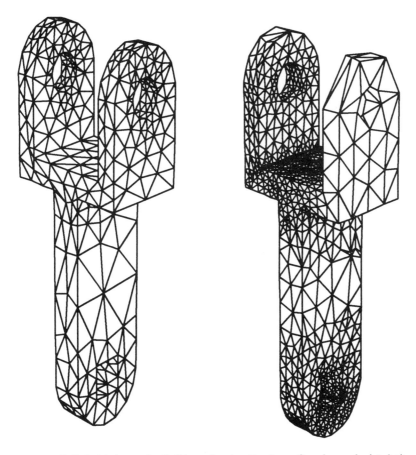

Figure 3.6 Initial mesh (left) and adaptively refined mesh (right) for the second automated adaptive example.

both the potential users of visualization in engineering analysis, as well as the results data that must be communicated to these users.

From the most general perspective the information available to the visualization process consists of the geometric description of the domain, the analysis attributes of loads material properties and boundary conditions defined in terms of that domain, and the distribution of the solution results of interest over that domain. What is actually available to the visualization process are two descriptions: the problem specification and attributes in terms of the original geometric model (e.g., CAD model), and the analysis results tied in a discrete manner to the computational mesh (e.g., finite element mesh).

The discussion given here focuses on the computational mesh description of the domain and attributes, and the results defined in terms of the mesh. An alternative approach is to visualize results data in terms of the original geometric description of the domain. Although we do not discuss this approach here, the basic idea is to perform an inverse mapping from the results data of the mesh to the original geometry. In either case the computational mesh, analysis attributes, and results data necessarily serve as the starting point for visualization.

3.5.1 Goals of Visualizing Results

The goal of the visualization process is to effectively communicate the potentially large data available from the engineering analysis process. Typical users of engineering analysis tools often fall into one of two categories: the *design* or *product* engineer, and the *methods* engineer or analyst.

The design engineer is generally interested in synthesis of function. Engineering analysis and visualization is used to perform overall evaluation of the product. The design engineer is typically looking for an understanding of a design or product in order to improve it. A typical example is designing a compressor blade in a jet engine. The design engineer looks carefully for stress concentrations and vibration response, and may adjust the structure to avoid resonance conditions or material fatigue problems. Numerical values are often required to characterize a particular design point, such as determining the peak magnitude of the stress, or to compare the natural frequencies of the compressor blade to upstream stimulus. The actual solution process of the engineering analysis is of little concern to the design engineer, as long as the solution is accurate enough for his needs.

In comparison, the analyst is generally interested in the details of the engineering analysis. Often the analyst is responsible for creating analysis tools for the design engineer to use, or performs analysis of particularly challenging analytical problems. Hence the primary concern of the analyst is the accuracy of results, and the sensitivity of results to variations in input parameters. This requires detailed understanding of the solution process. The analyst may also require information to guide the solution process, that is adjusting model and simulation inputs to provide proper convergence to solution. As a typical example, an analyst might evaluate the location of shock fronts in a supersonic flow analysis around a compressor blade in a jet engine. Effective visualization provides enough insight into the solution process to adjust parameters controlling numerical stability and modify analytical models as necessary.

3.5.2 Types of Analysis Variables to Be Visualized

The data available for visualization from engineering analysis can be roughly categorized into *mesh geometry* and the *solution data* associated with the mesh geometry. Although this classification is obvious in light of the previous discussion of engineering analysis techniques, this distinction between geometry and data is blurred in many visualization applications. In volume visualization the geometry is completely implicit, and the data available for visualization is assumed to be a series of values implicitly associated with a regular array of points. In finite difference analysis, the topology is implicitly assumed; (i.e., a regular array of points in conjunction with i-j-k dimensions), and the geometry is specified as an (implicitly) ordered sequence of coordinate locations.

Mesh geometry is the computational mesh including intermediate mesh geometry and topology hierarchy. For example, in three dimensions tetrahedral or hexahedral elements are often used to discretize the domain. Many visualization techniques require the triangle and quadrilateral faces of these elements for viewing results, or may require the ability to move across element boundaries (as in streamline generation). Mesh geometry also includes intermediate meshes from any enriched mesh overlays (s-refinement), or may be *time* dependent due to adaptive solution techniques or a truly transient analysis. Mesh geometry is generally used to form the viewing context for visualization techniques such as mapping color corresponding to stress level on the surface, or deforming the geometry according to the displacement field.

Solution data consists of both primary and secondary solution variables. The primary variables result directly from the solution process of the system of global equations (e.g., displacements in structural analysis), while secondary solution variables are typically related to derivatives of the primary variables (e.g., stresses or strains). In some cases, results data includes surface fluxes that may be associated with a particular face or edge of the element.

Visualization techniques are often characterized according to the form of solution data. Typical classifications include scalar data, vector data, and tensor data. Scalar data is an array of scalar (i.e., single-values, each value uniquely associated with a point in space. Examples include temperature or pressure data. Vector data is an array of n-dimensional vectors, where n is the dimension of the computational domain. Example vector data includes velocity, displacement, or momentum fields. Tensors are generalized specifications of data in the form of matrices. Common tensors include the second-order stress tensor (a 3×3 matrix in 3-D) and the fourth-order elastic stress-strain tensor (a 9×9 matrix in 3-D). Scalar and vector data are zero-order and first-order instances of tensors, respectively.

3.6
REPRESENTATION OF MESH AND RESULTS DATA

A major issue facing implementors of 3-D visualization systems is the representation of data. On the one hand, visualization systems must be as general as possible, since they must interface to a broad range of data sources. Visualization systems are also constrained by limitations on computer performance. Computer hardware vendors offer efficient paths for 3-D graphics by providing hardware-accelerated graphics primitives such as points, lines, and polygons. Using these primitives as compared to generating visualizations in software produces order of magnitude differences in speed. On the other hand, modern analysis systems depend upon sophisticated mathematical techniques for modelling complex physics. The result is that most visualization systems make significant compromises in both the representation and mapping of results data into visual representations in order to facilitate the interactive exploration of data.

This section describes a data structure that explicitly represents computational meshes and results data. This structure is not typical of most visualization systems. Some use structures quite similar to the hierarchical structures described here, and require limited mapping from one form to the next. Other visualization methods (e.g., volume visualization) represent data in terms of structures completely independent of the computational mesh. These methods may be properly referred to as sampling techniques, and the representation of this data is not treated here.

3.6.1 Mesh Geometry

Representations of mesh geometry are dependent upon the particular analysis techniques employed. For example, finite difference techniques use a topologically regular grid in conjunction with an ordered list of point coordinates to specify geometry. In the discussion that follows, mesh geometry is assumed to be of a finite element type. This type is the most general form, and other geometry types can be mapped into it.

Historically, the representations of a finite element mesh consisted of a *list of element connectivities and node point coordinates* (Figure 3.7 (a)). In particular, a type flag is used to represent the topology of the element, and an ordered list of nodes in combination with a list of nodal point coordinates is used to specify the geometry of the mesh. This information, combined with the knowledge of how to employ the element type flag, can be used to construct any information regarding the shape of an element. Although it is a compact structure, it lacks the generality needed for some of the more advanced finite elements and their combination with adaptive analysis procedures. A more general approach is to consider the hierarchy of topological entities and describe the finite elements in terms of these entities and their adjacencies.

Topological hierarchies provide a general framework for engineering analysis [23, 28, 29]. This means that topology is an explicit abstraction, which serves as an organizing structure for data. In engineering analysis, topology serves as the link between geometrically specified computational models (Figure 3.1) and the numerical methods (e.g., the mesh) necessary to solve these problems (Figure 3.2). Organizing data according to topology shields the user from the details of the geometric representation (splines, implicit surfaces, etc.) and computational mesh, while providing a mechanism to map information from one representation to the other.

A simple hierarchical structure for mesh geometry is shown in Figure 3.7(b). The topology of each n-dimensional element is defined in terms of its $(n - 1)$-dimensional boundaries. Each n-dimensional topological entity may also have a geometric specification (i.e., shape and location) associated with it. For example, a vertex is associated with a position in space, an edge with a parametric space, and a face with a spline surface.

Advanced modeling of composite structures, evolving and or non-manifold geometry, and adaptive analysis techniques benefit greatly from the addition of additional *classification, adjacency,* and *use* information. Classification is a necessary step for rigorous generation of finite element meshes, and is simply an association of each entity in the mesh topological hierarchy with a corresponding topological entity in the original geometric model [19, 21]. Classification information is the hook that allows mapping problem specifications in terms of geometry to a discretized computational model, and then back again to visualize results. Adjaceny information is the relationship in terms of physical proximity and order of one topological entity to another. An example of one adjacency relationship is the group of faces in cyclic order around an edge. Use information is a modeling convenience that specifies the way one topological entity is used in the

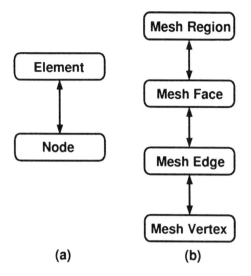

(a)   **(b)**

Figure 3.7 Traditional mesh structure (a)
and hierarchical structure(b).

definition of another; (e.g., the direction or orientation of the defining topology). Both adjacency and use information are useful in complex analytical problems such as evolving geometry, where boundary contact occurs and modification to the underlying geometric representation is required.

3.6.2 Data Representation

As described previously the results data from a finite element analysis may consist of scalar (zero order tensor), vector (1st order tensors), or tensor information. The location of this information may be on element nodes, within the element at interior points, or possibly on the element boundary.

The hierarchical mesh geometry representation is a convenient structure in which to house this information. Scalar, vector, or tensor data located at element nodes is associated with the mesh vertices. Surface or edge fluxes are associated with the faces or edges. Interior element data are associated with the region. In some cases the interior element data may be extrapolated to, and stored with, the mesh vertices.

A particularly important issue is the native representational form of the analysis results. That is, if the analysis system generates results in double precision form, the visualization system should represent data in native form as well. This is particularly important when the results are of small size (byte or short), since representing a small type with a large type can unnecessarily consume enormous memory resources. Related to this issue is computational form: visualization algorithms should use enough accuracy to produce correct visualizations.

Probably the overriding issue in representing analysis results is choosing a compact representational form. Since the expressed purpose of visualization is to effectively communicate information, visualization systems are most effective when they can treat large data.

3.7
MAPPING ANALYSIS RESULTS TO VISUALIZATIONS

Producing visualizations requires mapping results data into visual representations. Typical procedures involve either sampling the results data on a regular grid (i.e., volume visualization), or conversion of analytical forms (nodes and elements) into graphical forms (points, lines, polygons). Once this mapping is accomplished, the techniques described in later chapters of this book are applied to generate the visual images. The remainder of this chapter provides an overview of the mapping from results data into forms necessary for visualization. Particular emphasis is placed on the approximations and potential errors involved in the mapping process.

3.7.1 Extrapolation and Interpolation

Because of the nature of engineering analysis, solution data is available at a finite set of points within the computational mesh. Primary solution variables are typically available at node points of the mesh, while secondary variables are often calculated at points interior to the element where they are known to be more accurate. The discrete nature of solution data is of major concern in the visualization process, because information is frequently required at locations other than that directly available from the solution. Hence this information must be derived by performing both interpolation or extrapolation, depending upon the location of the solution data. Generally this mapping process requires an intimate knowledge of the analysis technique, and should be carried out using the same element approximation functions used for formulation of the system equations.

Extrapolation is used when results data is available interior to mesh elements, and a data value is desired in outer regions such as element node locations. Results data is frequently available only at select interior points, because solution accuracy is known to be greatest there. Extrapolating stresses from integration points to element nodes is a typical example.

A simple extrapolation scheme is based on normalizing the element shape functions so that the integration points are located at the corners (i.e., at $\xi = (\pm 1)$), and then evaluating the data at the element node points. Another common extrapolation scheme is based on the least squares process. Typically, interior values are known interior to an element on a small array of points (e.g., $2 \times 2 \times 2$ or $3 \times 3 \times 3$) located in the parametric space of the element. Stresses are assumed to vary as a product of low order polynomials (usually linear or quadratic), and the least squares coefficients are generated from the integration point values and evaluated at the element nodes.

There are two major difficulties with extrapolation. When extrapolating from the element interior to the node points, different values for each node will be generated from each of the elements that use that node. The usual approach in this situation is to average the contributions from each element to generate a single value. Extrapolation may also produce errors as a result of the difference between the order of the approximation function in the element and the actual physics of the problem. In elliptic partial differential equations the maximum value will always occur at the domain boundary and extrapolation techniques produce results that underestimate peak values. Analytic solutions of stress concentrations around geometric features clearly show polynomial rates of stress increase much higher than the extrapolation equations above.

Interpolation is used when results data is available throughout a region of the element, and a data value is desired within that region. The most common case arises when results data is available at the element nodes, and an interior element data value is required. Interpolation is based on the element shape functions of Equation 3.1, where in this case U represents results data available at the element nodes.

A common problem with both extrapolation and interpolation techniques is that they require specifying locations (where a data value is desired) in terms of the element coordinate system. Unfortunately many visualization algorithms specify point location in global coordinates. Hence the use of interpolation and extrapolation techniques frequently requires transforming a global coordinate into an element coordinate. This process involves identifying the particular element the point is in, as well as solving Equation 3.25 for the element coordinates ξ. Because the element geometry functions are typically products of polynomials, closed-form solutions are generally not available. Instead, numerical techniques such as Newton's method can be used to solve the systems of equations for the element coordinates [6].

3.7.2 Mapping to Visualization Forms

There are two common approaches to mapping engineering analysis data into visualizations. These are 1) data sampling and 2) conversion of mesh geometry and results data directly into graphical primitives.

Data sampling is a conceptually simple process (Figure 3.8(a)). Results data are sampled on a structured array of points using interpolation and/or extrapolation. The user need only specify the resolution and position of the sampling array, taking care to sample at a high enough frequency to capture the details of the solution. Standard volume visualization techniques (Chapter 6) are then used to generate the visual images.

Data sampling is particularly useful for visualizing analysis results based on higher-order shape functions, or for selected regions within the domain. A significant problem with this method is that the data size of the sampled data grows with the cube of the sampling density, since current techniques are not adaptive. Hence, the danger is that limitations on computer resource may result in errors due to undersampling the results data.

Conversion of results data to graphics primitives is another common mapping technique. This process involves matching element types to available graphics primitives (Figure 3.8(b)). For a small set of linear element types (i.e., points, lines, triangles, and quadrilaterals) this mapping is direct, as long as results data is available at the element nodes, otherwise extrapolation needs to be employed. Other linear 3-D elements such as hexahedra and tetrahedra can be decomposed by

79

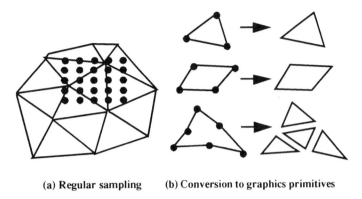

(a) Regular sampling   (b) Conversion to graphics primitives

Figure 3.8 Sampling data (a) and primitive conversion (b).

mapping the element faces to triangles and quadrilaterals. Higher order elements are often broken into many primitives depending upon the topology of the elements and possibly the nature of the solution within the element.

Mapping to graphics primitives is the most common technique today, since it provides information that graphics hardware can efficiently process. This results in highly interactive visualization systems. The basic problem with this approach is that decomposing non-linear elements into linear graphics primitives results in significant loss of accuracy. Decomposition of higher order elements is particulary difficult because of the complex topology of the element. The decomposition should also be driven by the particulars of the analytical solution, which is rarely performed in practice.

Another important effect during the mapping of results data to visualizations is due to the linear interpolation schemes employed during the rendering process. This effect is common to both data sampling and primitive conversion techniques (Figure 3.9). Data sampling techniques depend upon volume rendering to gener-

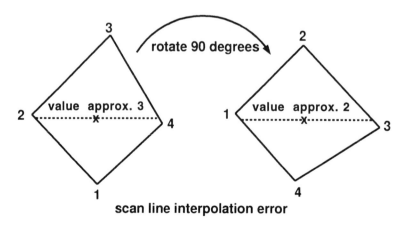

Figure 3.9 The application of basic linear interpolation

ate the image. Volume rendering in turn uses nearest neighbor or tri-linear interpolation methods to generate data values. These methods generate interpolated values different from that obtained by using element shape functions, especially for higher order elements such as those employed in the adaptive *p-refinement* finite element method. The primitive conversion technique suffers a similar problem, since a linear interpolation scheme is employed during the rendering (i.e., scan conversion) process. Also, because the relative orientation of the graphics primitives may vary with respect to the direction of the scan conversion, the interpolation process will generate different visualizations depending upon the orientation of the primitives.

3.8
SUMMARY

Typical modern engineering and analysis techniques are based upon discretizing a problem domain into small pieces, or elements. Over each element an approximation function is used to represent the behavior of the element in terms of unknown solution variables. These variables are gathered into large systems of equations and then solved on a computer. The results of this computation can be further processed to yield derivatives and other related solution variables. The forms of these data are usually scalar, vector, or arbitrary tensor. Visualization techniques are then used to map the solution information back into the original problem domain.

Visualization is a relatively young field, and significant improvements are needed to better support engineering analysis. A major problem is that analysis and visualization are often viewed as disconnected activities. Visualization techniques must be tightly coupled with engineering analysis to accurately convey the full form and range of results data. Computer graphics vendors also must be encouraged to directly support advanced visualization functionality such as higher-order graphics primitives and/or programmable interpolation functions. New visualization techniques must be developed to extend current scalar and vector techniques, and to provide effective tensor visualization.

3.9
APPENDIX: CONSTRUCTION AND DISCRETIZATION OF WEAK FORM OF THE GOVERNING EQUATIONS

Weak forms representing the mathematical description of a physical problem can either be directly stated in terms of some integral principal, or can be constructed from the governing differential equations. Assume the mathematical description of a boundary value problem of interest is given as a second order partial differential equation form as[2]:

---

2. Consideration of higher order partial differential equations, and initial value problems where time is also an independent variable, adds to the terms considered here. However, the primary issues discussed are the same. Specific comments on accounting for time are given in later sections.

Given $f : \Omega \rightarrow \Re, g : \Gamma_g \rightarrow \Re$, and $\underline{h} : \Gamma_h \rightarrow \Re$, find $\underline{u}$ such that $\qquad$ [3.9]

$$\mathcal{D}^2\left(\underline{u}\right) - \underline{f} = 0 \text{ on } \Omega$$

$$\underline{u} = \underline{g} \text{ on } \Gamma_g \qquad\qquad\qquad [3.10]$$

$$\mathcal{B}^1\left(\underline{u}\right) = \mathcal{F}\left(\underline{\sigma}\right) = \underline{h} \text{ on } \Gamma_h$$

where $\underline{u}$ is the primary dependent variable, f is the forcing function, g are pre-scribed boundary conditions, $\underline{h}$ are prescribed flux conditions, $\mathcal{D}^2$ is a second order differential operator, $\mathcal{B}^1$ is a first order differential operator, $\mathcal{F}(\underline{\sigma})$ is an algebraic operator acting on the fluxes $\underline{\sigma}$, Ω is the domain of the analysis, Γ_g is the portion of the boundary on which the prescribed boundary conditions are prescribed, and Γ_h is the portion of the boundary on which the prescribed flux conditions are prescribed.

Solid mechanics is one such problem area where the dependent variables, $\underline{u}$, are the displacements, the forcing functions, $\underline{f}$, are body loads, the prescribed boundary conditions are displacements, g, and tractions, $\underline{h}$, and the secondary variables of interest are the stresses, $\underline{\sigma}$. As discussed later, the users of the finite element analysis procedures are interested in visualization of both the primary and secondary variables of interest.

A common method to construct a weak form of the partial differential equations (see Equation 3.9), begins by multiplying the domain equation by a weighting function, integrating over the domain, and setting that to zero.

$$\int_{\Omega} \underline{w}\left(\mathcal{D}^2(\underline{u}) - \underline{f}\right) d\Omega = 0 \qquad\qquad [3.11]$$

If Equation 3.11 is satisfied for all admissible weighting functions $\underline{w}$, and the boundary conditions of Equation 3.10 are satisfied, the exact solution to the problem is obtained. Obtaining this solution is as difficult as solving the original system Equations 3.9 and 3.10. The advantage of the weak form comes when finite dimensional spaces are used for the weighting and trial functions, $\underline{w}$ and $\underline{u}$, respectively. In this case the solution to Equation 3.11 provides only a weighted integral solution to Equation 3.9, since Equation 3.11, which is only an approximate solution, will not in general be satisfied at all points.

Although it is possible to directly construct approximate numerical solutions to the basic weighted integral form of Equation 3.11, it is not a convenient form for two major reasons. It requires trial and weight functions that must satisfy all boundary conditions as does Equation 3.10 in their full and homogeneous form, respectively. Commonly applied weighted residual methods perform mathematical manipulations which yield more convenient integral forms. For example, by the proper application of integration by parts and the divergence theorem, Equation 3.11 can be manipulated to produce an equivalent, but more useful, weak form:

Given $\underline{f} : \Omega \to \Re$ and $\underline{g_i} : \Gamma_i \to \Re$, $\underline{u} = \underline{g}$ on Γ_g, $\qquad$ [3.12]

and $\underline{w} = 0$ on Γ_g, find $\underline{u}$ such that

$$\int_\Omega \mathcal{H}^1(\underline{w})(G^1(\underline{u})) d\Omega = \int_\Omega \underline{wf} d\Omega + \int_{\Gamma_h} \underline{w\underline{h}} d\Gamma$$

for all admissible weight functions $\underline{w}$, where $\mathcal{H}^1$ and G^1 are first order differential operators which depend on $\mathcal{D}^2$ and the mathematical manipulations. In Equation 3.12 it was assumed that the mathematical manipulations were performed such that the last integral did recover the natural boundary condition term, $\underline{h}$.

It is convenient at this point to introduce the commonly used abstract operators, with specific properties, for the individual terms in Equation 3.12. This allows the direct application of the discretization procedure outlined below to any class of problem which satisfies the operators' properties [13, 26]. For the current example define

$$a(\underline{w},\underline{u}) = \int_\Omega \mathcal{H}^1(\underline{w})(G^1(\underline{u})) d\Omega \qquad [3.13]$$

$$(\underline{w},\underline{f}) = \int_\Omega \underline{wf} d\Omega \qquad [3.14]$$

$$(\underline{w},\underline{h})_\Gamma = \int_{\Gamma_h} \underline{w\underline{h}} d\Gamma \qquad [3.15]$$

With this notation Equation 3.12 becomes

$$a(\underline{w},\underline{u}) = (\underline{w},\underline{f}) + (\underline{w},\underline{h})_\Gamma \qquad [3.16]$$

Following Reference [13], the discretization of Equation 3.16 to yield the form used by numerical methods begins by approximating the infinite dimensional spaces for $\underline{u}$ and $\underline{w}$ with finite dimensional spaces $\underline{u}^h$ and $\underline{w}^h$. To satisfy non-zero essential boundary conditions while selecting functions from spaces satisfying the appropriate boundary conditions, it is convenient to write

$$\underline{u}^h = \underline{v}^h + \underline{g}^h \qquad [3.17]$$

The terms $\underline{v}^h$ and $\underline{w}^h$ must satisfy homogeneous essential boundary conditions, $\underline{w}^h = \underline{v}^h = 0$ on Γ_g, and $\underline{g}^h$ must satisfy, at least approximately, the essential boundary conditions, $\underline{g}^h = \underline{g}$ on Γ_g. Substitution of these functions into Equation 3.16 yields

$$a(\underline{w}^h,\underline{v}^h) = (\underline{w}^h,\underline{f}) + (\underline{w}^h,\underline{h})_\Gamma - a(\underline{w}^h,\underline{g}^h) \qquad [3.18]$$

which must hold for any admissible weighting functions $\underline{w}^h$.

In the finite element method the domain being analyzed is discretized into a set of finite elements over which the functions $\underline{v}^h$ and $\underline{w}^h$ are written in terms of degrees of freedom (**dof**) times piecewise functions that are nonzero over only a small subset of the finite elements, typically those that share the **dof**. In equation form these functions can be written as[3]

$$\underline{w}^h = \sum_{A \in n - n_g} N_A c_A \qquad [3.19]$$

and

$$\underline{v}^h = \sum_{A \in n - n_g} N_A d_A \qquad [3.20]$$

where N_A are shape functions, typically piecewise polynomials, c_A are constants and d_A are the **dof** that are to be determined. The use of capital subscripts indicates a function or multiplier associated with the global system.

Since $\underline{v}^h$ and $\underline{w}^h$ satisfy only the homogeneous version of the essential boundary conditions, and the trial functions, $\underline{u}^h$, must satisfy the essential boundary conditions, it is convenient to expand the function $\underline{g}^h$ as

$$\underline{g}^h = \sum_{A \in n_q} N_A g_A \qquad [3.21]$$

where N_A and g_A are constructed to satisfy the essential boundary exactly, in a pointwise sense, or in an integrated sense.

Substitution of Equations 3.19, 3.20 and 3.21 into Equation 3.18 yields

$$a \left(\sum_{A \in n - n_g} N_A c_A, \sum_{B \in n - n_g} N_B d_B \right) = \left(\sum_{A \in n - n_g} N_A c_A, \underline{f} \right) + \left(\sum_{A \in n - n_g} N_A c_A, \underline{h} \right)_\Gamma \qquad [3.22]$$

$$- a \left(\sum_{A \in n - n_g} N_A c_A, \sum_{B \in n_g} N_B g_B \right)$$

Based on the properties of the operators used Equation 3.22 can be rewritten as

$$\sum_{A \in n - n_g} c_A \qquad [3.23]$$

$$\left[\sum_{B \in n - n_g} a(N_A, N_B) d_B - (N_A, \underline{f}) - (N_A, \underline{h})_\Gamma + \sum_{B \in n_g} a(N_A, N_B) g_B \right]$$

$$= 0$$

Since the weighting functions are arbitrary, the individual multipliers c_A in

---

3. In the simplified expressions given here the vector expressions are directly expressed in terms of the element shape functions. In a more detailed explanation of the finite element method it is common to write the expansions in terms of the individual vector components.

Equation 3.23 can take on any value. This means the term in the square brackets must be equal to zero for all values of A. That is:

$$\sum_{B \in n - n_g} a\left(N_A, N_B\right) d_B = \left(N_A, \underline{f}\right) + \left(N_A, \underline{h}\right)_\Gamma - \qquad [3.24]$$

$$\sum_{B \in n_g} a\left(N_A, N_B\right) g_B, A \in n - n_g$$

which represents a set of algebraic equations which can be written in matrix form

$$\mathbf{Kd = F} \qquad [3.25]$$

where the terms in the vector $\mathbf{d}$ are the unknown degrees of freedom, and the terms in the stiffness matrix, $\mathbf{K}$, and load vector, $\mathbf{F}$, are given by

$$K_{PQ} = a\left(N_A, N_B\right) \qquad [3.26]$$

and

$$F_p = \left(N_A, \underline{f}\right) + \left(N_A, \underline{h}\right)_\Gamma - \sum_{B \in n_q} a\left(N_A, N_B\right) g_B \qquad [3.27]$$

The subscripts P and Q range over the number of **dof** in the problem and are related to the subscripts A and B through a mapping process that tracks the fact that some of the possible **dof** are associated with **dof** in the final problem and other potential **dof**, $A, B \in n - n_g$, are used to account for the essential boundary conditions, $B \in n_g$.

A key to the effective application of finite element methods is the ability to calculate the terms in the stiffness matrix of Equation 3.25 with element contributions. To give an indication of the key aspects of that process, consider the case where the individual **dof**, d_P corresponds to the nodal values of the unknown field, the finite element mesh consists of three-noded triangles, and the global shape function, N_A is a piecewise linear function which has a value of **one** at the node of interest and **zero** at the edges opposite the vertex (left side of Figure 3.10). In

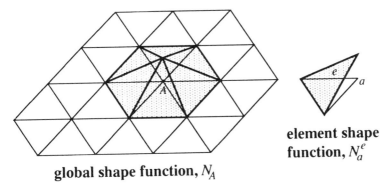

global shape function, N_A

**element shape
function,** N_a^e

Figure 3.10 Global shape function and one of its elemental contributions

finite element methods the global shape function is constructed as the appropriate sum of elemental shape functions, N_a^e, (right side of Figure 3.10) where the superscript identifies an element and the lowercase subscript identifies the degrees of freedom on the elemental level.

The integral operators, Equations 3.10–3.15, can be written one element at a time to yield the elemental stiffness matrix, $\mathbf{k}^e$ and load vector $\mathbf{f}^e$, where the individual terms are given in terms of the elemental **dof** as

$$k_{pq}^e = a\left(N_a, N_b\right) \qquad [3.28]$$

and

$$f_p^e = \left(N_a, \underline{f}\right) + \left(N_a, \underline{h}\right)_{\Gamma} - \sum_{b \in n_q} a\left(N_a, N_b\right) g_b \qquad [3.29]$$

here the integrations are over the domain of the element and its appropriate boundary segments. Since the local **dof** have an equivalence to the global **dof**, and the properties of the integral operators and shape functions are such that the integral of a sum of element contributions is equal to the sum of the integrals of the element contributions, the global equations can be constructed by the appropriate summation of element contributions represented by

$$\mathbf{K} = \overline{\sum_{e=1}^{nel} \mathbf{k}^e} \,,\, \mathbf{F} = \overline{\sum_{e=1}^{nel} \mathbf{f}^e} \qquad [3.30]$$

where the summation process adds the terms for the element matrices into the correct locations of the global matrices based on the mapping of local to global **dof** labeling.

3.10
REFERENCES

[1] I. Babuska, O. C. Zienkiewicz, J. Gago, and d. A. Oliveria, editors. *Accuracy Estimates and Adaptive Refinements in Finite Element Computations.* John Wiley, Chichester, 1986.

[2] T. J. Baker. Automatic mesh generation for complex three-dimensional regions using a constrained Delaunay triangulation. *Engineering with Computers, 5:* pages 161–175, 1989.

[3] T. D. Blacker and M. B. Stephenson. Paving: "A new approach to automated quadrilateral mesh generation." *Int. J. Numer. Meth. Engng.,* 32(4): pages 811–847, 1991.

[4] E. K. Buratynski. "A fully automatic three-dimensional mesh generator for complex geometries." *Int. J. Numer. Meth. Engng.,* 30: pages 931–952, 1990.

[5] J. C. Cavendish, D. A. Field, and W. H. Frey. "An approach to automatic three-dimensional mesh generation." *Int. J. Numer. Meth. Engng.,* 21: pages 329–347, 1985.

[6] S. D. Conte and C. de Boor. *Elementary Numerical Analysis.* McGraw Hill Book Co., New York, NY, 1972.

[7] J. E. Flaherty, P. J. Paslow, M. S. Shephard, and J. D. Vasilakis, editors. *Adaptive Methods for partial Differential Equations.* SIAM, Philadelphia, PA, 1989.

[8] R. H. Gallagher. *Finite Element Analysis: Fundamentals.* Prentice Hall, Englewood Cliffs, NJ, 1975.

[9] P. L. George. *Automatic Mesh Generation.* John Wiley and Sons, Ltd, Chichester, 1991.

[10] W. J. Gordon and C. A. Hall. "Transfinite element methods: Blending function interpolation over arbitrary curved element domain." *Int. J. Numer. Meth. Engng.,* 21: pages 109–129, 1973.

[12] H. N. Gursoy and N. M. Patrikalakis. "Automatic interrogation and adaptive subdivision of shape using medial axis transform." *Advances in Engineering Software,* 13: pages 287–302, 1991.

References

[13] T. J. R. Hughes. *The Finite Element Method: Linear Static and Dynamic Finite Element Analysis.* Prentice Hall, Englewood Cliffs, NJ, 1987.

[14] A. Kela. "Hierarchical octree approximations for boundary representation-based geometric models." *Computer Aided Design,* 21: pages 355–362, 1989.

[15] R. Löhner and P. Parilch. "Three-dimensional grid generation by the advancing front method." *Int. J. Num. Meths. Fluids,* 8: pages 1135–1149, 1988.

[16] A. K. Noor, editor. *Adaptive, Multilevel and Hierarchical Computational Strategies.* ASME, 345 East 47th Street, NY, NY, 1992.

[17] J. T. Oden, editor. *Computer Methods in Applied Mechanics and Engineering,* volume 82. North Holland, 1990. Special issue devoted to the reliability of finite element computations.

[18] J. T. Oden and L. Demkowicz, editors. *Computer Methods in Applied Mechanics and Engineering,* volume 101. North Holland, 1992. Second special issue devoted to the reliability of finite element computations.

[19] W. J. Schroeder. *Geometric Triangulations: with Application to Fully Automatic 3D Mesh Generation.* PhD thesis, Rensselaer Polytechnic Institute, Scientific Computation Research Center, RPI, Troy, NY 12180-3590, May 1991.

[20] W. J. Schroeder and M. S. Shephard. "A combined octree/Delaunay method for fully automatic 3-D mesh generation." *Int. J. Numer. Meth. Engng.,* 29: pages 37–55, 1990.

[21] W. J. Schroeder and M. S. Shephard. "On rigorous conditions for automatically generated finite element meshes." In J. turner, J. Pegna, and M. Wozny, editors, *Product Modeling for Computer-Aided Design and manufacturing,* pages 267–281. North Holland, 1991.

[22] M. S. Shephard. "Approaches to the automatic generation and control of finite element meshes." *Applied Mechanics Review,* 41(4): pages 169–185, 1988.

[23] M. S. Shephard and P. M. Finnigan. "Toward automatic model generation." In A. K. Noor and J. T. Oden, editors, *State-of-the-Art Surveys on Computational Mechanics,* pages 335–366. ASME, 1989.

[24] M. S. Shephard and M. K. Georges. "Automatic three-dimensional mesh generation of the Finite Octree technique." *Int. J. Numer. Meth. Engng.,* 32(4): pages 709–749, 1991.

[25] M. S. Shephard and M. K. Georges. "Reliability of automatic 3-D mesh generation." *Comp. Meth. Appl. Mech. Engng.,* 101: pages 443–462, 1992.

[26] B. A. Szabo and I. Babuska. *Finite Element Analysis.* Wiley Interscience, New York, 1991.

[27] T. K. H. Tam and C. G. Armstrong. "2-D finite element mesh generation by medial axis subdivision." *Advances in Engng. Software,* 13(⅚): pages 313–324, 1991.

[28] K. J. Weiler. *Topological Structures for Geometric Modeling.* PhD thesis, Rensselaer Design Research Center, Rensselaer Polytechnic Institute, Troy, NY, May 1986.

[29] K. J. Weiler. "The radial-edge structure: A topological representation for non-manifold geometric boundary representations." In M. J. Wozny, H. W. McLaughlin, and J. L. Encarnacao, editors, *Geometric Modeling for CAD Applications,* pages 3–36. North Holland, 1988.

[30] O. C. Zienkiewicz and R. L. Taylor. *The Finite Element Method—Volume 1.* McGraw Hill Book Co., New York, 4th edition, 1987.

CHAPTER

Scalar Visualization Techniques

RICHARD S. GALLAGHER

THE DISPLAY OF a single variable in space represents one of the earliest applications of computer graphics to the display of behavior. These techniques have evolved from simple color coding and contour displays to newer 3-D visualization techniques. The trends in this area are toward a better understanding of scalar variables throughout a full 3-D domain. Most scalar visualization techniques use a consistent approach across one-, two-, or three-dimensional fields. Practical application of these in analysis problems often requires adapting these approches to irregular, discrete geometric fields such as finite element and boundary element models. This chapter explores the most common approaches currently used to visualize scalar variables within these fields.

4.1
INTRODUCTION

One of the most common operations in the three-dimensional display of behavior is the display of a single variable within a three-dimensional field.

Quantities such as equivalent stress, temperature, or the estimated error of a solution itself are generally represented as two- or three-dimensional fields of a single variable. These scalar visualization techniques help engineers and analysts answer some of the basic questions of analysis, such as "Did it fail?" or "Is it experiencing too high a temperature?"

A scalar variable is any single quantity which can be expressed as a function of its position in space and time, as in Equation 4.1. For a constant point in time, engineering analysis problems tend to represent scalar values as a set of result values at the vertices of coarse, irregular elements connected at these vertices.

$$\sigma = F(x,y,z,t) \qquad\qquad [4.1]$$

In the general case, a scalar field of this form can be visualized using local operations on elements, or global operations on the field itself. Local techniques, which are by far the most common, generate displays on an element-by-element basis using discrete symbols or field and isovalue displays across the element.

Global techniques, by comparison, operate on the overall scalar field. Such techniques can involve reducing the field to a volume continuum for visualization, or more specific approaches such as following the path of constant scalar values from element to element. Methods for the visualization of a global volume field are discussed in more detail in Chapter 6. Other examples of global field visualization include topology analysis, where local saddle points and critical points are determined within the field, and by *data probes,* which sample a field at points selected by the user.

Analysis display techniques for scalar variables once revolved around simple color-coding or the *contour plot,* where results are displayed as colored lines or regions painted on the exterior visible surfaces of a structure. More recent techniques attempt to show the full three-dimensional variation of a scalar variable within a volume field. These techniques include isosurfaces, particle clouds, volume slicing and sampling planes. These methods can be combined to allow analysts to see far beyond what is discernable from actual test data, and they are a logical step in the ultimate purpose of numerical methods in analysis—an evaluation of the true three-dimensional state of behavior within a model.

4.2
ONE-DIMENSIONAL SCALAR FIELDS

The most simple case of a scalar variable is a one-dimensional distribution of values. This can be represented physically as the variation of a scalar value along a parametric line, e.g., a single path in space. As with scalar fields of higher dimension, one can display the overall field, or individual isovalues (points of constant value) along the path.

Color coding, one of the more common methods for displaying a one-dimensional field, involves displaying sub-segments of the line with colors corresponding to the scalar value. In the limit, as these segments become infinitesimally small, this representation becomes a continuous tonal variation of color corresponding to the one-dimensional scalar field. An example of this is shown in Figure 4.1(a).

Normally, a color spectrum from blue to red is chosen, representing a natural variation from "cool" to "hot," showing critical values brightly visible in red. The mapping of such a contour spectrum to result values is expressed in Table 4.1.

The hue-lightness-saturation (HLS) model of color allows a direct mapping of the result value to a linear variation of hue, with fixed lightness and saturation values. These colors show the full, continuous hue range excluding the range from red to magenta to blue. Use of the RGB color model requires a discrete set of variations of red, green and blue values to produce the same color range.

The display of an individual value on a one-dimensional path is simply a matter of displaying a point on this path, interpolated between the endpoint

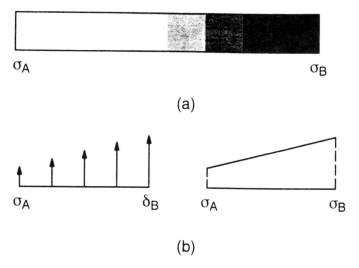

Figure 4.1. Methods of showing the variation of a scalar value in a one-dimensional field include color variation (a) and discrete symbols of off-path displays (b).

values. Alternatively, techniques such as discrete symbols or off-path displays of the scalar value can be used for a more direct physical representation of either individual regions or the overall field magnitude. Examples of these displays are shown in Figure 4.1(b).

4.3
TWO-DIMENSIONAL SCALAR FIELDS

Scalar fields in two parametric dimensions effectively represent a variable across one or more surfaces or subsegments of these surfaces. The display of such a field shows its variation over these surfaces. The simplest cases of this are techniques such as the display of a color-coded symbol at the centroid of each element,

TABLE 4.1   Color Values for Standard Result Range

Normalized result value	Hue(degrees)	RGB values	Color
0.000	0	0.0, 0.0, 1.0	Blue
0.125	30	0.0, 0.5, 1.0	Blue-Cyan
0.250	40	0.0, 1.0, 1.0	Cyan
0.375	90	0.0, 1.0, 0.5	Cyan-Green
0.500	120	0.0, 1.0, 0.0	Green
0.425	150	0.5, 1.0, 0.0	Green-Yellow
0.750	180	1.0, 1.0, 0.0	Yellow
0.875	210	1.0, 0.5, 0.0	Orange
1.000	240	1.0, 0.0, 0.0	Red

representing the average scalar value; the more general case displays a discrete or continuous scalar field across the domain.

Surface visualization techniques are important for three-dimensional domains as well. For many forms of engineering analysis, such as linear structural behavior, there is a truism that the most critical behavior occurs on the exterior of a structure. As a result, techniques described in this section remain in common usage for the visible surfaces of three- as well as two-dimensional problems.

The following sections describe the most common techniques used in engineering analysis for display of a two-dimensional scalar field, from the display of a single color value per element face, to discrete contour lines and regions, and finally the continuous tonal display of the field itself.

4.3.1 Element Face Color Coding

A quick overview of a scalar variable across the exterior of a model can be produced by setting the color of each visible element face of the model to correspond to the average scalar value across this face. This technique was particularly common with early computer graphics hardware platforms, on which the speed of displaying a single colored polygon from hardware far outstripped the speed at which more continuous displays could be computed and displayed. It is still used for a quick, general overview of a state of behavior.

Usually the original computed results are at vertices of elements, and these values are averaged to create a single centroidal value per face.

$$\sigma_c = \frac{\displaystyle\sum_{i=1,n} \sigma(i)}{n} \qquad\qquad [4.2]$$

where n is the number of vertices in the element and $\sigma(i)$ are the vertex result values. This value is then used to create a normalized value used to interpolate a color value from a color table ranging from a color for the minimum result value to a color for the maximum result value.

$$\text{color} = \frac{(\sigma_{\max} - \sigma_c)}{(\sigma_{\max} - \sigma_{\min})} \qquad\qquad [4.3]$$

where $\sigma_{\min}$ and $\sigma_{\max}$ represent the global maximum and minimum result values for the entire model, and the color value represents a normalized point on a color spectrum as described earlier. An example of this color coding is shown in Figure 4.2.

One noteworthy drawback to this technique is an accuracy problem that often occurs because of the nature of analysis result data. Color coding of polygons requires a single value for each visible element face, yet techniques such as the finite element method rarely compute such single values. More commonly, results are computed at face vertices, or at specified interior locations, such as the Gauss points located at specified interior parametric locations of the element.

Averaging these values to produce a single centroidal value, or directly computing a centroidal value using the element's shape functions, can result in a loss of extreme vertex or interior result values. Figure 4.3 shows the effects of aver-

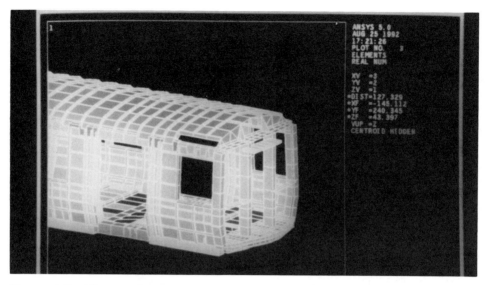

Figure 4.2. Element face color coding of results (Courtesy Bombardier, Inc. and H. G. Engineering).

aging vertex values to element centroids, resulting in a lower value for the apparent maximum result. Because of this phenomenon, analysis results, color coded by face, must be viewed as being conservative.

Light Source Shading of Color Result Values

Another common problem with scalar color-coded result values is the loss of three-dimensional perspective in the model. When all faces of a common discrete result range have the same color regardless of their orientation in space, it is easy to lose a sense of depth trying to view the model, as shown in Figure 4.4.

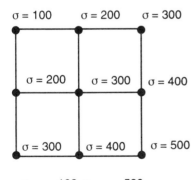

$\sigma_{MIN} = 100, \sigma_{MAX} = 500$

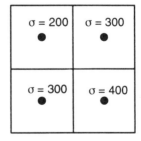

$\sigma_{MIN} = 200, \sigma_{MAX} = 400$

Figure 4.3. Effect of centroid averaging on result range values. Note that the minimum and maximum nodal values reflect the true range more accurately than the centroidal values.

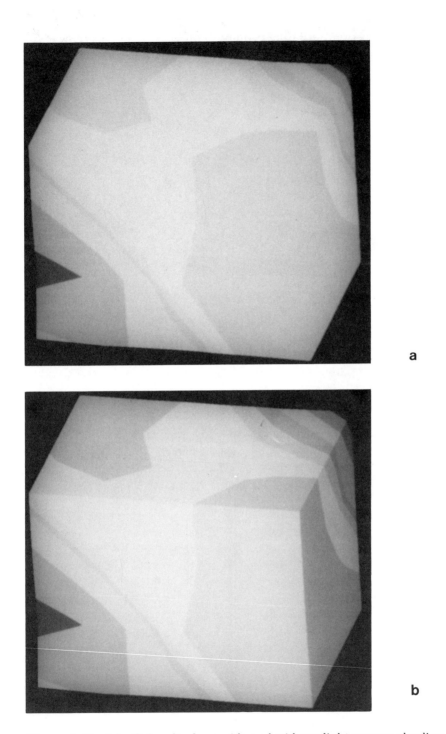

a

b

Figure 4.4(a, b). Color displays with and without light source shading (Courtesy Swanson Analysis Systems, Inc.).

Within the limits of computer graphics equipment, it is possible to show the effects of light-source shading on a color-coded result model through the use of a color table keyed to both result values and polygon surface normals. This is best expressed using the HLS color scheme discussed above, where hue continues to correspond to the scalar value, and the lightness value varies based on a normalized value described as

$$l = \cos\theta \qquad\qquad\qquad [4.4]$$

where θ is the angle between the polygon surface normal and the light source vector from the observer. The saturation value remains constant in this case. In the case of a single polygon, with a base color of red corresponding to maximum result value, the displayed HLS color of this polygon will vary from full red (HLS = (240.0, 0.5, 1.0)) for a light angle $\theta = 0$, through dark red (HLS = (240.0, 0.25, 1.0)) for $\theta = 45$ degrees, and finally to black (HLS = (240.0, 0.0, 1.0)) for $\theta = 90$ degrees, perpendicular to the polygon.

Since this technique expands the number of colors needed from the number of contour colors n_{color} to the number of contour colors times the number of light source gradations ($n_{color} \times n_{shading}$), limits on either or both color sets are generally required for display platforms with a small, fixed number of display colors. A platform supporting 256 simultaneous colors, for example, can theoretically support 14 light source gradations of 14 base result colors.

4.3.2 Contour Display

Contour-oriented techniques are among the most common methods for displaying a result across a surface. They are based around *contour lines,* which are

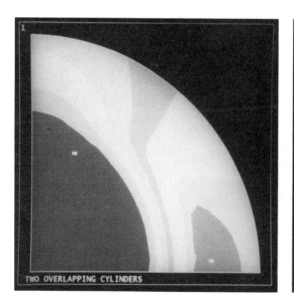
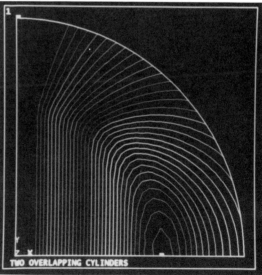

Figure 4.5(a, b). Contour displays (Courtesy Swanson Analysis Systems, Inc.).

more properly defined as isovalue lines, or lines representing a constant value across a surface field. These contour displays share much in common with methods used to create topographic maps, in which isovalue contour lines of constant elevation values above sea level are created.

Contour displays are most useful as a visualization technique by which a state of behavior can be accurately represented as a display on the exterior visible surfaces of a structure. Essentially, they limit the display of scalar variables to two parametric dimensions, although 3-D extensions such as the carpet plot are possible, as in Figure 4.6. These images display the contoured result with a depth in the third dimension, proportional to the value of the scalar result. Such displays are useful for showing the rate of change (i.e., the gradient) of a scalar variable as well as its value.

In general, contour displays are useful on models composed of surfaces or solid analysis models where the exterior results can be shown to govern. As this has often been the case with simple geometric models and basic forms of analysis, contour displays have been one of the most popular ways of showing discrete levels of scalar analysis results.

Basic Linear Interpolation of Contour Levels

The exact location of contour lines within a model of analysis elements depends a great deal upon the assumptions which are made about the varation of the result within that element. In the most general case, contour lines represent the locations where an isovalue is computed from the shape functions describing the interpolation of the element's geometry and results. From this general case, assumptions can be made to simplify the display of an approximation to the result distribution.

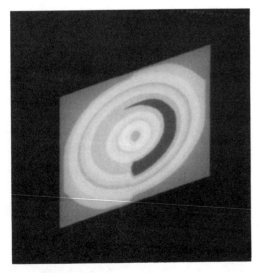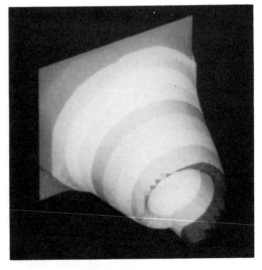

Figure 4.6(a, b). Carpet plot (Courtesy Swanson Analysis Systems, Inc.). (See color plate 4.6)

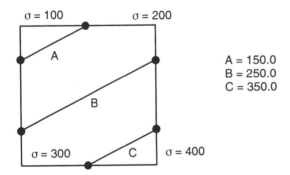

Figure 4.7. Linear interpolation of contour levels across a 4-vertex element.

One of the most common simplifications in commercial analysis software, particularly in the case of linear elements, is that of contour isolines being linear across the element. In actual shape functions, as described in a subsequent section, isolines more commonly display some curvature—even with linear shape functions. A common philosophy assumes that the variation of a variable within a single element is considered less important than the overall variation of the scalar value across the element field. Therefore, the most basic kind of contour line display represents isovalue lines as linear segments, with one line segment for every pair of isovalue points along the element edges. Given the convex 4-vertex quadrilateral element in Figure 4.7, with scalar values σ_1, σ_2, σ_3 and σ_4, the isovalue lines of value σ_{iso} can be determined as follows

1. If all vertex values are less than the isovalue, or if all vertex values are greater than the isovalue, stop processing—there will be no isovalue lines passing through the element.

2. Start at the first pair of vertices of the element, and determine if the isovalue exists along this edge. This will be the case when one vertex is less than the isovalue while the other vertex is greater than the isovalue, in either order. If no isovalue exists along this edge, proceed in either a consistent counterclockwise or a clockwise direction until an edge containing the isovalue is found.

3. Once an edge containing an isovalue is found, between vertices i and j, compute the isovalue location along the edge by linear interpolation:

$$x = x(i) + fac * (x(j) - x(i))$$ [4.5]
$$y = y(i) + fac * (y(j) - y(i))$$
$$z = z(i) + fac * (z(j) - z(i))$$

where

$$fac = \left(\frac{\sigma(j) - \sigma_{iso}}{\sigma(j) - \sigma(i)} \right)$$

This isovalue location will be the first point of the contour line.

4. Examine each subsequent edge until the next edge containing an isovalue is found, and repeat step 3 on this edge to compute the second endpoint of the contour line. Connect these two points to form the contour line.

5. Continue this process for the remaining edges if at least two edges remain. Subsequent points found will become the first and second endpoints of the next contour line.

A four-vertex quadrilateral can have a maximum of two such contour lines in the case where the isovalue exists on each of the four edges. Except for the degenerate cases of an isovalue occurring at a vertex or along an edge, the isovalue will always occur in an even number of points along an element edge.

Piecewise Contour Interpolation on Isoparametric Elements

In the mid 1970s, Meek and Beer [10] proposed a scheme that expanded the above linear contour calculations to approximate the true variation of an isovalue contour curve across higher-order elements such as quadratic elements. This is an important consideration for analysis methods for what is known as the *P-version* of the finite element method, where solutions are converged by increasing the order of the equations in the element. In cases of P-version or higher-order elements, which generally work with a smaller number of large elements, the variation of the contour line within an element itself may have significance to the analyst.

This approach involves creating a parametric unit square or triangle, which is mapped to the actual element by use of the element shape functions shown in Figure 4.8. These shape functions, expressed in parametric coordinates, interpolate defined result values such as those at vertices to other locations within the element.

The variation of the isovalue curve across the element is then determined in a piecewise fashion by subdividing this unit square or triangle into subareas, and following the path of the contour curve from the isovalue points on the edges. This method first looks at a subarea containing an isovalue point along an element edge, and then uses element shape functions to generate a linear interpolation of the vertices of the element to the vertices of the subarea.

A result value at a parametric location (r, s) on the element can be described as

$$\sigma(r,s) = \left[H(r,s) \right] \sigma^* \qquad [4.6]$$

where the matrix H represents the known interpolation functions, such as the element shape functions described above, and σ^* represents the vector of vertex values. For a linear 4-vertex surface function, this interpolation function becomes

$$\sigma(r,s) = \sum_{i=1,4} 1/4\, \sigma(i)\left[\left(1 + rr(i)\right)\left(1 + ss(i)\right) \right] \qquad [4.7]$$

while the shape functions for a 4-vertex quadratic (second-order) surface element are:

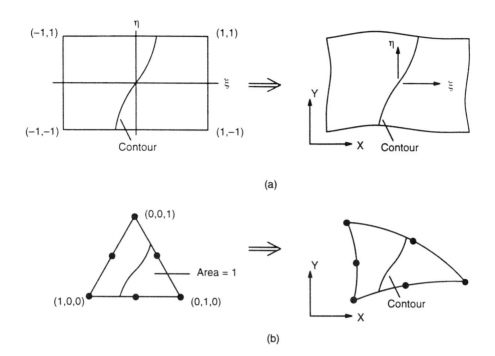

Figure 4.8. Parametric mapping of contour lines for quadrilateral and triangular surface areas (From Meek and Beer, reference 10, copyright 1974. Reprinted by permission of John Wiley & Sons, Ltd.)

$$\sigma(r,s) = \sum_{i=1,4} 1/4\,\sigma(i)\left[\left(1+rr(i)\right)\left(1+ss(i)\right)\left(rr(i)+ss(i)-1\right)\right] \qquad [4.8]$$

for vertex nodes

$$+\sum_{i=1,2} 1/2\,\sigma(i)\left[\left(1-r^2\right)\left(1+ss(i)\right)\right] \text{ for } r(i)=0 \qquad [4.9]$$

$$+\sum_{i=1,2} 1/2\,\sigma(i)\left[\left(1+rr(i)\right)\left(1-s^2\right)\right] \text{ for } s(i)=0$$

for midside nodes.

These relations are used to interpolate the known result values at element vertices i to the vertices of the subarea's parametric r and s locations on the element.

Once the vertex values are interpolated to the subarea, linear interpolation, previously described for the simple contour line case, is performed to produce a contour line segment across the subarea, as shown in Figure 4.9. The next computed endpoint of this contour line is then used as a starting point to compute a contour line segment in the adjacent subarea. This process continues until a contour line endpoint is computed on another edge of the element—or until one

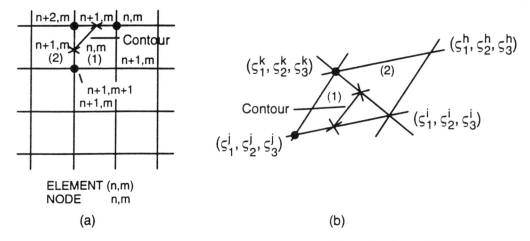

ELEMENT (n,m)
NODE   n,m

(a)   (b)

Figure 4.9. Contour interpolation across subarea (From Meek and Beer, reference 10, copyright 1974. Reprinted by permission of John Wiley & Sons, Ltd.)

of the previously computed subareas is revisited, indicating the much less common case where a contour line becomes a closed loop within the element.

Direct Contour Generation on Isoparametric Elements

Both of these methods for generating contour lines presume that a piecewise linear approximation will adequately represent the actual isovalues, and differ largely in the refinement of this linear approximation. An alternate approach by Akin and Gray [1] uses both the result field and its derivatives for direct generation of contour lines on an isoparametric surface. This method begins with a starting point σ_0, which can be computed along an edge as done for previous methods, and then uses a predefined step size to determine the next point along the contour line. By definition, a contour line represents a path of zero variation in sigma with respect to the parametric coordinates r and s, or

$$d\sigma = 0 \qquad [4.10]$$

which can be expressed in (r, s) space as

$$0 = \left(\frac{\partial \sigma}{\partial r}\right) * dr + \left(\frac{\partial \sigma}{\partial s}\right) * ds \qquad [4.11]$$

where dr and ds are the components of the line tangent to the contour line for the known constant step size dL. Figure 4.10 shows the tangent segment dL forming an angle θ with the parameteric r axis in (r, s) space, and τ can be solved by combining equation 4.11 with the relations

$$dR = dL \cos\theta \qquad [4.12]$$
$$dS = dL \sin\theta$$

100

and the solution of $\partial\sigma/dr$ and $\partial\sigma/ds$, using the derivatives of the shape functions

$$\frac{\partial\sigma}{dr} = \left(\frac{\partial H}{dr}\right)\sigma^* \qquad\qquad [4.13]$$

$$\frac{\partial\sigma}{ds} = \left(\frac{\partial H}{ds}\right)\sigma^*$$

Once a value for the angle θ is obtained, the next point on the contour path is computed to be at a distance dL along a tangent line at the angle θ within (r, s) space.

The success of this algorithm, i.e., how accurately a piecewise step along the tangent from a contour point will remain on the actual contour path, depends on the choice of a proper step size—with too large a step, the lines computed will diverge from the actual contour. Smaller steps are clearly more accurate, but at a cost in computing time. In the original work on this technique, a step size of $\frac{1}{140}$th of the perimeter length was used.

Another potential problem with a direct computational approach is the possibility of an endless loop, in which a closed contour path within a region never reaches an edge and thereby terminates. In this case, a maximum number of path points may be used to limit the path computation.

Direct computational techniques such as these can be particularly useful when working with more large-scale, parametric surfaces as the basic analysis data. At the same time, difficulties such as path divergence and looping make basic linear approximation within elements or subelements more popular for many cases, particularly when the elements themselves are linear.

Extension of Contour Lines to Color-Filled Regions

One of the more common types of contour displays is the *contour fringe plot,* the color fill analogy to contour line displays, where discrete color-filled regions correspond to ranges of the result value.

Such displays are conceptually straightforward—color-filled regions are generated between the isovalue lines at the boundaries of result value ranges. In

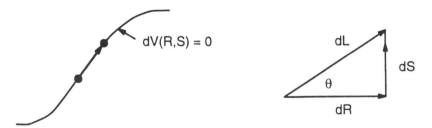

Figure 4.10. Tangent to contour line used in step calculation (From Akin and Gray, reference 1, copyright 1977. Reprinted by permission of John Wiley & sons, Ltd.)

practice, however, simple linear approaches of fitting polygons to vertices and edge intersection points, as is often done with contour lines, can lead to overlapping or ambiguous regions when several result ranges occur in an element with four or more vertices.

A common method of generating linear color polygons within an element involves computing a point location and interpolated value at the element centroid, and then subdividing the element into triangles defined by the element edges connected to this centroid. These triangles can be subdivided further into polygons using an approach such as the following:

1. Determine if all vertex values of the polygon fall within a single contour level range. If so, the polygon is displayed as a single color corresponding to this range.

2. Take the first pair of vertices (i, j) within the polygon, and determine which contour level values fall within the result range σ_i to σ_j. Compute the points along this edges corresponding to these individual contour level values.

3. Proceed in a consistent counter-clockwise or clockwise direction, and repeat step 2 for the remaining two edges of the polygon.

4. Starting at one vertex, find the points for the contour range values containing this vertex, to form an n-vertex polygon. Continue in each direction from this vertex and find subsequent contour level points and vertices within these contour levels to form adjacent polygons. This process produces a set of disjoint polygons encompassing the element shown in Figure 4.11.

As in directly color coded elements, these polygons can be rendered either directly with a color corresponding to the contour result range, or with a color incorporating both the result range and the light source shading component from the 3-D angle made between the polygon and the light source.

Optimizing Free Faces for Solid Element Contour Displays

Surface-oriented visualization techniques such as contour or fringe displays will be visible only on the exterior surfaces of an analysis model. When this analysis is composed purely of surface elements, it generally means that all elements are processed and rendered. On the other hand, analyses performed using 3-D solid elements involve polyhedra in which many result vertices may be completely interior to the model. For these elements, it is desirable to optimize the model so that only visible exterior faces are processed and displayed.

Such an optimization of exterior or *free* faces involves an up-front cost in computation and storage in return for what is often an order of magnitude increase in the speed of computing and displaying the image.

There are at least two optimization techniques which can be applied to a group of element polygons prior to display computations:

1. *Removal of Duplicate Interior Faces.* Polygons from elements in an analysis model are generally defined by numbered vertices rather than by direct coordinate locations. Such polygons can be sorted easily to remove faces which are

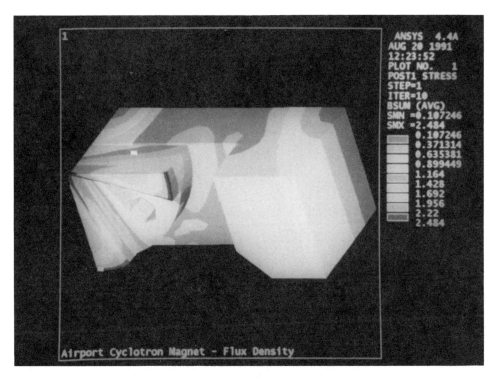

Figure 4.11. Contour fringe display, with discrete color filled result regions (Courtesy MSV National Superconducting Cyclotron Laboratory).

interior to the model by sorting each polygon by the sum of its vertex numbers, and then comparing polygons with the same sum. Such an approach generally requires knowing whether the polygons come from surface or solid elements. In the case of solid elements, all polygons sharing common vertices will be interior to the model and can be removed. In the case of surface elements, optimization is generally not performed because either polygon may be visible—examples of this include the case where surfaces of two adjacent materials are joined for reinforcement purposes in a structural analysis.

2. *Display-Time Culling of Rearward Faces.* When solid elements are defined in a consistent vertex order, as is generally the case in finite element analysis, the polygon normal can be used to determine whether the element is facing forward or rearward. Rearward-facing polygons from solid elements are never visible, and can be removed. This technique is view-specific, and must be repeated whenever there is a change of viewing direction.

Using the right-hand normal rule, the polygon normal can be defined as shown in Figure 4.12 by obtaining the cross product of the first and last non-degenerate adjacent edges

$$n = e_{1,2} \, X \, e_{1,n} \qquad\qquad [4.14]$$

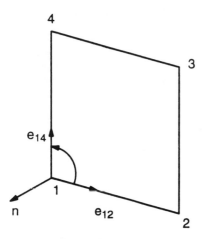

Figure 4.12. Right-hand normal rule
for polygon orientation.

where the two edges share a common vertex location, this common vertex is
the first one of each edge, and the order of the cross product is the first edge
followed by the last one. If the Cartesian Z component of the normal is negative in the viewing coordinate system, the polygon is facing rearward and can be
removed.

4.3.3 Direct Color Interpolation of Scalar Results

Displays showing scalar results as a continuous tonal variation of color across
a surface have a physical appearance similar to a smoothed version of a contour
display, but have little in common with contour methods from an algorithmic
standpoint.

While contours are used as a starting point to generate polygonal color representations across a surface, accurate color rendering of surface results involves
a more direct transformation of the result field into screen space and a color field.
At the same time, a continuous color display of a result value can function like a
discrete contour display by variations in the color map—mapping results to a set
of discrete color regions will produce an area of color fill whose boundaries are
analogous to isovalue contour lines.

The two approaches are separated by the change in focus from finding the first
occurrence of an isoline within an element to rendering every point on the elements containing the isovalue. If one tried to create the effect of contour lines by
setting up a color table consisting only of single, discrete colors at isovalue levels,
the isovalues would interpolate to produce thicker or thinner lines as the individual
isovalue locations are computed on each surface.

For a model composed of polygonal faces, the generation of a continuous tonal
display begins with a mapping of the scalar result value to color values at polygon

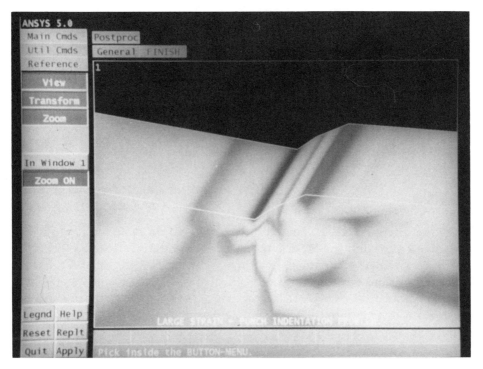

Figure 4.13. Continuous tonal color representation of a scalar result (Courtesy Swanson Analysis Systems, Inc.).

vertices. From this point, the display generation is almost identical to the process of Gouraud polygon shading, where color values derived from a light source are interpolated across the polygon. For continuous tonal result display, result-based values are instead interpolated from the polygon vertices.

The interpolation itself is performed in a similar fashion to Gouraud shading. Each polygon is projected into screen space, and a technique known as Bresenham's algorithm can be used to evaluate the pixels making up each scan line through the projected polygon. The color values for these pixels are then interpolated from the color values obtained where endpoints of the scan line cross the polygon.

As with contour displays, the base colors corresponding to the scalar result can be combined with a light source-based lightness component to preserve the three-dimensional appearance of an image. Similar to contour polygons, this lightness is computed at each pixel location as a normalized value

$$I_{pixel} = \cos\theta \qquad\qquad [4.15]$$

where θ is the angle between the normal to the model surface and the light ray, whose position is usually directly into the Z direction of the screen.

One drawback that inhibits light source shading of continuous tonal displays is that most analysis models are polygonal representations of an underlying model.

The use of polygon normals can cause sharp visual discontinuities in lightness across polygon boundaries, although the result values themselves should appear continuous.

The large number of colors required to accomplish light source shading raises another problem. While a range of 256 simultaneous colors is generally considered sufficient for displaying the scalar result itself, this range must be multiplied by the number of lightness variations used, generally making true light source shading of continuous results the domain of hardware supporting "true" color variation based on actual RGB or HLS values at each pixel.

Correcting for Hardware Interpolation of Scalar Color Values

Continuous tonal result images can be generated on most surface topology representations, as long as these surfaces can be projected into the pixel space of a graphics display. In practice, however, these surfaces are generally divided into polygons, and graphics hardware polygon shading capabilities are often used to interpolate the color across the polygons. Because graphics hardware often breaks polygons into triangles for shading and rendering, there is an important possible inaccuracy which can occur when sending polygons with four or more vertices to such hardware. Since each triangle is rendered independently, the order of triangulation makes a difference in the distribution of color, as in Figure 4.14.

When results are computed on polygons with four or more vertices, such a triangulation will still produce correct results across element boundaries and vertices. To produce a more accurate and consistent result within the elements themselves, they can be subdivided into a more regular pattern of triangles, or into subpolygons based on the color distribution within the element.

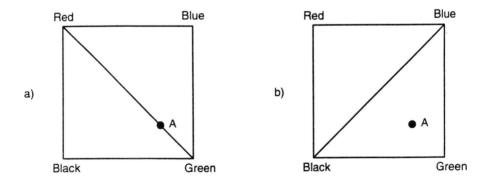

Figure 4.14. Effect of triangulation on rendering a result polygon. Note that point A will be a shade of orange (RGB = (0.25, 0.75, 0.0)) in the first case, and a shade of cyan (RGB = (0.0, 0.5, 0.5)) in the second case.

4.4
THREE-DIMENSIONAL SCALAR FIELDS

As with one-dimensional and two-dimensional scalar fields, one can idealize the display of a three-dimensional scalar field using discrete symbols at specific locations in space, or use techniques which show the overall variation of the field.

One requirement unique to the display of a three-dimensional scalar field is the need to see information which is not on the exterior visible surfaces of the field. This means that the techniques which work for displaying lower-order fields often display confusing or obscured information in 3-D, and, in the limit, the display of a continous volume field only reveals its outside surfaces.

As a result, numerous techniques have been specifically developed in recent years for displaying volume scalar fields. While many of these methods can be generalized to lower dimensions, they share the common denominator of operating on discrete volume components to produce comprehensible imagery of a 3-D state of behavior.

4.4.1 Isosurface Techniques[1]

An isosurface is the 3-D surface representing the locations of a constant scalar result value within a volume. Every point on the isosurface has the same constant value of the scalar variable within the field. As such, isosurfaces form the three-dimensional analogy to the isolines that form a contour display on a surface.

Although contour displays were generally developed directly for use with analysis results, the generation of isosurfaces has its roots in fields such as medical imaging, on which surfaces of constant density must be generated from within a volume continuum. These techniques were generally implemented to process an ordered, regular array of volume elements that are comparatively very small relative to the overall volume.

One of the difficulties of adapting isovalue display methods to analysis data involves applying algorithms designed for a continuum field to coarse, irregular volume elements arrayed randomly in 3-D space. While it is possible to convert a volume field of analysis results to a continuum field representation and apply the same methods—a topic discussed in more detail in a separate chapter—it is generally much more computationally efficient to generate isosurface segments directly from coarse volume elements such as finite elements.

Early Isosurface Generation Techniques

Many of the early techniques for generating isosurfaces began as three-dimensional extensions to the image processing problem of finding constant-valued curves within a 2-D field of points. Generally, these involved fitting curves to points of constant density within a slice through the volume, and then connecting these curves across adjacent slices to form the surfaces.

---

1. Selected material in this section is adapted from reference [6], with the permission of the American Society of Mechanical Engineers.

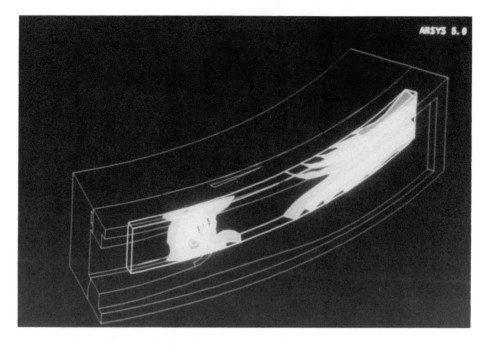

Figure 4.15. Isosurfaces of stress within a compressive seal (Courtesy Dedo Sistemi–Italcae SRL, Italy). (See color section, plate 4.15)

These approaches were well suited to applications in medical imaging, whose raw data generally consisted of progressive slices of 2-D imagery from sources such as computer tomography (CT) or nuclear magnetic resonance (NMR) scans of the human body. This data formed a regular array of 3-D points, as ordered slices of *n*-by-*m* 2-D point arrays. Gray scale points on each slice represented densities of features such as human tissue and bone, and points on density boundaries could be used with curve-fitting techniques to generate contour curves.

Methods published by researchers such as Christiansen and Sederberg [3] and Ganapathy and Dennehy [7] attempted to fit 3-D polygons between points on adjacent contour curves on each slice to form the segments of an isosurface of constant density along the region boundaries. The end result of this polygon fitting became a 3-D image of the boundary of an artifact such as a tumor, or organ.

A later approach developed by Artzy et al. [2] sought to fit surfaces to adjacent volume elements into the full 3-D space. Here, a graph theory representation was used to link the adjacent 3-D volume elements. This paper was one of the first to use the term *voxel*—now the common term for a basic unit of volume data, much the same as a pixel represents the basic component of a raster computer graphics display.

These approaches required substantial computational logic, and not all of these algorithms were "foolproof"—situations such as diverging result paths might cause a pure surface-fitting algorithm to fail. More important, most were calculated around regular ordered arrays of volume elements, and could not be applied directly to random 3-D volume components such as finite elements. More recently, these approaches have been replaced by techniques which are algorithmic rather than heuristic, and can generally guarantee a correct rendering of a volume array so long as each volume element, or voxel, is considered within the algorithm.

These discrete or surface-fitting methods generally consider each volume element or data point's contribution to a surface of constant value, or isosurface, through the volume. These methods originated largely in the medical area for detection of the exterior of known-density areas such as tumors and organs. In one of the earliest approaches Höhne and Bernstein [8] computed the gradient of the scalar value in adjacent volume elements as a basis for the display of surfaces.

Newer approaches include the popular Marching Cubes algorithm for generating isosurface polygons on a voxel-by-voxel basis (Cline et al. [4]), an extension to Marching Cubes for fitting surfaces within each voxel by use of a smoothing scheme (Gallagher and Nagtegaal [5]), and the Dividing Cubes approach of subdividing threshold voxels into smaller cubes at the resolution of pixels (Cline et al. [4]), each of which are described hereafter.

These techniques are easily extended for use with numerical analysis data, subject to certain constraints. In their most basic form, they presume linear volume element topologies such as bricks, wedges or tetrahedra. While extensions can be developed to account for issues such as quadratic and higher-order edge curvature or mid-face vertices, in practice linear assumptions are generally used.

The Marching Cubes Algorithm

One of the key developments in volume visualization of scalar data was the Marching Cubes algorithm of Lorensen and Cline [9], which was patented by the General Electric Company in 1987. This technique examines each element of a volume, and determines, from the arrangement of vertex values above or below a result threshold value, what the topology of an isosurface passing through this element would be. It represents a high-speed technique for generating 3-D isosurfaces whose surface computations are performed on single volume elements, and are almost completely failure-proof.

This technique was one of the first to reduce the generation of isosurfaces to a closed form problem with a simple solution. It processes one volume element at a time, and generates its isosurface geometry immediately before moving to the next volume element. Its basic approach involves taking an n-vertex cube, looking at the scalar value at each vertex, and determining if and how an isosurface would pass through it.

The first step in the algorithm is to look at each vertex of the volume element, and to determine if its scalar result value is higher or lower than the isovalue of interest. Each vertex is then assigned a binary (0 or 1) value based on whether that scalar value is higher or lower. If an element's vertices are classified as all zeros or all ones, the element will have no isosurface passing through it, and the algorithm moves to the next element.

For the remaining case where the element will contain an isosurface, these binary values are arranged in vertex order to form the bits of a binary number—for example, an 8-vertex cube will produce a number between 0 and 255. Then, this number is used to look on a pre-defined table which enumerates (a) how many triangular polygons will make up the isosurface segment passing through the cube, and (b) which edges of the cubes contain the polygon vertices of these triangles, and in what order. This process is shown in Figure 4.16.

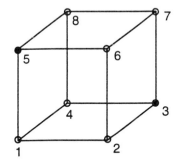

o = less than result value

● = greater than result value

1. Set Vertex Flags

| 0 | 0 | 0 | 1 | 0 | 1 | 0 | 0 | = 20

2. Construct Bit String

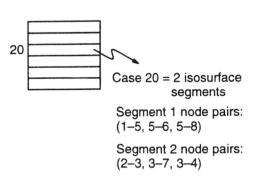

Case 20 = 2 isosurface segments

Segment 1 node pairs: (1–5, 5–6, 5–8)

Segment 2 node pairs: (2–3, 3–7, 3–4)

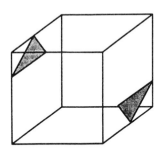

3. Look Up Isosurface Segments

4. Generate Isosurface Segments

Figure 4.16. The Marching Cubes algorithm. Vertices above and below an isovalue are used to construct the bits of a value, which point to a table defining isosurface segments within the solid. (From Gallagher, reference 6, copyright 1991. Reprinted by permission of the American Society of Mechanical Engineers.)

In this example, the ordered binary vertex values produce a value of 20. This value is used to look at location 20 on the Marching Cubes table, which reveals that 2 isosurface segments will be created, and that they will be created from intersections along edges [(1, 5),(5, 4),(5, 8)], and [(2, 3),(3, 7),(3, 4)], respectively.

Finally, the exact locations of these isosurface segments are computed along the specified edges, the same as is done for contour line isovalue points, using a simple linear interpolation of the isovalue between the values at vertices i and j

$$x = x(i) + fac * \left(x(j) - x(i) \right)$$ [4.16]

$$y = y(i) + fac * \left(y(j) - y(i) \right)$$

$$z = z(i) + fac * \left(z(j) - z(i) \right)$$

where

$$fac = \left(\frac{\sigma(j) - \sigma_{iso}}{\sigma(j) - \sigma(i)} \right)$$

These isovalue polygons may then be sent to a graphics display, or saved for later rendering.

As the name implies, the Marching Cubes algorithm was originally designed to generate isosurface polygons from regular 8-vertex cubes (or other hexahedra) of volume data. This method is easily extended to other volume element topologies such as 4-vertex tetrahedra or 6-vertex wedges by the construction of a separate polygon definition table for each kind of topology. This extension is very important for most analysis applications, in which various element types are often needed to define an analysis model.

A more subtle point is that the same kind of algorithm can also be applied to two-dimensional and even one-dimensional topologies. Consulting the same kind of table for individual intersections, this approach can yield isovalue lines from two-dimensional elements, and isovalue points within one-dimensional ones.

These tables themselves are defined ahead of time, with each containing 2^n table entries, where n is the number of vertices in the element. Therefore, a table for 6-node wedges will support 64 possible combinations, and a table for 4-noded tetrahedra requires only 16 cases. An example of marching tetrahedra is shown in Figure 4.17.

The general 8-vertex case of this table will have 256 possible isosurface polygon combinations, reducing by symmetry to 128 different combinations. This can be reduced further to 15 distinct topology combinations by rotational symmetry, shown in Figure 4.18. Extending this to lower dimensions, a three-noded triangle produces eight possible combinations for generating isovalue lines, and a two-noded line has four possible combinations—which clearly reduce by symmetry to the cases of one isovalue point, and none.

Within the volume domain, 8-noded hexahedral analysis elements can be used as a larger and more coarse case of a voxel. The result produces facets, corresponding to the size of the elements, approximating an isosurface within the

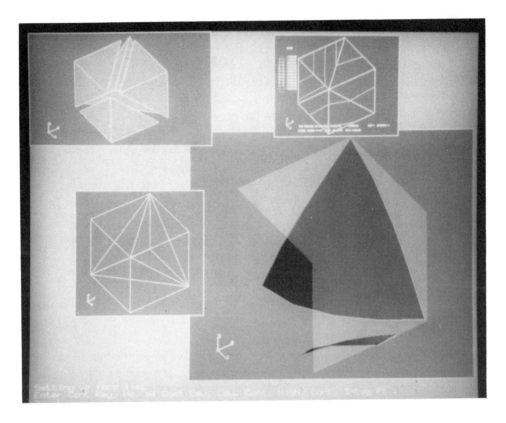

Figure 4.17. Marching tetrahedra

structure. Smooth shading of these isosurface segments requires the normal to the isosurface, at each vertex of the isosurface polygons. Physically, this surface normal represents the gradient of the scalar result

$$\left[\frac{dF(x,y,z)}{dx}, \frac{dF(x,y,z)}{dy}, \frac{dF(x,y,z)}{dz}\right]$$ [4.17]

or the vector of the result value's rate of change in the X, Y and Z directions.

In the medical implementation of Marching Cubes for an ordered array of small voxels, four adjacent XY planes of voxel data are kept in memory at the same time, to allow computation of these gradients at run time. On the other hand, finite elements, being randomly oriented in space, cannot take advantage of such an assumption. To perform smooth shading in this case, one needs to precompute gradient information at the nodes, and interpolate these gradients along with the scalar values as isosurface segments are computed.

Possible Discontinuities in Marching Cubes

Part of the elegance and simplicity of the Marching Cubes approach lies in its ability to generate polygons within each individual volume element, without

112

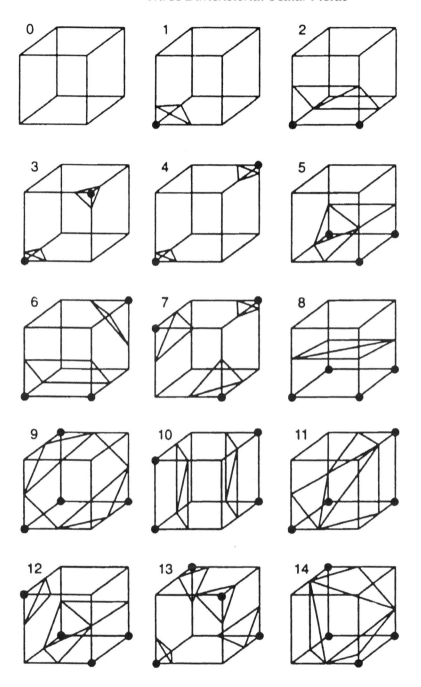

Figure 4.18. Marching Cubes topology combinations for an 8-vertex cube (From Lorenson and Cline, reference 9. Copyright 1987, Association for Computing Machinery, Inc. Reprinted by permission.)

regard to neighboring elements or the model as a whole, and which, in sum total, produce an approximation to the isosurface. At the same time, this independence of elements can lead to a few exceptional situations in which the isosurface polygons are discontinuous across two adjacent volume elements.

One of the more common occurrences is the first case shown in Figure 4.19, where isosurface segments in a hexahedron will be formed from eight points spanning two diagonally opposing edges. These two isosurface polygons can either be constructed from face pairs (1–2, 3–4), or equally correctly from face pairs (4–1, 2–3). Depending on the polygons in the adjacent elements, one or the other choice will produce a "hole."

This case is easily dealt with, at a cost of a small number of extra polygons, by constructing all four polygons corresponding to both cases. A more general, and hard to correct, case occurs when two adajcent volume faces share two opposing in or out vertices, shown in Figure 4.20.

Such ambiguities are present, but not common, in the general case of Marching Cubes. There are a number of ways to deal with these ambiguities; the simplest is to subdivide each 8-noded polyhedron into tetrahedra prior to generating isosurface polygons. Although accurate, this method produces a larger number of isosurface polygons.

Nielson and Hamann [11] developed a more general solution to this problem, using an approach called the *asymphtotic decider*. It uses the bilinear variation of the scalar variable in parametric directions r and s across a potentially ambiguous face—results above the isovalue only occurring on two opposing vertices—to determine how edges of isosurface polygons on this face should be connected. Using the bilinear interpolation function

$$B(r,s) = (1-r,r)\begin{pmatrix} \sigma_{00} & \sigma_{01} \\ \sigma_{10} & \sigma_{11} \end{pmatrix}\begin{pmatrix} 1-s \\ s \end{pmatrix} \qquad [4.18]$$

the bilinear interpolant of the intersection point of the asymphtotes of the function where $B(r, s)$ equals the isovalue σ_{iso} can be derived as

$$B(R_{iso}, S_{iso}) = \left(\frac{\sigma_{00}\sigma_{11} + \sigma_{10}\sigma_{01}}{\sigma_{00} + \sigma_{11} - \sigma_{01} - \sigma_{10}} \right) \qquad [4.19]$$

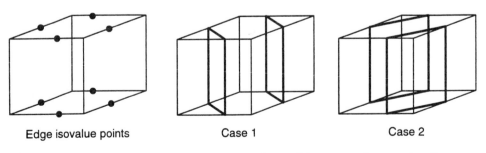

Edge isovalue points   Case 1   Case 2

Figure 4.19. This type of element can produce either one of two sets of isosurface polygons using the Marching Cubes algorithm.

114

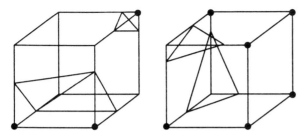

Figure 4.20. An example of a discontinuity between two elements. Note that the isosurface polygons are disjoint across the common element face (From Nielson and Hamann, reference 11, copyright 1991 IEEE.)

The criterion for connection, as shown in Figure 4.21, is

IF $\sigma_{iso} > B(R_{iso}, S_{iso})$ THEN   [4.20]
        connect $(R1, 1)$ to $(1, S1)$ and $(R0, 0)$ to $(0, S0)$
   ELSE connect $(R1, 1)$ to $(0, S0)$ and $(R0, 0)$ to $(1, S1)$
END IF

Parametric Cubic Isosurface Smoothing

The Marching Cubes approach produces flat facets of an isosurface from a field of volume elements. It is presumed that, if these volume elements are small and regularly arranged, their final image will approximate the true isosurface by use

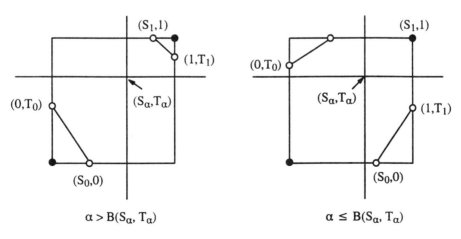

Figure 4.21. Asymphtotic decider criteria for connecting ambiguous edges from Marching Cubes (From Nielson and Hamann, reference 11, copyright 1991 IEEE.)

of shading. On the other hand, analysis data such as finite elements represent very coarse, irregular groups of volume data, when direct application of Marching Cubes can lead to a noticeably faceted isosurface. In 1989, Gallagher and Nagtegaal [5] developed an extension to the Marching Cubes approach which produces a smooth, visually continuous isosurface directly from a group of finite elements. Its key points are:

• The gradients and location of each Marching Cubes isosurface segment are used to construct a bi-cubic surface within the isosurface segment.
• The triangular polygons of Marching Cubes are replaced with quadrilateral surfaces wherever possible, to produce smoother bi-cubic surfaces.
• Separately, the gradients are used to construct a distribution of surface normals across the surface segment for shading.
• Each surface segment is then tesselated, or divided into small planar polygons, and these polygons and their interpolated normals are used to generate smooth shaded images of the isosurface.

Figure 4.22. Isosurface smoothing—two element test case (Courtesy Gallagher and Nagtegaal, reference [5]. Copyright 1989, Association for Computing Machinery, Inc. Reprinted by permission). (See color section, plate 4.22)

This approach produces an isosurface throughout the structure which appears smooth and free of visual artifacts such as creases. Figure 4.22 illustrates isosurfaces from a two element test case.

The equations of the bi-cubic surface segments can be described in the following matrix equation

$$x_i(r,s) = \sum_{j,k} f_i(r) B_{ijk} f_k(s) \qquad [4.21]$$

that describes the global *XYZ* coordinates of any point in the parametric space of the surface, ranging from (0, 0) to (1, 1) in parametric space. The function vector *f* represents the standard Hermite functions of

$$f_1 = 2\xi^3 - 3\xi^2 + 1 \qquad [4.22]$$
$$f_2 = 2\xi^3 + 3\xi^2$$
$$f_3 = \xi^3 - 2\xi^2 + \xi$$
$$f_4 = \xi^3 - \xi^2$$

where ξ is the parametric component to be evaluated in *r* or *s*, while the matrix B_{ijk} describes the individual surface itself, in the following form

$$B_{ijk} = \begin{bmatrix} x(i) & \dfrac{dx(i)}{ds} \\ \dfrac{dx(i)}{dr} & \dfrac{d^2x(i)}{dr\,ds} \end{bmatrix} \qquad [4.23]$$

Here, the upper left matrix terms represent the coordinates of the surface; each of the four upper left components contain the Cartesian *X*, *Y* and *Z* components of its corner vertices. The lower left and upper right terms represent tangents computed from the gradients at each vertex; these form the *X*, *Y* and *Z* components of the first derivative of the surface with respect to each of its two parametric directions.

To ensure tangent continuity between adjacent elements, tangents are computed in the plane formed between two adjacent vertex normals along the shared edge of the isosurface segment. Alternatively, tangents along exterior free faces are computed to lie within the plane of the free face.

The lower right quadrant terms represent the second derivative terms of the surfaces. These are known as the *twist* vectors, as they describe interior surface topology analogous to the effects of twisting the edges of the surface inward or outward. These terms are set to zero to form a surface known as a Ferguson patch or F-patch, which maintains as little curvature as possible given the topology of its outer edges.

Coordinates and gradients alone are insufficient to produce C1-continuous isosurface segments with bi-cubic functions. To accomplish smooth shading, separate normals to the isosurface polygons are computed by substituing the matrix

$$B_{ijk} = \begin{bmatrix} n(i) & \dfrac{dn(i)}{ds} \\[2ex] \dfrac{dn(i)}{dr} & \dfrac{d^2 n(i)}{dr\,ds} \end{bmatrix} \qquad\qquad [4.24]$$

into the Hermite functions described above for interpolation of normals across the isosurface. The vertex normal vectors $n(i)$ are obtained separately at element vertices as the gradient of the scalar result

$$n(i) = \left(\frac{d\sigma}{dx}, \frac{d\sigma}{dy}, \frac{d\sigma}{dz} \right) \qquad\qquad [4.25]$$

and are interpolated to the corners of that element's isosurface polygons employing the same Marching Cubes approach used for interpolating result values. To insure continuity of normals across isosurface segments of adjacent elements, the normal derivative terms $dn(i)/dr$ and $dn(i)/ds$ are computed so that normals along polygon edges will lie in the plane between their vertex normals.

One subjective issue which must be taken into account with this technique is the fact that a linear element result function is being smoothed into a bi-cubic surface. Here, the tradeoff is a certain degree of accuracy within the element versus a smooth isosurface which is free of edge artifacts.

Rendering of Isosurfaces

After polygons corresponding to an isosurface are generated, they can be treated for display purposes, from a graphics display standpoint, like any other geometric polygon. In general, isosurface polygons are color coded according to the value of the scalar result, in much the same manner as contour lines or polygons. Other rendering techniques can be applied, such as texture mapping, shading or even the contouring of a second variable to convey information about the nature of the isovalue. The shading of isosurface polygons in particular depends a great deal on underlying assumptions. The computation of shading components depends in large part on the normal to an isosurface polygon, which may or may not correspond to the actual normal of the isosurface itself, shown in Figure 4.23.

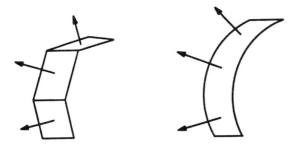

Figure 4.23. Normals of isosurface polygons versus normals of actual isosurface.

Both the Marching Cubes and cubic smoothing approaches discussed above make assumptions regarding these normals which have the effect of smoothing the data. In many cases, this is desirable, because it gives an approximation to a true isosurface which is free of visible discontinuities between adjacent polygons. On the other hand, as noted previously in the case of cubic smoothing, smoothing techniques will not reflect actual behavior with 100 per cent precision.

In either case, a key factor is how exact an interpolation of behavior is desired. In many engineering analysis problems, which are themselves approximations, behavior within an element is not as important as the overall distribution of the result in the model, and smoothing provides a useful overview. When a more exact picture of results within individual elements is important, implicit methods such as ones discussed in the next section may be more appropriate.

Translucency represents another useful rendering technique for displaying volume data—inherently, one must be able to see within a 3-D volume to evaluate it. Since the late 1970s, several techniques have existed in both software and hardware to simulate translucent objects that tint, but still display, objects behind them in 3-D space. While the more correct approach involves applying a tint function to pixels covered by a translucent object, another popular technique involves simply drawing every *n*th pixel of a translucent object, with the undrawn pixels remaining as originally set. This latter technique is known as *screen-door* translucency because of its analogy to a mesh screen.

There are at least two key uses of translucency in the display of isosurfaces: (1) as a means of displaying the exterior of the 3-D volume around the isosurfaces, and (2) as an independent variable, in which the degree of translucency in an isosurface corresponds to the scalar value. An example of this with stress results appears in Figure 4.24.

4.4.2 Particle Sampling and Implicit Isosurfaces

Isosurface techniques such as the ones discussed above generate polygons or surfaces that approximate the actual location of a 3-D surface of constant result value. An alternative approach, that is more computationally expensive, but more exact, is to compute the actual points of constant result value within the entire 3-D volume.

Such methods produce an *implicit* isosurface, in the sense that the result display consists of a dense group of points which imply the surface, but in sum total have no surface relationship. This can be seen as a 3-D analogy to directly generating continuous color information versus a contour plot on a two-dimensional field.

This technique is part of the more general case of particle sampling, where the volume is sampled at regular points, and the results of this sampling are displayed as dots or symbols. Both the color and density of points displayed can vary with the magnitude of the result value, and points are often limited to those falling within a specified result range. An example of particle sampling, using the Data Visualizer system from Wavefront Technologies, is shown in Figure 4.25.

When a very dense array of points are sampled, and only those points corre-

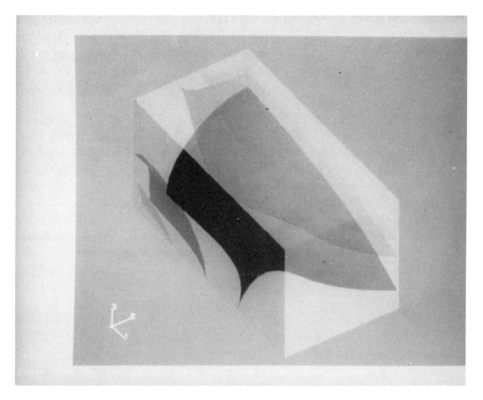

Figure 4.24. Translucent isosurfaces (From Gallagher and Nagtegaal, reference 5. Copyright 1989, Association for Computing Machinery, Inc. Reprinted by permission.) (See color section, plate 4.24)

sponding to locations of an isovalue are displayed, these points become an implicit isosurface in the limit. Unlike most polygon-based generation techniques, an implicit set of points will produce a true variation of the result in the equational order of the element—for example, a quadratric or cubic element will display an apparent quadratic or cubic variation of behavior.

The Dividing Cubes approach of Cline et al. [4] is one example where subpoints within a regular array of volume elements are computed to produce such isosurfaces. In Dividing Cubes, each voxel is subdivided to sub-voxels on the isosurface which, when projected to the space of the display screen, are at or below the resolution of a screen pixel. These isovalue locations can then be displayed directly, without the need for surface fitting.

Methods such as Dividing Cubes are particularly useful for high-speed or large dataset applications such as medical imaging, where the direct display of point values bypasses the need to scan-convert the polygons which result from techniques such as Marching Cubes. For engineering applications, which tend to deal with much more coarse volume datasets, implicit isosurfaces offer more accuracy than speed advantages, compared with polygon-based methods.

The shape functions of an analysis element can also theoretically be used to

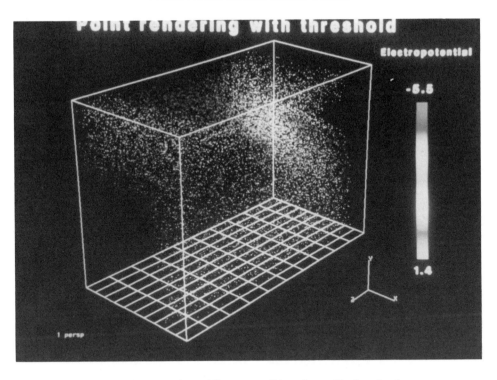

Figure 4.25. Particle sampling (Courtesy Wavefront Technologies—
Data Visualizer).

generate a continuum of points at any desired density by using a sufficiently small
increment in the parametric r, s and t values computed. In the most general—and
computationally expensive—case, these functions would be evaluated for each
element at a density which was equal to or greater than the volume element
density needed to produce adjacent points in screen space. For example, the shape
functions of a linear 8-vertex hexahedron

$$\sigma(r,s,t) = \sum_{i=1,8} 1/8\ \sigma(i)\left[\left(1+rr(i)\right)\left(1+ss(i)\right)\left(1+tt(i)\right)\right] \qquad [4.26]$$

would be evaluated for σ at r, s and t values finely spaced enough to approximate
an adjacent set of points. A more coarse spacing of r, s and t would produce a
display of discrete points along the isosurface.

This general case can quickly involve a very large number of points, easily
reaching six to eight orders of magnitude. Moreover, most resulting points will
not contain a given isovalue. Therefore, in practice, shape function interpolation
should only be applied after a check that the element itself will contain a given
isovalue, and, ideally, after further subdividing the element and evaluating those
polyhedra containing the isovalue.

Implicit isosurfaces can be generated as an extension to creating isovalue lines
in two dimensions. Upson [13] describes an approach of creating what are called

vector nets, that are a three-dimensional set of isolines computed on orthogonal planes through the volume. As with Dividing Cubes, this approach presumes a regular array of volume elements, rather than the irregular volume elements found with a finite element model.

4.4.3 Volume Slicing

Most techniques for displaying scalar states of behavior in a volume carry the risk of obscuring critical information. Contour displays show only exterior visible surfaces, isosurfaces can hide other isosurfaces, and other displays can become crowded and complicated. Thus, the ability to cut away part of a volume to see what is behind it forms an important tool in the visualization process. Volume slicing is a general term which encompasses the removal of part of a volume to observe the rest of its contents. It represents the intersection of a model with a half-space, a predefined visible portion of 3-D display space composed of the volume to one side of a cutting plane or surface. There are three common forms of volume slicing:

1. Clipping. Here, a 3-D model is cut by a slicing plane to reveal a hollow interior. After removing geometry in front of the clip surface, it displays the interior of individual elements, or, by using only the exterior free faces of the volume, the volume as a whole. It is performed by evaluating each volume element against the boundary of the half-space to see if it is inside, outside, or partially contained.

In the case of a planar clipping surface described by a point and a normal vector, the test for clipping a volume element is as follows:

> IF
> all points of volume element are inside the half-space, display the element.
> ELSE IF
> all points of volume element are outside the half-space, discard it.
> ELSE
> volume element is partially contained in half-space:
> DO FOR each face of the volume element:
> IF
> all points of face are inside the half-space, display the face.
> ELSE IF
> all points of face are outside the halfspace, discard face.
> ELSE
> intersect face polygon with half-space to create subpolygon,
> display subpolygon.
> END IF
> END DO
> END IF

For a convex volume element, the actual intersection of a partially contained element face with a linear clipping half-space simply becomes a matter of evalu-

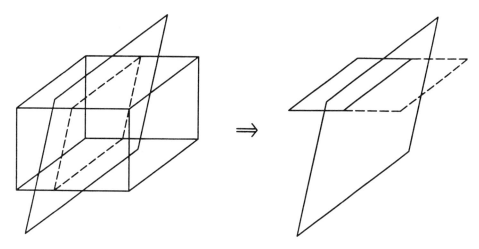

Figure 4.26. Clipping of a volume element by operating on individual polygons.

ating each polygon edge, subdividing lines crossing the half-space boundary, and forming a new polygon from the contained edge(s), subdivided edge segments, and a new edge connecting the intersection points, shown in Figure 4.26.

2. Clipping with Capping. A more useful operation for visualization of behavior is to clip a model, with a display of the scalar result on the clip surface. The result has the visual effect of cutting through the solid itself to display its interior behavior. This operation of displaying the clip surface is known as *capping*. Clipping with capping is shown in Figure 4.27.

These capped surfaces are produced by generating additional display polygons for each volume element, bounded by the edges connecting the intersection points between the volume element's edges and the half-space. The scalar result values are interpolated from the vertices of the volume element, providing vertex values for rendering the polygon with result surface techniques such as contour or continuous tonal display.

One graphics display problem concerning clipping with capping is that while clipping alone can often be performed in graphics hardware, clipping with capping generally must be performed in software. Clipping itself, as a display operation, is self-contained to individual polygons, and can therefore take advantage of 3-D polygon clipping capabilities on a polygon-by-polygon basis in hardware.

Capping, on the other hand, requires knowledge of the entire volume element to interpolate vertex values and form the capping polygon and its scalar values. The need to decompose this data into individual polygons before displaying them in hardware requires that this operation be performed in software, under current 3-D display architectures. This means that operations such as animating the motion of a capping plane relies heavily on the refresh rate of re-computing and re-drawing the entire model.

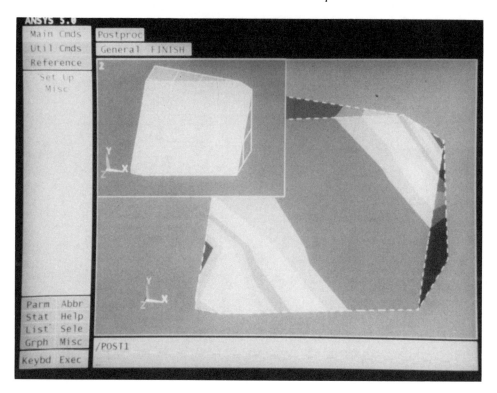

Figure 4.27. Volume slicing, using clipping with capping, of a solid model with interior scalar results.

3. Sampling Planes. An increasingly common operation in interactive visualization involves combining the capping portion of one or more volume slicing operations with a wireframe outline of the model. This allows the simultaneous display of scalar results at multiple locations within the volume, and can provide a clear overview of how the result varies across regular intervals in space. An example of sampling planes is shown in Figure 4.28.

Volume slicing does not, by necessity, imply a purely planar intersection between a clipping or capping surface and a 3-D model. The same technique can be applied using the general intersection of any surface with a volume dataset.

Ferguson [14] has used an isosurface as a clipping and capping surface, as shown in Figure 4.29. This combines a view of an internal state of behavior with the nature of the isovalue, particularly when animated over time with a varying isovalue. Further extensions to this concept include the intersection of isosurfaces from different scalar fields to determine points satisfying multiple constraints, and the use of a trimmed isosurface as a sampling plane from element to element.

Another example, in Figure 4.30, implemented by the Data Visualizer software package from Wavefront Technologies, is the generation of an isovolume display. This is produced as an image of an implicit bounded volume within the model, excluding volume regions above or below a specified threshold value.

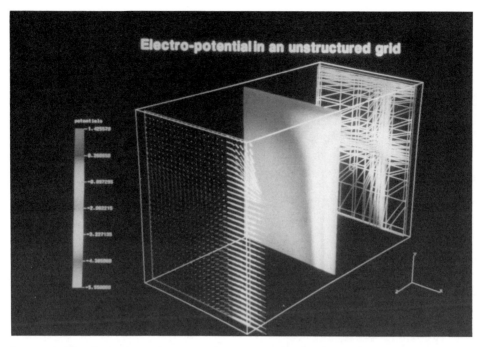

Figure 4.28. Sampling planes, with continuous tonal and particle results displayed across the slice planes (Courtesy Wavefront Technologies— Data Visualizer). (See color section, plate 4.28)

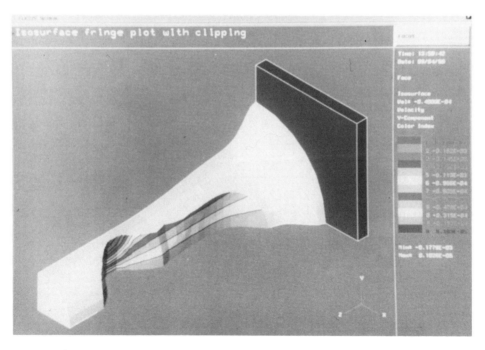

Figure 4.29. Isosurface used as a clipping and capping surface. (Courtesy Visual Kinematics, Inc.) (See color section, plate 4.29)

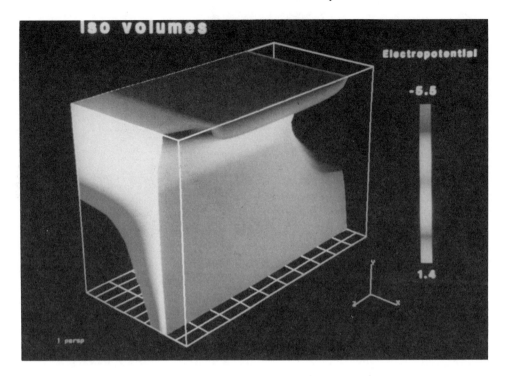

Figure 4.30. Isovolume display (Courtesy of Wavefront Technologies—Data Visualizer)

4.5
SUMMARY

The display of a scalar variable in one, two or three dimensions generally takes one of a few basic forms, where color, symbols or boundary lines and surfaces are used to convey both the location and the magnitude of the scalar field.

There has been an evolution in scalar variable display from single-dimensional representations such as the contour line, to two-dimensional surfaces such as fringe or shaded result displays, and beyond to three-dimensional representations such as isosurfaces, point sampling and volume slicing. This trend extends logically to the display of multiple variables, geometrically and over time. This is discussed in subsequent chapters.

This evolution has been driven in part by the development of algorithmic methods of generating these displays, but equally by the applications themselves. Declining computer hardware costs and increasing capabilities have resulted in more complicated and sophisticated 3-D analysis problems, increasing the need for ways to visualize the resulting scalar fields. Techniques such as these, outlined in this chapter, are part of a continuing process to make this increasingly complex behavior clear to the analyst.

4.6
REFERENCES

[1]. Akin, J.E. and Gray, W.H., "Contouring on Isoparametric Surfaces," International Journal of Numerical Methods in Engineering, Vol. 11 pp. 1893–1897, 1977

[2]. Artzy, E. Frieder, G., and Herman, G., "The Theory, Design, Implementation and Evaluation of a Three-Dimensional Surface Detection Algorith, " Proceedings of SIGGRAPH '78, in Computer Graphics 14,3, July 1980

[3]. Christiansen, H.N., and Sederberg, T.W., "Conversion of Complex Contour Definitions Into Polygonal Element Mosiacs," Proceedings of SIGGRAPH '78, in Computer Graphics 12,3

[4]. Cline, H., Lorensen, W., Ludke, S., Crawford, C. and Teeter, B., "Two Algorithms for the Three-Dimensional Reconstruction of Tomograms," Medical Physics, Vol. 15, No. 3, May 1988

[5]. Gallagher, R.S. and Nagtegaal, J.C., "An Efficient 3-D Visualization Technique for Finite Element Models and Other Coarse Volumes," Proceedings of SIGGRAPH '89, Computer Graphics 23,3, July 1989

[6]. Gallagher, R.S., "Direct Generation of Isosurfaces From Finite Element Models," PVP Vol. 209, ASME, New York, 1991

[7]. Ganapathy, S. and Dennehy, T.G., "A New General Triangulation Method for Planar Contours," Proceedings of SIGGRAPH '82 in Computer Graphics 16,3 July 1982

[8]. Höhne, K. and Bernstein, R., "Shading 3-D Images from CT using Gray-Level Gradients," IEEE Transactions on Medical Imaging, Vol. 5, No. 1, 1986, pp. 45–47

[9]. Lorensen, W. and Cline, H.E., "Marching Cubes: A High Resolution 3-D Surface Construction Algorithm," Proceedings of SIGGRAPH '87, in Computer Graphics 21,4, July 1987

[10]. Meek, J.L. and Beer, G., "Contour Plotting of Data Using Isoparametric Element Representation," International Journal of Numerical Methods in Engineering, Vol. 10, pp. 954–957, 1974.

[11]. Nielson, G.M. and Hamann, B., "The Asymphtotic Decider—Resolving the Ambiguity in Marching Cubes," Proceedings of Visualization '91, IEEE Computer Society Press, October 1991.

[12]. Sunguruff, A., and Greenberg, D.P., "Computer Generated Images for Medical Applications," Proceedings of SIGGRAPH '78, in Computer Graphics 12,3, August 1978.

[13]. Upson, C., "The Visualisation of Volumetric Data," Proceedings of Computer Graphics 89, Blenheim Online Publications, Pinner, Middlesex UK, 1989.

[14]. Visual Kinematics, Inc. (Mountain View, CA USA), FOCUS User Manual, Release 1.2, October 1992.

[15]. Winget, J.M., "Advanced Graphics Hardware for Finite Element Display," PVP Vol. 209, ASME, New York, June 1988.

C H A P T E R

A Unified Framework for Flow Visualization

THIERRY DELMARCELLE AND LAMBERTUS HESSELINK

FLOW VISUALIZATION PLAYS an important role in science and engineering. Its applications range from the highly theoretical—such as the study of turbulence or plasmas—to the highly practical—such as the design of new wings or jet nozzles. Besides, the problems tackled by flow visualization have far-reaching implications in areas that are well beyond fluid mechanics. Indeed, the main challenge of flow visualization is to find ways of representing and visualizing large (multidimensional and multivariate) data sets, and to do so in a fashion that is both mathematically rigourous as well as perceptually tractable. More precisely, flow data in a N-dimensional space can be either N-dimensional scalar fields (univariate), vector fields (N-variate), or even second-order tensor fields (N^2-variate). Data of this type are not peculiar to fluid flows, and occur commonly in many branches of physics and engineering.

In general, multivariate data sets are more difficult to visualize as the number of variables increases. In this chapter, we adopt the theoretical standpoint of representation theory, and we develop a unified framework for the visualization of vector and tensor fields. We discuss many different representations in terms of both their spatial domain and their embodied information level. This allows us to show the connections between various a priori unrelated vector and tensor visualization techniques, and to point out areas where research must be undertaken. Although we illustrate the concepts mainly by examples of aerodynamical flows, the methodology applies to a much wider variety of data.

5.1
INTRODUCTION

Flow visualization motivates much of the research effort recently undertaken in scientific visualization. Indeed, continuously increasing resources for computing and data acquisition allow researchers and engineers to produce large multivariate 3-D data sets with improving speed and accuracy. Simulated aerodynamical flows, for example, typically involve five, possibly time-dependent, scalar quantities defined over more than a million grid points; but, analyzing and interpreting such volumes of information without appropriate tools is beyond the processing capability of the human brain.

Scientific visualization in general and flow visualization in particular aim to provide such tools. Without attempting to construct an exhaustive list, we recognize at least three areas where they are indispensable:

Experimental and computational steering. By examining results at intermediate stages of a simulation, researchers can refine a mathematical model, evaluate more accurately heuristic parameters, or make decisions related to the convergence of their algorithms. Figure 5.1 represents such a "steering loop" together with the main computing resources that are required for each step of a simulation or an experiment. Computing resources include storage space, processing time, and transmission time. The dotted box positions the visualization process inside the loop.

Understanding of physics. Flow visualization is useful for improving knowledge of the physical principles that underlie simulated or measured phenomena; in this respect, visualization idioms[1] that extract structural information from vector and tensor fields are particularly useful.

Validation of flow solvers. Flow visualization allows fluid dynamists to compare solutions obtained with different flow solvers, therefore assessing their respective validity and performances.

Visualization idioms have progressively evolved from techniques that mimic experimental methods—i.e., that produce continuous representations of physically measurable quantities—to more abstract depictions of the data. The underlying reasons for this evolution are twofold. First, many important flow quantities such as helicity density or viscous stress tensor are not currently directly accessible through experiment; second, in order to represent the highly multivariate information contained in vector and tensor fields while at the same time avoiding cluttered images, it becomes necessary to simplify the display by extracting and rendering only the relevant features of the data.

5.1.1 Flow Data

Physical variables in fluid flows are scalar, vector, or tensor quantities. (Useful background information on vector and tensor fields can be found in Borisenko and Tarapov [5].) Techniques for displaying 3-D scalar fields—such as contour lines, isosurfaces [6], or volume rendering [7, 8]—are not specific to flow visualization and are described elsewhere in this book. We therefore restrict our discussion to vector and tensor fields defined, in most cases, on volumetric domains.[2]

We discuss many vector visualization techniques and we generalize some of them to symmetric tensor fields U whose nine individual components U_{ik} are related by

---

1. A visualization idiom is any sequence of operations that produces an abstract display of data sets. Specific operations are discussed in Section 5.1.2.

2. Unless otherwise specified, in this chapter the term "tensor" stands specifically for "second-order tensor"—i.e., a tensor characterized by two indices.

$$U_{ik} = U_{ki} \qquad\qquad [5.1]$$

for $i, k = 1, 2, 3$. We develop a framework for analyzing and classifying diverse, a priori–unrelated, methods. The reader can refer to References [9, 10] for the more complex task of visualizing general unsymmetric tensor fields whose components do not especially obey Equation 5.1. Briefly, we can uniquely decompose the data into the sum, or the product, of a symmetric tensor field and a vector field. Thus, we can visualize unsymmetric tensor data by combining various visualization techniques that apply to vector and symmetric tensor fields discussed in this chapter.

Tables 5.1 and 5.2 (see page 152) list some important vector and symmetric tensor fields in fluid flows. Both are examples of highly multivariate data, equivalent to three and six independent scalar functions, respectively. While increasing multivariability amounts to increasing complexity of the visualization process, it also denotes larger information content. For example, the Navier-Stokes equations expressing momentum conservation in steady inviscid flows involve only one tensor variable. Indeed, these equations can be written as

$$\sum_{i=1}^{3} \frac{\partial \Pi_{ik}^{r}}{\partial x_i} = 0 \qquad\qquad [5.2]$$

where $1 \leq k \leq 3$ and Π_{ik}^{r} is the reversible momentum flux density tensor given in Table 5.2. Π_{ik}^{r} is made up of diverse contributions such as pressure, kinetic energy density, and velocity—all of which can be correlated in a single tensor display.

5.1.2 The Visualization Process

Visualization idioms transform raw experimental or simulated data into a form suitable for human understanding; they can take on many different forms, depending on the nature of the original data and the information that is to be extracted. As shown in Figure 5.1, however, visualization idioms can generally be subdivided into three main stages—*data preprocessing, visualization mapping,* and *rendering* [2, 3, 11].

Data preprocessing involves such diverse operations as interpolating irregular data to a regular grid, filtering and smoothing raw data, or deriving functions of measured or simulated quantities. Visualization mapping—in many ways the most crucial and least automated stage of the visualization process—involves designing an adequate representation of the filtered data, an icon,[3] which efficiently conveys the relevant information. This often involves first deciding what aspects of the data carry meaningful information and then extracting data features such as singularities, vortex cores, etc. The resulting icon is generally geometrical, but it can assume other forms; for example, turbulent flow audiolization—the mapping of turbulence into a sound stream—is discussed in Reference [12]. Finally, the icon must be rendered (visually and/or aurally) to communicate information to the human user.

---

3. The precise meaning of the term "icon" in this chapter is discussed in Section 2.1.

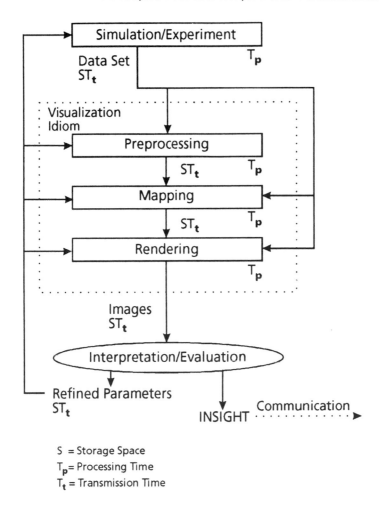

Figure 5.1. Experimental and computational steering. (Adapted from P. Ning and L. Hesselink [4]. Copyright 1993 IEEE)

5.1.3 Chapter Content

The scope of this chapter is the second stage of the visualization process—namely visualization mappings of vector and tensor data in flow fields. In Section 5.2, visualization mappings and resulting icons are discussed from the standpoint of representation theory, and several of their important properties are identified. The discussion provides a theoretical basis and a unified framework for analyzing diverse vector and tensor mappings in Sections 5.3 and 5.4, where the various concepts are illustrated mainly by examples from aerodynamics (other important areas in flow visualization that are not discussed in this text include visualization of jets [13, 14, 15] and of atmospheric simulations [16, 17]). Finally, the interested reader will find in appendix a discussion of some recently developed visualization software environments.

5.2
VISUALIZATION MAPPINGS OF FLOW DATA

Since scientific visualization is a new discipline, the correlations between various techniques are little understood—a fact mainly due to the lack of a conceptual model for thinking about multivariate data visualization [18]. However, the problem of representation tackled by scientific visualization—i.e., creating a mental image of the data—is hardly a new subject; its theoretical and practical implications have been studied extensively in various disciplines such as logic, linguistics, psychology, and sociology.

The following discussion analyzes visualization mappings from the standpoint of representation theory and identifies general properties of related icons. The purpose of this framework is twofold: first, it allows scientific visualization to be conceptually distinguished from other applications of computer graphics; second, it provides a natural categorization of numerous a priori–unrelated visualization mappings to be examined in the next sections.

5.2.1 Icons

In scientific visualization, icons are often defined as geometrical objects that encode the data at a given point either through geometric characteristics such as lengths or angles, or through other visible attributes such as color or opacity [19]. In this chapter, however, we expand this typical notion of "icon" to a more general concept borrowed from theories of the semiotics of data representation.

Visualization mappings extract a psychologically meaningful representation from the data; thus, they always posit a relation between an object (data) and its interpretant (psychological imprint of the data), i.e., a semiological sign [20]. In his work on logic, C.S. Peirce identifies several classes of signs [21]. A sign relates to the object in three different ways: as an icon, an index, or a symbol. This subdivision of signs—formerly applied to medical imaging [22]—is relevant to all branches of scientific visualization, including flow visualization. According to Peirce:

An *icon* is based on a resemblance between the object and its representation; it is not, however, affected by the object and has no "dynamic" connection to it. Examples are chemical diagrams that represent molecules. On the other hand,

An *index* "is a sign which refers to the object that it denotes by virtue of being really affected by that object [21];" typical examples include a clock indicating the time of the day and the photograph of an object. In fact, an index is essentially causal whereas an icon is mainly mimetic [23]. Finally,

A *symbol* relates to the object by virtue of an arbitrary convention; for example, the correspondence between the shape of letters in the roman alphabet and their sound is largely arbitrary.

In order to characterize the nature of signs used in scientific visualization, consider, for example, representing a vector at a given point in space by an arrow. The arrow in itself is an icon, since it has qualities in common with the data—i.e., direction and length. However, for the visualization mapping to be useful, the orientation and length of the arrow must be determined by the data. In other words, the representation is causal and the arrow, as it relates to the data, is indexical. However, this index involves an icon to "embody" the information.

Many more examples of such combined signs are reviewed in this chapter. For simplicity, we conform to the prevailing usage of the term "icon." It should be kept in mind, however, that "icons" here are in fact "indices-involving-icon" in respect to their semiological functions. The use of these complex signs is a common property shared by diverse scientific visualization systems, and helps distinguish the discipline from other applications of computer graphics which usually produce pure icons—as in architectural design or photorealistic studies.

5.2.2 Attributes of Icons

Important features of visualization mappings are derived from the attributes of the associated icons—i.e., *object, spatial domain,* and *embodied information level.*

Object. Icons of flow data are characterized by their object—i.e., scalar, vector, or tensor data. Object contraction consists in simplifying the visualization mapping by displaying derived data of lower multivariability, such as representing a vector field by its scalar magnitude. Object contraction implies a loss of information which is compensated, however, by a considerable simplification of the visualization mapping.

Spatial domain. Icons represent their object across a spatial domain; an arrow, for example, displays vector information at a single point. Overall, there are point, line, surface, and volume icons.

Embodied information level. Perhaps the most fundamental attribute of icons is the information level embodied in the representation—which we characterize as elementary, local, or global:

> *Elementary icons* represent their object strictly across the extent of their spatial domain (point, line, etc.) For example, an arrow is an elementary point vector icon.
> *Local icons* represent—in addition to elementary information—a local distribution of the values of the data around the spatial domain. Practically, this means that local icons display, at least partially, data gradients which are scalar, vector, or tensor gradients. Finally,
> *Global icons* show the structure of the complete data field.

Global icons of multivariate data are typically obtained by feature extraction. What makes them "global" is, therefore, problem-specific since it requires distinguishing parts of the data that carry structural information from those that can be neglected. Designing global icons for data visualization is a complex but worthwhile challenge. Because they represent multivariate information by means of a few carefully selected points, lines, or surfaces, global icons result in significant data compression.

Embodied information levels correspond closely to those suggested by Bertin [24, 25] in his work on the semiology of graphics, and were used recently by Robertson [26] in choosing an adequate methodology for representing 2-D bivariate data.

Figure 5.2 summarizes various vector and tensor icons together with their attributes. We discuss these icons in detail in Sections 5.3 and 5.4, respectively.[4] First, we illustrate the former concepts by an example of turbulent flow visualization [27].

3-D turbulent flow dynamics tends to produce a hierarchy of interacting coherent structures. Large-scale structures can be studied by simulating the evolution of vortex tubes; i.e., tubes of concentrated vorticity. A mechanism known as vortex-stretching is responsible for the collapse and entanglement of vortex tubes together with a cascade to small-scale vortex debris.

The tubes shown in Figure 5.3 are surfaces of constant vorticity magnitude, and their color indicates locally the velocity (red corresponds to the highest velocity). The time-dependent stretching of the tubes is described by the equation

$$\frac{\partial \bar{\omega}}{\partial t} + \left(\bar{v}.\vec{\nabla}\right)\bar{\omega} = \left(\bar{\omega}.\vec{\nabla}\right)\bar{v} + v\Delta\bar{\omega} + \text{ forcing} \tag{5.3}$$

which governs the evolution of the vorticity vector $\bar{\omega}$ (Table 5.1 on page 152); $\bar{v}$ is the velocity and v the kinematic viscosity. The left-hand side of Equation 5.3 represents advection of the vorticity due to the velocity field and the right-hand side describes both vortex-stretching $((\bar{\omega}.\vec{\nabla})\bar{v})$ and dissipation at small scales $(v\Delta\bar{\omega})$. Vortex-stretching is the main cause of the complex non-linear interaction of the vortex tubes. Initially, they are orthogonal to each other, but, as time proceeds, complex secondary finger structures appear in what becomes an intricate entanglement.

Several authors studied this phenomenon for various initial configurations of the two vortex tubes [28, 29, 30]. In addition, a technique for visualizing spatial variations of the vorticity magnitude near the extrema is given in References [31, 32].

In the simulation of Figure 5.3, two vector fields ($\bar{v}$ and $\bar{\omega}$) are computed, but the complex structure of the flow is better represented by a scalar field, the vorticity magnitude $|\bar{\omega}|$ obtained by object contraction. Then, an isosurface $|\bar{\omega}| = \text{constant}$ is extracted from the scalar field for subsequent rendering. The isosurface is not a pure icon since its time-dependent stretching is determined by the data. It is, again, another example of "index-involving-icon." In general, isosurfaces embody only elementary information.[5] In this case, however, the surface constant is chosen in order to elucidate the topology of the entanglement process and to reveal the relevant structures in the scalar field; it follows, then, that this particular isosurface is a global icon.

---

4. Vector gradients are, in general, tensor fields. Local vector icons therefore display elementary tensor information. However, we do not define them as tensor icons because important attributes, such as position of critical point glyphs or trajectory of streamribbons and streamtubes, are determined by the vector field. Tensor icons can visualize tensor fields that are not vector gradients.

5. It might be argued that an isosurface is a local icon since information about the scalar gradient is included in the shading [6], but this is relevant only to the rendering step and is not a property of the visualization mapping.

Information Level

Spatial Domain	Elementary	Local	Global
Point	arrows wedges hedgehogs	critical point glyphs	
Line	streamlines streaklines particle traces	streamribbons streamtubes	vortex cores
Surface	streamsurfaces		2-D vector topology skin-friction topology
Volume			skin-friction topology and separation surface, helicity density,* or vortex cores

VECTOR FIELDS

Information Level

Spatial Domain	Elementary	Local	Global
Point	ellipsoids tensor glyphs		
Line	tensor field lines* hyperstreamlines		
Surface			
Volume			collective behavior of hyperstreamlines

TENSOR FIELDS

Figure 5.2. Vector and tensor icons. See Sections 5.3 and 5.4. (*) denotes object contraction.

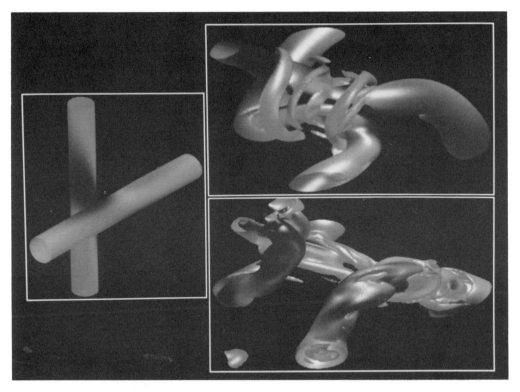

Figure 5.3. Entanglement of vortex tubes. Tubes are initially orthogonal *(left)* and are represented at time $t = 1.5$ *(top)* and at time $t = 2.6$ *(bottom)*. (From Briscolini and Santangelo, reference 27. Copyright 1991 by International Business Machines Corporation; reprinted by permission.)

5.3
VECTOR MAPPINGS

In this section, various elementary, local, and global icons of vector fields are discussed. These icons and their corresponding attributes are summarized in Figure 5.2 (left). Elementary icons typically mimic experimental flow visualization techniques while local and global icons are more abstract representations.

5.3.1 Elementary Icons

Elementary vector icons represent vector information strictly across their spatial domain—which can be points, lines, or surfaces. First, point icons and their limitations are described; then, line and surface icons are discussed that provide a continuous representation of the vector field, therefore improving perception of the data.

5.3.1.1 Point icons

The most straightforward vector mapping consists in drawing point icons such as arrows at selected points in the flow—a technique analogous to tufts or vanes used by experimentalists [33]. Different point icons—such as wedges or bulb-shaped hedgehogs—are sometimes used, but a comparative study shows that simple arrowheads are most efficient at conveying vector information from volumetric data sets [34].

Arrows are useful in visualizing 2-D slices of 3-D vector fields such as cutting planes [35]; yet, they are impractical when applied to the entire volume. To avoid visual clutter, the density of displayed arrows must be kept very low. However, it is not possible to comprehend the underlying structure of the vector field by mentally interpolating adjacent arrows, except for very simple objects.

Figure 5.4, for example, shows the velocity field in the flow past a cylinder. For improved perception, color maps the kinetic energy density. Although valuable information is represented, the display of merely 4% of the arrows renders the image overly cluttered. Point icons do not represent the intrinsic continuity of the data, and the displayed information is too poor in spatial resolution for elucidating important flow features such as vortices.

5.3.1.2 Particle traces, streaklines, and streamlines

Line icons are more efficient in the sense that they provide a continuous representation of the data, therefore avoiding mental interpolation of point icons.

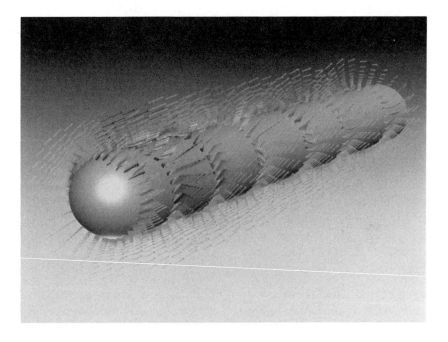

Figure 5.4. Arrows depict the velocity field in the flow past a cylinder. Blue, green, yellow, and red correspond to increasing kinetic energy density.

Consider a vector field $\bar{v}(\bar{x}, t)$ where $\bar{x}$ is the position in space and t is the time. We discuss particle traces, streaklines, and streamlines below—all of them are line icons that emphasize different aspects of the flow.

Particle traces are trajectories traversed by fluid elements over time. They are visualized experimentally by injecting instantaneously a dye or smoke in the flow and by taking a long exposure photograph. Numerically, the trace $\bar{x}(t)$ of the particle originally at position $\bar{x}_o$ is the curve obtained by integrating the equation

$$\frac{d\bar{x}}{dt} = \bar{v}(\bar{x}, t) \qquad\qquad [5.4]$$

with the initial condition $\bar{x}(0) = \bar{x}_o$. A collection of particle traces therefore gives a sense of the complete time evolution of the flow.

The *streakline* $\bar{x}(\bar{x}_o, t_o)$ passing through the point $\bar{x}_o$ at time t_o is formally defined as the locus at time t_o of all the fluid elements that have previously passed through $\bar{x}_o$. Streaklines are obtained experimentally by injecting continuously at the point $\bar{x}_o$ a non-diffusive tracer—such as hydrogen bubbles—and by taking a short exposure photograph at time t_o. Numerically, streaklines are computed by linking the endpoints of all the trajectories obtained by integrating Equation 5.4 between times t_i and t_o for every value of t_i such that $0 \le t_i \le t_o$ and with initial conditions $\bar{x}(t_i) = \bar{x}_o$. Thus, streaklines at time t_o give information on the past history of the flow.

Finally, *streamlines* at time t_o are integral curves satisfying

$$\frac{d\bar{x}}{ds} = \bar{v}(\bar{x}, t_o) \qquad\qquad [5.5]$$

where t_o is held constant and is a parameter measuring distance along the path. Streamlines at time t_o are everywhere tangent to the steady flow $\bar{v}(\bar{x}, t_o)$, and a collection of such streamlines therefore provides an instantaneous "picture" of the flow at time t_o. Streamlines in unsteady flows are by nature transitory but they can be visualized experimentally by injecting a large number of tracer particles in the flow and taking a short-time exposure photograph.

In general, particle traces, streaklines, and streamlines are distinct from each other, but these three families of trajectories coincide in steady flows. Streamlines of the flow in Figure 5.4 are represented in Figure 5.5 (top); the display shows two pairs of vortices hidden in Figure 5.4. The same streamlines are rendered as tubes of small radius in Figure 5.5 (bottom) in order to improve perception of the spatial arrangements of the trajectories. Comparing Figures 5.4 and 5.5 shows that line icons reveal more of the flow structure than point icons. As we show in Section 5.3.3.3, however, important flow features are still hidden in Figure 5.5.

Accuracy and interactivity. The simulation of the planet Jupiter for the movie "2010" required the computation of approximately 10 million 2-D particle traces that were blended in a moving texture [36, 11]. Fortunately, realism and abstraction are not incompatible in scientific visualization and a more modest number of particles—say a few tens to a few hundreds—suffices for representing fluid flows. Accuracy and interactivity, on the other hand, are primary concerns.

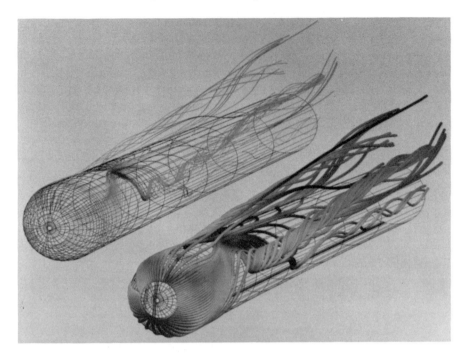

Figure 5.5. Streamlines of the steady flow in Figure 5.4. Color maps kinetic energy density according to the scale in Figure 5.21.

The complexity of most interesting 3-D flows is reflected by intricate trajectories and integration must be handled with care in order to avoid excessive numerical errors. This is especially relevant in turbulent flows where the distance between adjacent fluid elements is known to grow exponentially with time [37]. Any numerical error is therefore dramatically enhanced as integration proceeds.

The integration scheme is an important source of numerical errors. Straightforward integration techniques, like the simple (but fast) Euler explicit scheme, are inadequate. Acceptable results, however, are found using a second-order Runge-Kutta algorithm with step size based on cell dimensions and the inverse of the vector magnitude [38]. Higher-order integration techniques, such as fourth-order adaptive Runge-Kutta, are more accurate but lead to increased computational loads.

Numerical errors also occur due to vector field interpolation between grid nodes. In fact, simple trilinear interpolation is the main source of errors in turbulent flows [39] and higher-order interpolation schemes such as cubic splines, though more accurate, impose a strong performance penalty.

Researchers in flow visualization are exploring new hardware configurations that improve both speed and accuracy. An example is distributed particle tracing, where trajectories are computed with a supercomputer and communicated to a front-end workstation handling all the graphics operations [40]. This configuration, now being implemented in virtual reality-based systems such as the Virtual Windtunnel [41], leads to speedups by an overall factor of 7 during typical visualization sessions.

Recent algorithmic enhancements also improve speed and accuracy. These algorithms exploit the fact that streamlines of 2-D incompressible flows can be computed as contour lines of a stream function [42] and that streamlines of 3-D steady flows are intersection curves of the isosurfaces of two stream functions [43]. In both cases, streamlines are quickly obtained by means of scalar mappings that do not require any error-prone numerical integration of trajectories. An obvious drawback of these methods is the need to precompute the stream functions.

Textures for streamline rendering. We can generate anisotropic textures to render 2-D streamlines directly, without integrating the vector field [44, 45]. Compared to conventional line drawings, the resolution of the display is not improved. However, anisotropic textures produce space-filling images that are difficult to obtain using the techniques mentioned above. In addition, because they are visually appealing, textures are particularly suitable for non-scientific purposes, such as presentations outside the scientific community.

Figure 5.6, for example, represents the 2-D flow tangent to the surface of the cylinder in Figure 5.4. The cylinder surface is shown unfolded. The anisotropic texture reflects local vector direction and color encodes vector magnitude. Here, the visualization idiom does not include a mapping step. The texture is created directly during rendering by convolving an input image with a spatial filter kernel. The input image is the band-limited noise shown in Figure 5.7. We can obtain such an image by using a 2-D version of Perlin's noise function [46]. For nonuniform vector data, the filter kernel is space-variant; i.e., its size and orientation changes across the image. We simply use for filter the sum of two short line segments. One

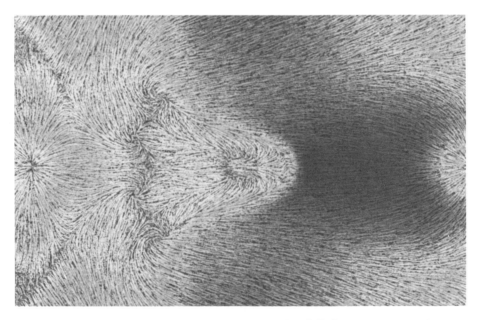

Figure 5.6. Anisotropic texture representing the 2-D flow tangent to the cylinder in Figure 5.4. The cylinder surface is shown unfolded. Blue, green, yellow, and red correspond to increasing velocity magnitude.

141

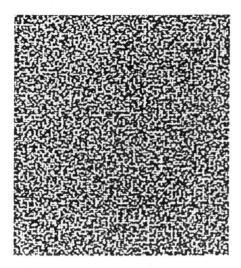

Figure 5.7. Band-limited noise used
to generate Figure 5.6.

segment is locally aligned with the vector field and the other lies in the opposite
direction. Other kernels can be used, such as ellipses or curved streamline segments.
Reference [45] further discusses texture rendering of volumetric vector data.

5.3.1.3 Streamsurfaces

Because they do not require a mental interpolation of adjacent point icons,
streamlines improve the perception of the flow and emphasize the continuity of
the vector field. The next logical step is to design surface icons—or streamsurfaces—that are tangent to the vector field at each of their points. Similar to
streamlines which are created by advecting one fluid particle, streamsurfaces are
obtained by advecting a material line segment; i.e., a front of particles.

Figure 5.8 shows a streamsurface and its polygonal tiling in the flow around
a post. The original line segment is made up of six fluid particles, and is drawn in
black at the bottom of the figure. The algorithm, which is discussed in detail in
Reference [47], models the surface as a collection of ribbons obtained by building a polygonal tiling of pairs of adjacent streamlines. As opposed to earlier
algorithms which typically postprocess previously computed streamlines [48, 49],
tiling is performed during advection of the particle front.

As pointed out earlier, adjacent streamlines in divergent flows tend to spread.
The algorithm then adaptively adds particles to the advancing front so oversized
polygons can be avoided. A few instances of these "ribbon splitting" events can
be seen in Figure 5.8. Also, the front is severed into two independent advancing
fronts wherever it becomes too stretched, for example at the boundary of an obstacle. Finally, the tiling of individual ribbons is done with care to avoid long and
skinny polygons in sheared flows, in which neighboring particles are advected at
substantially different speeds.

Generating streamsurfaces does not especially require a polygonal tiling. For

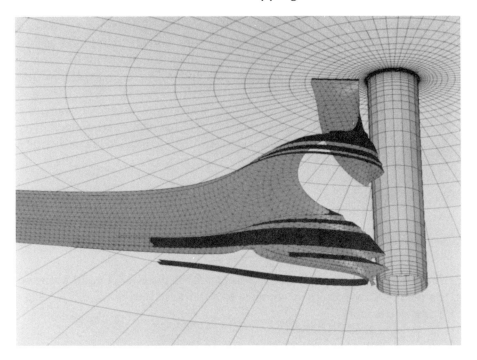

Figure 5.8. Streamsurface in the flow around a post. (Courtesy Jeff Hultquist, NASA Ames Research Center)

example, we can render directly an advected front of surface particles; i.e., small facets modeled as points with a normal vector [50]. Surface particles are shaded according to their normal vector. Then, each particle is blurred, filtered, and scan-converted. No geometry is generated. A large number of surface particles gives the appearance of a continuous surface. However, holes can appear if there is no adaptive control of the density of particles.

5.3.2 Local icons

Local vector icons represent information about vector gradients. Existing local vector icons include point icons such as critical point glyphs and line icons such as streamribbons and streamtubes.

5.3.2.1 Critical points and their glyphs

Phase-space techniques [51, 52] used in analyzing differential equations can be applied to visualize fluid flows. Among these techniques, important features of vector fields are critical points; i.e., points in the flow where the magnitude of the vector field vanishes and where the slope of the streamline is locally indeterminate. Indeed, streamlines never cross each other except at critical points [53, 54, 55].

Critical points are rarely used by themselves for visualization purposes; they are generally embedded in a topological representation of vector fields—a global icon discussed in Section 5.3.3. However, as primary constituents of vector field topology, they are often displayed together with a glyph representing vector field gradients. In this respect, critical points are local icons, and are therefore discussed in this section. We start with 2-D critical points which are important for both 2-D vector fields (Sections 5.3.3.1 and 5.3.3.2) and 3-D vector fields (Section 5.3.3.3). Then, we extend the discussion to 3-D critical points.

2-D critical points. Since the vector field vanishes at a critical point, the behavior of nearby streamlines is determined by the first order partial derivatives of the vector field. More precisely, the 2-D vector field $\bar{v} = (v_1, v_2)$ near a critical point is given by the first-order expansion

$$v_1(dx_1, dx_2) \approx \frac{\partial v_1}{\partial x_1} dx_1 + \frac{\partial v_1}{\partial x_2} dx_2 \qquad [5.6]$$

$$v_2(dx_1, dx_2) \approx \frac{\partial v_2}{\partial x_1} dx_1 + \frac{\partial v_2}{\partial x_2} dx_2$$

where dx_1 and dx_2 are small distance increments from the critical point position. Thus, the nearby flow pattern is completely determined by the 2×2 Jacobian matrix J whose elements

$$J_{ij} = \frac{\partial v_i}{\partial x_j} \qquad [5.7]$$

are evaluated at the critical point position.

Different patterns arise that are characterized by the invariants of the matrix J, or equivalently by its eigenvalues. Figure 5.9 shows how the eigenvalues of J classify a critical point as an *attracting node,* a *repelling node,* an *attracting focus,* a *repelling focus,* a *center,* or a *saddle.* Real eigenvectors of J are tangent to the streamlines ending at the critical point. A positive eigenvalue defines an outgoing direction and a negative eigenvalue corresponds to an incoming direction. When the eigenvalues are complex, the streamlines circulate about the critical point; the direction of the motion is inward if the real part of the eigenvalues is negative, and outward if it is positive.

Critical points sometimes occur so close together that it is difficult to distinguish among them. In fact, they act as elementary building blocks of the vector field, meaning that a combination of critical points looks like a single critical point when observed from a far enough distance. For example, the combination [node, saddle, node] which occurs frequently is similar to a pure node in the far field.

3-D critical points. The former classification of 2-D critical points can be extended to 3-D vector fields $\bar{v} = (v_1, v_2, v_3)$ defined over 3-D domains. The Jacobian J is now a 3×3 matrix whose elements are still given by Equation 5.7. However, J has three eigenvalues and three eigenvectors. Again, real eigenvectors are tangent to streamlines ending at the critical point and complex eigenvalues, that always occur in pairs, denote circulation. Thus, possible 3-D patterns include *repelling nodes* (eigenvalues are all real and positive) appearing as 2-D repelling nodes in each of the three planes spanned by pairs of eigenvectors; *attracting nodes*

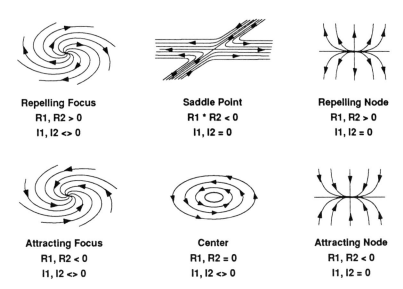

Figure 5.9. 2-D critical points. R1 and R2 denote the real parts of the eigenvalues of **J**, I1 and I2 the imaginary parts. (From Helman and Hesselink, reference 48, copyright 1991 IEEE)

(eigenvalues are all real and negative) appearing as 2-D attracting nodes in each of the planes; *saddle/saddle/nodes* (eigenvalues are all real but one has a different sign) appearing as 2-D saddles in two planes and as a 2-D node in the third plane; and spiral nodes (one real and two complex conjugate eigenvalues) with an attractive or repelling third direction. Figure 5.10, for example, shows a saddle/saddle/ node which plays an important role in flow separation (Section 5.3.3.3). An algorithm for locating and extracting critical points is detailed in Reference [56].

3-D critical point glyphs. We usually display critical points together with a glyph that characterizes local flow patterns [56, 48]. An example is given in Figure 5.11 which shows some of the 3-D critical points in the velocity field of Figure 5.4.

The arrows are oriented in the direction of the real eigenvectors of and show incoming or outgoing directions corresponding to negative or positive eigenvalues, respectively. The disks are in planes spanned by pairs of complex eigenvectors where circulation occurs. Dark blue or yellow disks represent positive or negative real parts. Light blue or red disks represent imaginary parts.

The glyphs in Figure 5.11 are point local icons that visualize the vector field gradients J_{ij} at critical points (where $\bar{v} = \bar{0}$). In addition we can use these glyphs to represent J_{ij} at other points in the flow where $\bar{v}$ does not vanish. In this case, the glyphs represent the local flow patterns that are seen by a massless observer moving with the flow. That is, they encode the behavior of neighboring streamlines relative to the observer's own trajectory.

Unsteady flow fields. Critical points in unsteady vector fields move, and eventually merge or split. These phenomena are studied by tracking and representing their trajectories over time [57] or by locating interactively critical points in nearby space-time regions [58].

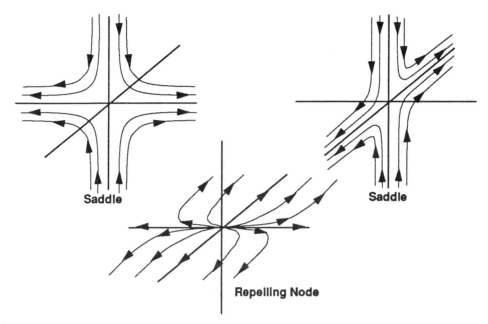

Figure 5.10. 3-D saddle/saddle/node. (From Helman and Hesselink, reference 48, copyright 1991 IEEE)

5.3.2.2 Streamribbons and streamtubes

Fluid elements moving along streamlines of nonuniform vector fields undergo local deformations due to vector field gradients. These deformations are expressed mathematically by the components of the matrix J (Equation 5.7) along the trajectories. Two distinct additive deformation mechanisms arise: strain and rigid body rotation. Strain changes the shape and the volume of fluid elements, and is expressed locally by the symmetric part of J; i.e., the rate-of-strain tensor (Table 5.2 on page 152). Rigid body rotation, on the other hand, is described by the antisymmetric component of J, which is equivalent to the vorticity vector $\bar{\omega}$ (Table 5.1 on page 152).

The critical point glyphs of Section 5.3.2.1 represent J in isolated points. Hereafter, we discuss streamribbons [59, 60, 61, 62] and streamtubes [61, 62], both of which are local line icons representing, at least partially, deformations along streamlines. More complex tensor icons must be used for a complete depiction of the deformations [9].

Streamribbons. Streamribbons are narrow surfaces defined by two adjacent streamlines. An example is given in Figure 5.12, where streamribbons are used to visualize the flow near the surface of the cylinder in Figure 5.4 (The cylinder is represented outlined by dots.).[6]

---

6. A streamribbon is usually a polygonal tiling obtained from simplified versions of the streamsurface algorithm discussed in Section 5.3.1.3. An alternate technique detailed in reference [60] consists in interpolating the two constituent streamlines for additional intervening lines that are clustered together to give the appearance of a surface. This technique is useful for drawing streamribbons 1) that are transparent and 2) with plotting devices capable of line plots only.

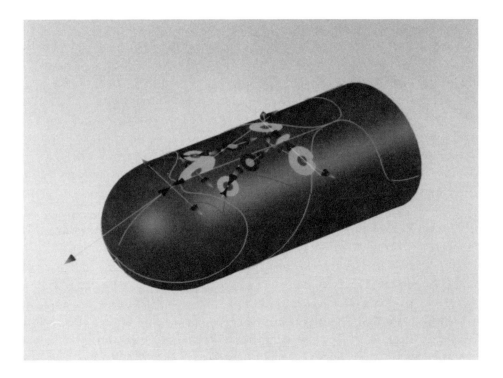

Figure 5.11. Local characterization of the velocity field in Figure 5.4. (From Helman and Hesselink, reference 48, copyright 1991 IEEE) (See color section plate 5.11)

Streamribbons are, in fact, streamsurfaces built from a front of only two particles. They nevertheless are local icons, since their width reflects the flow divergence and their twist rate encodes the local streamwise vorticity. Indeed, the rotation of a ribbon sheet per unit length is given by

$$\frac{d\phi}{ds} = \frac{1}{2}\frac{\bar{\omega}.\bar{v}}{|v|} \tag{5.8}$$

where s is the distance along the streamline and the right-hand side is half the streamwise vorticity. Adjacent streamlines in vortical regions wrap around each other, therefore creating streamribbons with high twist rate.

Streamribbons in divergent flows may become too wide; in this case they must be discarded since the twist rate no longer reflects correctly the streamwise vorticity along the trajectory. To remedy this, streamribbons in Figure 5.12 are built by adding to a single streamline a narrow strip of polygons whose twist is obtained by integrating Equation 5.8 along the trajectory. This avoids problems related to flow divergence and produces streamribbons that always have the correct twist [62].

Streamtubes. Combined effects of the streamwise vorticity and the transverse strain can be visualized by linking N streamribbons and forming a streamtube as in Figure 5.13 (top) where $N = 4$. The technique amounts to sweeping along a

Figure 5.12. Streamribbons of the flow near the surface of the body in Figure 5.4. The twist of the ribbons encodes streamwise vorticity and the width reflects cross-flow divergence. (Courtesy of G. Volpe [60])

streamline a N-sided polygon[7] that is deformed locally by the matrix **J**. In a streamtube, the rotation of the edges reflects both streamwise vorticity and transverse strains[8] whereas the expansion of the cross-section encodes cross-flow divergence. Figure 5.13 (bottom) compares a streamline, a streamribbon, and a streamtube with $N = 6$, respectively. Alternate faces of the streamtube are colored with flow temperature and flow pressure.

Again, problems in diverging flows can be avoided by computing only one streamline and surrounding it by a tubular surface whose cross-section varies as a function of the cross-flow divergence along the trajectory [61, 62].

5.3.3 Global Icons

As earlier shown in Figure 5.4, arrows must be coarsely distributed in space to avoid visual clutter. Comprehending the global structure of the vector field is then difficult because of the need to interpolate the displayed information. In this respect, line icons such as streamlines are more appropriate. Understanding complex flows, however, requires many streamlines which clutter the display without guaranteeing the detection of all important features of the flow.

These problems typically arise from using elementary icons. With global icons, we render the structure of the complete data field by producing a simplified and more abstract representation. We prevent visual clutter by discarding unnecessary information, while keeping only those features that are structurally relevant. By using global icons and reducing the multivariate data field to a set of points, lines, or surfaces, we therefore achieve significant data compression. Also, due to their simplicity and abstract nature, global icons are suitable input to automated data analysis systems [63].

---

7. Hence the name "streampolygon" of this technique [61].

8. Discriminating between both effects is somewhat difficult. A palliative solution consists in adding to the surface a narrow colored stripe with techniques similar to those in Reference [61]. If the stripe is forced to rotate according to Equation 5.8, the effect of streamwise vorticity can be isolated.

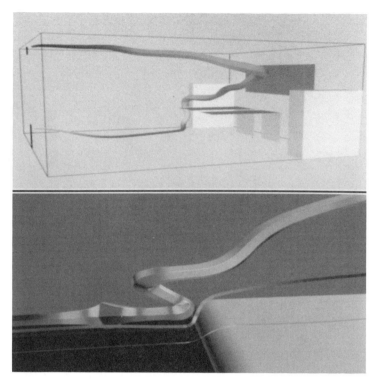

Figure 5.13. Streamtube colored with air pressure visualizing the flow in a room *(top);* comparison of a streamline, a streamribbon, and a streamtube *(bottom).* (From Schroeder et al., reference 61, copyright 1991 IEEE)

There is no universal method for designing global icons, and each solution is problem-specific. In Section 5.2.2, surfaces of constant vorticity magnitude were shown to adequately represent a class of 3-D turbulent flows. In the following, we focus on flows past a body, that play a central role in aerodynamics, and we discuss their topological representation.

5.3.3.1 2-D Vector field topology

Vector field topology is conceptualized as a schematic depiction of the behavior of a large collection of streamlines. The basic constituents of vector field topology are

the critical points (Section 5.3.2.1) and
the set of their connecting streamlines.

Among critical points, the saddle points are distinct because there are only four tangent curves which actually end at the point itself (Figure 5.9). These tangent curves are called *separatrices* because streamlines that are arbitrarily close to each other on either side of a separatrix are diverted to very different regions in the

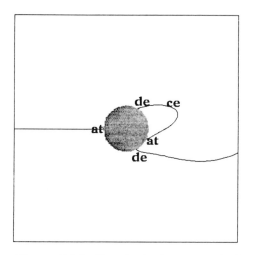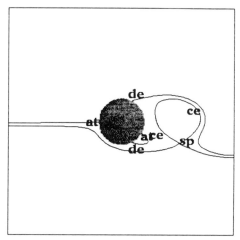

Figure 5.14. Topological representation of the 2-D flow past a circular cylinder at two different time steps. The flow is coming from the left; *at* = attachment point; *de* = detachment point; *sp* = saddle point; *ce* = center. (From Helman and Hesselink, reference 48, copyright 1991 IEEE)

flow. In 2-D flows, critical points near the surface of a body have a similar property. Indeed, near walls where the velocity is constrained to be zero[9] the flow is mainly tangential, and streamlines propagate parallel to the surface. However, there are points where the tangential velocity field vanishes and a streamline, instead of being deflected parallel to the body, suddenly originates or terminates on the surface. These points are known as *detachment* and *attachment* points, respectively [64]. They play the same role as saddle points in the sense that adjacent streamlines can be deflected in opposite directions.

Figure 5.14 shows topological skeletons of the 2-D flow past a cylinder at two different time steps. They are obtained by locating critical points and by integrating streamlines from the saddle, attachment, and detachment points along the principal directions of their respective Jacobian matrices **J** given by Equation 5.7. (streamlines in the incoming directions are integrated backward).

The topological skeletons divide the field into regions topologically equivalent to uniform flow. The representation is highly effective due to the ease of inferring the instantaneous behaviour of every streamline in the flow from these simplified graphs. Comparing the flow at different time steps is also greatly facilitated and can be automated using syntactic pattern recognition. The flow in Figure 5.14, for example, underwent a topological transition between the two time steps, the attachment-detachment bubble on the left having developed into a paired saddle and center on the right.

5.3.3.2 2-D Time-dependent vector field topology

Global icons of vector fields that depend on time, Reynolds number, or any other parameter, must represent not only the "instantaneous" structure of the flow

9. No-slip condition.

but also the topological transitions that may occur between consecutive steps. For 2-D vector fields, such icons are obtained by stacking the instantaneous topological skeletons [65].

Figure 5.15 evinces the complete spatiotemporal evolution of the flow previously shown at two individual time steps in Figure 5.14. Adjacent skeletons are joined by linking their corresponding critical points and connecting streamlines, and the stacked topologies are displayed as a set of surfaces with the third dimension corresponding to time. Yellow and blue surfaces correspond to incoming and outgoing separatrices of the saddle points, respectively; surfaces from attachment points are colored orange and those from detachment points are colored purple. The periodic vortex shedding can be seen in the repeated development and movement downstream of saddle-center pairs, therefore enlightening the spatiotemporal structure of the flow.

5.3.3.3 3-D separated flows

3-D separated flows play a significant role in aerodynamics because of the close relationship between separation and vortices, which are important structures of the flow far from the body [64].

As in the 2-D example of Figures 5.14 and 5.15, the fluid in 3-D separated flows moves parallel to the body, and then suddenly detaches from the surface, creat-

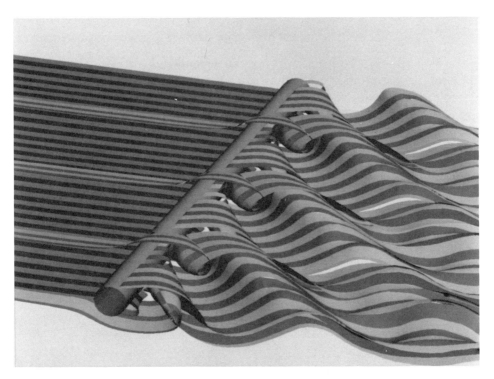

Figure 5.15. Topological surfaces depicting the time evolution of the 2-D flow past a circular cylinder. Time increases from back to front. (From Helman and Hesselink, reference 48, copyright 1991 IEEE) (See color section plate 5.15.)

TABLE 5.1. Vector fields in fluid flows.
ρ = mass density, p = pressure, and T = temperature.

$\bar{v}$	— velocity
$\bar{m} = \rho \bar{v}$	— momentum density
$\bar{\omega} = \text{curl } \bar{v}$	— vorticity
$\bar{g} = \text{grad } s$	— scalar gradient. $s = \rho, p, T$, etc.

ing vortices in the wake. The fluid can also reattach, causing recirculation regions similar to the bubble in Figure 5.14. However, detachment and attachment in 3-D flows do not arise in isolated points on the surface of the body but are distributed along entire lines that extend into surfaces in the flow. Theoretical papers have been written on the subject [64, 66, 67], but computer visualization techniques are necessary for accurately depicting both surface of separation and associated vortices.

In this section, we discuss several complementary global icons. First, we display

skin-friction topology that characterizes the flow near the surface of the body. Then, we represent

topological extensions in the flow, namely, the surface of separation and associated vortices.

Since there is no agreement on a universal definition of vortex and vortex core, the resulting visualization techniques are varied and numerous. Batchelor, for example, defines a vortex core as "a region with a finite cross-sectional area of relatively concentrated vorticity [68]," while Chong et al. [55] suggest that "a vortex core is a region of space where the vorticity (Table 5.1) is sufficiently strong to cause the rate-of-strain tensor [ε_{ik} (Table 5.2)] to be dominated by the rotation tensor—i.e., the [velocity gradient] has complex eigenvalues ." As pointed out by Yates and Chapman, "in [3-D] separated flows, there are no discontinuities that

TABLE 5.2. Symmetric tensor fields in fluid flows.
p = pressure, ρ = mass density, v_i and v_k = velocity components, and η = viscosity. δ_{ik} is the Kronecker symbol.

$\varepsilon_{ik} = \dfrac{\partial v_i}{\partial x_k} + \dfrac{\partial v_k}{\partial x_i}$	— rate-of-strain tensor
$\sigma'_{ik} = \eta \varepsilon_{ik}$ *	— viscous stress tensor
$\sigma_{ik} = -p\delta_{ik} + \sigma'_{ik}$	— stress tensor
$\Pi^r_{ik} = p\delta_{ik} + \rho v_i v_k$	— reversible momentum flux density tensor
$\Pi_{ik} = \Pi^r_{ik} - \sigma'_{ik}$	— momentum flux density tensor

* In compressible flows, there is an additional term involving the divergence of the velocity field.

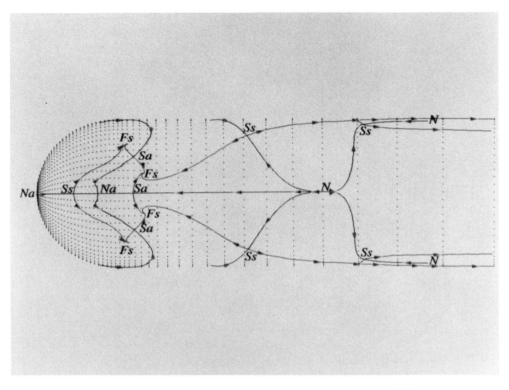

Figure 5.16. Skin-friction topology on the upper hemisphere of the cylinder in Figure 5.4. *Sa, Ss* = saddles of attachment and separation; *Na, Ns* = nodes of attachment and separation; *Fa, Fs* = spiral nodes of attachment and separation.

define the extent of the vortices and their cores [69]." The problem of detecting and representing vortices is therefore complex. We close the discussion on separation by two vortex detection techniques that are gaining wide acceptance:

- representation by means of *helicity density* (which involves object contraction), and
- line icons for vortex core tracing.

Skin-friction topology. The first step in visualizing 3-D separated flows consists in depicting the structure of the vector field near the body, for which an adequate description is inferred from the skin-friction field; i.e., the 2-D tangential velocity field one grid plane away from the surface of the body.[10]

Experimentally, the skin-friction field is studied by examining the streaks that form in an oil film on the surface of the body in a wind tunnel [33]. In computer visualization, similar information is derived by integrating 2-D streamlines of the skin-friction field or, preferably, by extracting its 2-D topological skeleton. The skin-friction topology of the flow in Figure 5.4 is represented in Figure 5.16

---

10. Velocity vanishes right on body.

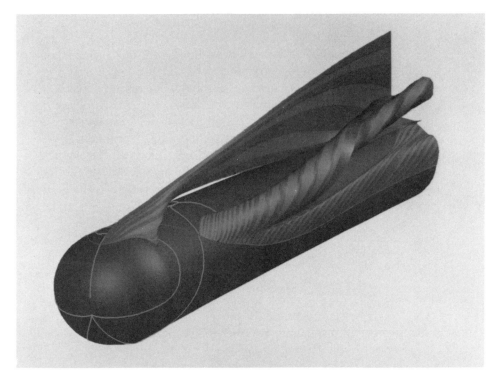

Figure 5.17. Streamsurfaces depicting separation topology. (From Helman and Hesselink, reference 48, copyright 1991 IEEE)

which shows outgoing separatrices, incoming separatrices, as well as 2-D nodes (*N*), foci (*F*), and saddles (*S*). The main difference from the former topological examples is that critical points are now truly three-dimensional. Hence, they always have a principal direction—cutting the surface—along which the flow is either outgoing (attachment points) or incoming (detachment or separation points).

The simplicity of topological representations appears clearly when comparing Figures 5.6 and 5.16 both of which display the same data.

Surface of separation. The surface of separation and the associated vortices are extensions in the flow of the skin-friction topology. Indeed, among skin-friction critical points, saddles of separation (*Ss*) play a particular role. As shown in Figure 5.10 their 3-D structure is really saddle/saddle/repelling node; hence, there is always a plane of outgoing trajectories emanating from them and leaving the surface of the body.[11] In fact, the surface of separation intersects the body along the outgoing separatrices of the saddles of separation, which are therefore called *lines of separation.* Note that these lines always connect saddle points to nodes or foci, but not to other saddles because such connections are structurally unstable.

---

11. The same situation arises for 3-D nodes and spiral nodes that are repelling in every direction; however, these nodes do not appear in incompressible or steady compressible flows because they are not compatible with the continuity equation.

The surface of separation is the streamsurface computed by advecting (as in Section 5.3.1.3) a front of particles initially positioned along the lines of separation. For example, Figure 5.17 shows parts of the surface of separation whose rolled up form delineates vortices (compare Figure 5.17 and Figure 5.5).

Object contraction and helicity density. Although efficient at detecting vortices, drawing the surface of separation is a complex process and requires critical points and lines of separation to exist in the skin-friction field—in which case the separation is termed *global*. As opposed to this, the skin-friction field in *local*[12] separations does not possess such features. The flow exhibits all the characteristics of separation downstream from the surface of the body, but not right on it. It is therefore not possible to compute surfaces of local separations with the aforementioned technique.

Object contraction offers a simple and reliable alternative. Instead of representing vector fields such as velocity $\bar{v}$ or vorticity $\bar{\omega}$, one can display a scalar function, the *helicity density* defined by Moffat [70] as

$$H_d = \bar{v} \cdot \bar{\omega} = |\bar{v}||\bar{\omega}|\cos\varphi \qquad [5.9]$$

where φ is the angle between $\bar{v}$ and $\bar{\omega}$. Contour lines of H_d are shown in Figure 5.18.[13] The advantage of displaying H_d rather than other scalar functions such as vorticity magnitude ($|\bar{\omega}|$) or enstrophy density ($\frac{1}{2}|\bar{\omega}|^2$) is that both its magnitude and sign are relevant. Indeed, large positive values of H_d reflect large velocity and vorticity magnitudes together with small values of φ—a configuration that denotes right-handed vortices. Conversely, large negative values of indicate left-handed vortices. The contour lines in Figure 5.18 allow discriminating between the primary and the smaller secondary vortices which have opposite swirl (color) and reveal structures hidden both in Figures 5.4 and 5.5. Figure 5.18 also illustrates the correlation between changes in swirl direction and skin-friction lines, a fact noted in Reference [71].

Line icons for vortex core detection. Instead of drawing the entire surface of separation, one can further simplify the display and draw only the vortex cores (or the vortex center lines). In global separations, vortex cores are the streamlines lying at the edges of the separation sheet and are often associated with spiral nodes (Section 5.3.2.1) either in the flow above the body[14] or on its surface.[15] In both cases, vortex cores are found by integrating from the spiral nodes streamlines in the direction of the real eigenvector. Vortex cores obtained by this technique are shown in magenta in Figure 5.18, and are in good agreement with the contour lines of H_d. However, no vortex core is found for the secondary separation, which is local and, therefore, not associated with any critical point. In this case, other core detection techniques are applicable. For example, streamlines can be integrated from points in the flow where scalar functions such as velocity magnitude, nor-

12. Also called cross-flow [67].

13. Using H_d is obviously not restricted to local separations and applies equally well to global separations such as the primary separation in Figure 5.18.

14. Type I separation [67].

15. Type II separation [67].

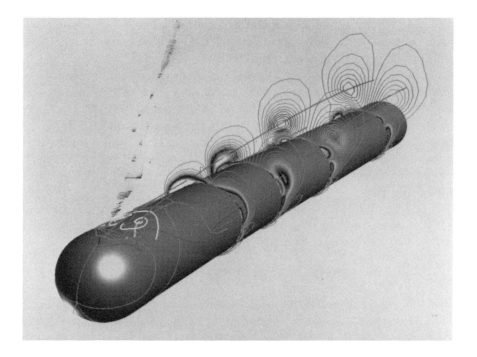

Figure 5.18. Contour lines of helicity density H_d (red/white = right-handed vortices; blue/black = left-handed vortices) together with skin-friction topology (blue and yellow lines) and vortex cores (magenta lines).

malized helicity,[16] or streamline curvature are extremum. Each method generally yields slightly different results [69], suggesting that a precise and universal definition as well as a method for detecting vortex cores is still open to question.

5.4
TENSOR MAPPINGS

Table 5.2 (see page 152) reveals that many physical quantities in fluid flows are tensor data. Visualizing tensor fields can therefore provide a significant insight into the physics of fluid flows. Not surprisingly, tensor visualization idioms are fewer—and newer—than their vector counterparts. Indeed, tensor data are two or three times more multivariate than vector fields—a fact resulting in greater complexity of the visualization process. For example, the simplest and most natural representation of tensor data is a set of three eigenvectors.[17] In spite of its simplicity, this representation is not as intuitive as the usual association of a vector with straightforward attributes, such as direction and magnitude. We are not used

---

16. The normalized helicity $H_n = H_d/|\bar{v}||\bar{\omega}|$ is discussed in Reference [71].

17. The individual scalar components U_{ik} of a tensor U are tight to a specific reference frame.

to forming mental images of tensor fields. Thus, abstraction is a necessary component of tensor mappings.

In this section, we discuss several elementary and global tensor icons that are summarized in Figure 5.2 (right).

Representation of symmetric tensor data. A symmetric tensor $\mathbf{U} = \{U_{ik}\}$ whose individual components obey Equation 5.1 is fully equivalent to three orthogonal vector fields. More specifically, $\mathbf{U}$ has, at every point $\bar{x}$, three real eigenvalues $\lambda^{(i)}$, $i = 1$, 2, or 3 as well as three real and orthogonal unit eigenvectors $\bar{e}^{(i)}$ [5]. We consider the three orthogonal vectors $\bar{v}^{(i)}$ given by

$$\bar{v}^{(i)} = \lambda^{(i)} \bar{e}^{(i)} \qquad\qquad [5.10]$$

where the eigenvalues are always ordered according to

$$\lambda^{(1)} \geq \lambda^{(2)} \geq \lambda^{(3)} \qquad\qquad [5.11]$$

Because of this particular ordering, $\bar{v}^{(1)}$, $\bar{v}^{(2)}$, $\bar{v}^{(3)}$ and are termed *major, medium* and *minor eigenvectors,* respectively.

Visualizing $\mathbf{U}$ is fully equivalent to visualizing simultaneously the three vector fields $\bar{v}^{(i)}$, since they include all the amplitude information (the eigenvalues $\lambda^{(i)}$) and all the directional information (the unit eigenvectors $\bar{e}^{(i)}$) represented in matrix notation by the components U_{ik}. Furthermore, visualizing the three vectors $\bar{v}^{(i)}$ allows one to understand the relative value of the six independent components U_{ik} with little or no training [10].

5.4.1 Elementary Icons

Elementary point and line icons that display tensor information strictly across the extent of their spatial domain are discussed below. To date, no surface tensor icon has been developed.

5.4.1.1 Point icons

Ellipsoids having the three vectors $\bar{v}^{(i)}$ for principal axes, are usually used to visualize $\mathbf{U}$ at coarsely spaced points. In addition, *tensor glyphs,* which are more sophisticated point icons designed to improve perception of the vectors $\bar{v}^{(i)}$, are discussed in References [2, 3].

Compared to vector arrows, problems of visual clutter in using point icons are even greater (imagine Figure 5.14 with ellipsoids instead of arrows). The density of displayed icons must be kept so low that the structure of the tensor field can not be perceived by mentally interpolating adjacent ellipsoids.

5.4.1.2 Hyperstreamlines

As for vector mappings, improved perception of continuous tensor fields is obtained using line instead of point icons. For example, one can apply object contraction and represent *tensor field lines;* i.e., streamlines of one of the vector fields $\bar{v}^{(i)}$ [72]. If tensor field lines emphasize the continuity of the data, they do not display the correlations existing between the three eigenvector fields $\bar{v}^{(i)}$. Thus, what is called for is a line icon that represents all the tensor information along a trajectory or, equivalently, one that encodes a continuous distribution of ellipsoids. For this purpose, we generalize vector streamlines to tensor *hyperstreamlines*, which are the simplest continuous tensor icons that can be extracted from volumetric tensor data.

We obtain hyperstreamlines as follows: a geometric primitive of finite size sweeps along one of the eigenvector fields $\bar{v}^{(i)}$ while stretching in the transverse plane under the combined action of the two other orthogonal eigenvector fields. A hyperstreamline is the surface obtained by linking the stretched primitives at the different points along the trajectory and is color coded by means of a user-defined function of the three eigenvalues, generally the amplitude of the longitudinal eigenvalue [9, 10].

The color and trajectory of a hyperstreamline fully represent the longitudinal eigenvector, and the cross-section encodes the two remaining transverse eigenvectors. Thus, hyperstreamlines form a continuous representation of the whole tensor data along their trajectory. They are called *major, medium,* or *minor* hyperstreamlines depending on the longitudinal eigenvector field.

To illustrate properties of hyperstreamlines, we first display two simple stress tensor fields in elastic materials in Figures 5.19, 5.20 and 5.21. Then, we apply the same methodology to more complex flow data.

Trajectory. Hyperstreamline trajectories show, for example, how forces propagate in a stress tensor field, and how momentum is transferred in a momentum flux density tensor field. Figure 5.19 illustrates this property for an elastic stress tensor field induced by two compressive forces on the top surface of the material.

Every line is color-coded according to the longitudinal eigenvalue. The lines propagating upward are along the most compressive direction—the minor eigenvector $\bar{v}^{(3)}$—and converge towards the regions of high stress where the forces are applied. Note the sudden divergence of close trajectories on each side of the plane of symmetry. Similarly, trajectories along the two other eigenvectors delineate a surface shown near the bottom face of the cube. This surface is everywhere perpendicular to the most compressive direction.

For an important class of tensor data, such as the stress tensor σ_{ik} in solids and the momentum flux density tensor Π_{ik} in steady fluids, encoding the longitudinal eigenvalue into the color of a hyperstreamline captures some of the geometric behavior; i.e., convergence or divergence of neighboring hyperstreamlines. We call such tensor fields *solenoidal,* by analogy with the properties of streamlines of *solenoidal* (divergence-free) vector fields [9, 5].

Cross-section. Hyperstreamlines are further characterized by the geometry of their cross-section; i.e., the geometric primitive that sweeps along the trajectory. We consider two types of primitives:

a *circle* that stretches into an ellipse while sweeping and that generates a hyperstreamline called a *tube;* and

a *cross* that generates a hyperstreamline called a *helix.*

Figure 5.20 shows two minor tubes propagating upward as well as four medium and major helices. In a tube, the principal axes of each elliptical cross-

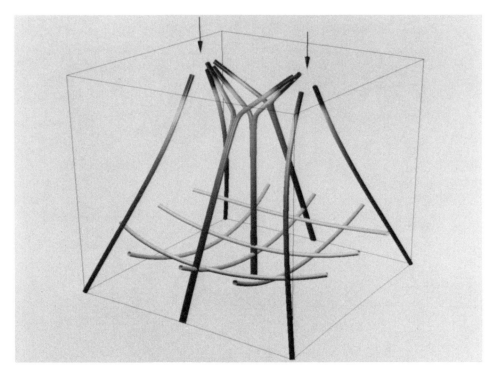

Figure 5.19. Stress tensor induced by two compressive forces. Hyperstreamline trajectories. Color scale is shown in Figure 5.2. (From Delmarcelle and Hesselink, reference 9, copyright 1993 IEEE)

section are along the transverse eigenvectors, and have a length proportional to the magnitude of the transverse eigenvalues. The same property holds for a helix, whose arms are proportional to the transverse eigenvectors (helices owe their name to the spiraling pattern of their arms that can be observed in some cases). In this manner, both directional and amplitude information are encoded along the trajectory. The local sign of the transverse eigenvalues can be detected by examining the singularities in the cross-section of the hyperstreamline. Indeed, the cross-section reduces to a single line or a point wherever one of the transverse eigenvalues changes sign.

Four different stages of a minor tube in a stress tensor field are displayed in Figure 5.21. The tensor field is similar to that of Figures 5.19 and 5.20, but an additional tension force is added. In the top-left, the cross-section is circular and the transverse stresses are equal in magnitude. The top-right shows an increasing anisotropy of the transverse stresses together with a decrease of the longitudinal eigenvalue (color). In the bottom-left, the cross-section is reduced to a straight line; one transverse eigenvalue is zero and the stresses are locally two-dimensional. In the bottom-right, the stresses are three-dimensional once again; the eigenvectors undergo a rapid rotation and a substantial stretching which reveals an important gradient of shear and pressure in the region.

Figure 5.20. Stress tensor induced by two compressive forces. Minor tubes, medium and major helices. Color scale is shown in Figure 5.21. (From Delmarcelle and Hesselink, reference 9, copyright 1993 IEEE) (See color section plate 5.20.)

We can modify the coloring scheme of hyperstreamlines to represent other aspects of the data. For example, we can color a tube in function of the angle between the radial vector $\bar{n}$ in the plane of the tube's cross-section and the force $\bar{f} = \mathbf{U}\bar{n}$ acting on a facet with normal $\bar{n}$. Color therefore discriminates among tensile, compressive, and pure shear transverse directions [9].

Reversible momentum flux density. A specific example of flow data illustrates how hyperstreamlines may be used to correlate several different physical quantities. For the reversible part of the momentum flux density tensor, Π^r_{ik} in Table 5.2 (see page 152) one may correlate pressure p, velocity direction $\bar{v}/|\bar{v}|$, and kinetic energy density k. Indeed, the major eigenvalue of Π^r_{ik} is $\lambda^{(1)} = p + 2k$, and the corresponding unit eigenvector is the velocity direction. The other eigenvalues are degenerate ($\lambda^{(2)} = \lambda^{(3)} = p$) in the whole space. It follows that only major tubes can be used. Tube trajectories are everywhere tangent to the velocity direction and are therefore streamlines of the velocity field. Cross-sections are circular, with a diameter proportional to the pressure. In addition, the color of the tubes is chosen as

$$\text{color} \sim \frac{\lambda^{(1)} - 0.5\left(\lambda^{(2)} + \lambda^{(3)}\right)}{2} = k \qquad [5.12]$$

so as to represent the kinetic energy density k. Thus, the trajectory, diameter, and

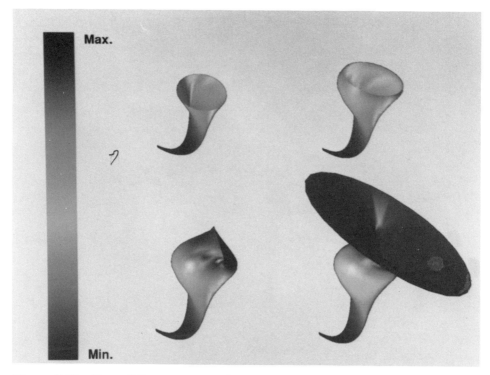

Figure 5.21. Four different stages of a minor tube in an elastic stress tensor field. (From Delmarcelle and Hesselink, reference 9, copyright 1993 IEEE) (See color section plate 5.21.)

color of the major tubes encode the velocity direction, pressure and kinetic energy density, respectively.

Figure 5.22 shows Π_{ik}^r in the flow past a hemisphere cylinder. The direction of the incoming flow is $5°$ to the left of the hemisphere axis. The detachment at the end of the cylinder is clearly visible. The pattern of hyperstreamlines indicates that the momentum is transferred fairly uniformly from the tip of the body to the end with a globally decreasing kinetic energy shown by color variations. However, there is a region on the front side of the body where direction, color, and diameter of the first five tubes vary suddenly. These variations indicate correlated changes in velocity direction, kinetic energy density, and pressure, respectively.

5.4.2 Global Icons

Global icons of vector fields, such as vector field topology and vortex cores, display the collective behavior of a large set of streamlines. By analogy, global icons of tensor data are obtained by encoding the behavior of a large number of hyperstreamlines.

Consider the collection $\mathcal{HS}^{(i)}$ of hyperstreamlines propagating along the eigenvector field $\bar{v}^{(i)}$ given by Equation 5.10. Important features exist in both the trajectory and the cross-section of these hyperstreamlines. For example, the locus

Figure 5.22. Reversible momentum flux density tensor in the flow past a hemisphere cylinder. Color scale is shown in Figure 5.21. (From Delmarcelle and Hesselink, reference 9, copyright 1993 IEEE) (See color section plate 5.22.)

$$\lambda^{(i)} = 0 \qquad\qquad [5.13]$$

is the set of the critical points in the trajectory of the hyperstreamlines $\mathcal{H}S^{(i)}$. (Here, we use "critical points" literally. They are points where the magnitude of the longitudinal eigenvector field $\bar{v}^{(i)}$ vanishes. We do not presuppose any specific pattern of the neighboring hyperstreamlines.) Further, the surface

$$\lambda^{(j)}\lambda^{(k)} = 0 \qquad\qquad [5.14]$$

where $\lambda^{(j)}$ and $\lambda^{(k)}$ are the transverse eigenvalues, is the locus of points where the cross-section of the hyperstreamlines $\mathcal{H}S^{(i)}$ is singular; i.e., reduced to a straight line or a point. In general, surfaces of constant eccentricity are loci where the cross-section of each hyperstreamline in $\mathcal{H}S^{(i)}$ has the same shape, regardless of its orientation and scaling. In particular, the locus

$$\lambda^{(j)} \pm \lambda^{(k)} = 0 \qquad\qquad [5.15]$$

is the set of points where the cross-section degenerates into a circle (zero eccentricity). We refer the reader to Reference [84] for a detailed discussion of the topology of tensor fields.

A global icon of the stress tensor of Figures 5.19 and 5.20 is given in Figure 5.23. The yellow surface is the locus of critical points of the medium eigenvector $\bar{v}^{(2)}$ and the green surface represents the critical points of the major eigenvector $\bar{v}^{(1)}$. On both of these surfaces, the cross-section of each minor tube—four of them are shown—reduces to a straight line. On the blue surface, the transverse eigenvalues are opposite to each other, and the cross-section is circular. Below the yellow surface, both transverse eigenvalues are positive and every transverse direction in the cross-section of the minor tubes is in tension. Above the yellow surface, the medium eigenvalue becomes negative and some transverse directions are in tension while others are compressive. Inside the green surface, however, every transverse direction is in compression.

Stresses and viscous stresses. The former concepts are applied to visualize the stress tensor σ_{ik} and viscous stress tensor σ'_{ik} in the flow past a hemisphere cylinder. As shown in Table 5.2 (see page 152), these two tensors differ only by an isotropic pressure component, implying that their unit eigenvectors are identical. However, the eigenvalues of σ_{ik} are equal to the eigenvalues of σ'_{ik} minus a large pressure component. Table 5.2 also shows that visualizing σ'_{ik} is equivalent to visualizing the rate-of-strain tensor e_{ik} in incompressible flows.

Hyperstreamlines of the stress tensor are shown in Figure 5.24 (top) (the flow

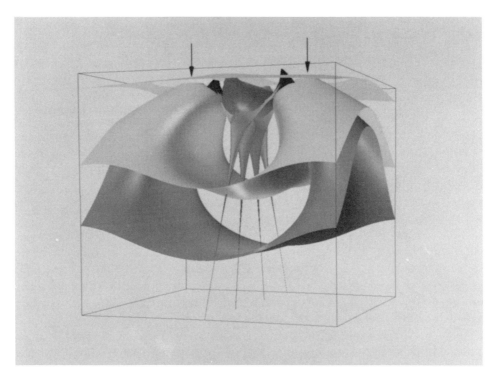

Figure 5.23. Global icon of the stress tensor of Figures 5.19 and 5.20. (From Delmarcelle and Hesselink, reference 9, copyright 1993 IEEE)

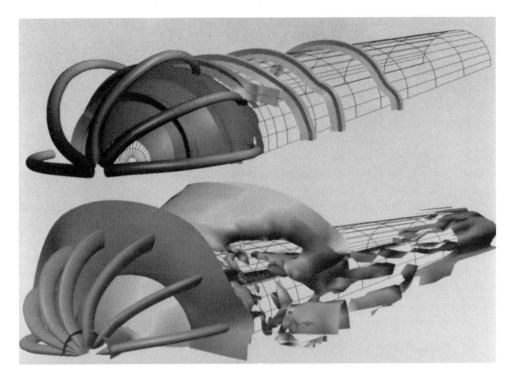

Figure 5.24. Stress tensor *(top)* and viscous stress tensor *(bottom)* in the flow past a hemisphere cylinder. Color scale is shown in Figure 5.21. (From Delmarcelle and Hesselink, reference 9, copyright 1993 IEEE)

is the same as in Figure 5.22). The major tubes in front are along the least compressive direction $\bar{v}^{(1)}$. Their trajectory show how forces propagate from the region in front of the cylinder to the surface of the body. The cross-section of the tubes is very circular, indicating, as expected, that the pressure component of the stresses is dominant. However, the viscous stresses close to the body create a slightly anisotropic cross-section. On the yellow surface, for example, the eccentricity is equal to 10%.

The helices are along the medium eigenvector field. They propagate mainly parallel to the cylinder surface, and the orientation of their arms indicates a fairly constant direction of the two transverse eigenvectors—respectively, the least and most compressive eigendirections. The third helix exhibits a more complex behavior, suggesting that the stress tensor is less uniform in the region of contact between the tubes and the body than in other parts of the flow.

Figure 5.24 (bottom) shows the viscous stress tensor σ'_{ik} in the same flow. As expected, the trajectories are similar to those in Figure 5.24(top), but removing the large isotropic pressure contribution dramatically enhances the anisotropy of the cross-section of the tubes. The surface corresponds to a constant eccentricity of 90 and is crossed twice by each tube.

5.5
CONCLUSIONS

A unified view of vector and tensor field visualization techniques in computational fluid dynamics has been presented in this chapter. Many diverse application-dependent visualization mappings are described in a unified framework by considering the semiotics of data representation and by identifying attributes of icons. Visualization mappings are classified as a function of their object, spatial domain, and information level. Line and surface icons improve the display of elementary information by using point icons. Local icons represent data gradients, and global icons reveal the complete structure of the data field. The concepts are illustrated here mainly by examples of aerodynamical flows, but apply to a much wider variety of data.

Undoubtedly, there are various types of icons suggested by our classification that are yet to be designed. For example, empty boxes in Figure 5.2 suggest that research be carried out in order to design local surface icons of vector fields, as well as elementary surface and local icons of tensor fields. In addition, global icons of vector and tensor data must still be improved and new mappings are to be designed.

5.6
APPENDIX:
SOFTWARE ENVIRONMENTS FOR
FLOW VISUALIZATION

This appendix completes the former theoretical discussion by describing actual implementations of various visualization mappings. Many different software packages for scientific visualization have appeared during the last few years, and extensive reviews are given, for example, in References [73, 74]. In the following, we first discuss FAST, a powerful visualization environment that includes facilities for computational aerodynamics. Then, we mention other visualization software capable of displaying scalar and vector fields. To our knowledge, tensor field mappings have not yet been implemented in multipurpose visualization packages, with the notable exception of NCSA's RIVERS project [2].

FAST. (Flow Analysis Software Toolkit)[18] is a flow visualization environment made up of several programs (modules) providing visualization tools for scalar and vector fields defined over single or multi-zoned grids [75]. The user commands the different modules by means of interactive graphical interfaces built with the Panel Library [76]. Every graphical object created with *FAST*, as well as grids, solution files, scalar and vector fields, are placed in shared memory and are accessible by all modules. *FAST* currently runs on Silicon Graphics 4D workstations. Its portability is enhanced, however, by the use of modular programming methods,

---

18. Contact Cosmic, The University of Georgia, 382 East Broad Street, Athens, GA 30602-4272 USA.

a graphics library standard, and common network communication protocols for the distribution of processing (Unix sockets). In addition, FAST is extensible and facilities are provided for implementing new modules and customizing the graphical interface.

FAST supports both structured and unstructured grid files and solution files, as well as any precomputed scalar or vector data in PLOT3D format. FAST is also capable of loading and rendering ArcGraph metafiles [77].

A calculator module computes various scalar and vector functions from the input data and performs different mathematical operations on the resulting fields. It has the appearance and functionality of real programmable calculators, but, instead of operating on numbers, it operates on fields of scalar numbers and vectors. More than a hundred scalar and vector functions are preprogrammed, but the user can interactively create and execute any formula that transforms scalar and vector fields.

Another module displays grid geometry and performs surface rendering of scalar and vector fields across grid planes; facilities include contour lines, arrows, displacement and polygonal surfaces. For example, this module was used to render the body in Figure 5.4 and 5.18, the arrow plot in Figure 5.4, and the helicity density contours in Figure 5.18. Most of the modalities for scalar fields are also available for unstructured grids. An additional module discussed in length in Reference [35] computes scalar isosurfaces and cutting planes of scalar and vector data.

Streamlines and rakes of streamlines can be computed interactively. Extraction and display of critical points, vortex cores, and skin-friction topology are performed by a topology module [56, 48], a unique feature of *FAST* that was used in Figures 5.16 and 5.18. The latest release of *FAST* includes an audio module, streamribbons, and streamtubes, which was used to create Figure 5.12.

Software for distributed computing. As mentioned in Section 5.3.1.2, distributed computing is being explored as an enabling technology for interactive flow visualization. Examples of NASA software linking Cray supercomputers and Silicon Graphics workstations include a distributed version of PLOT3D and RIP, a remote interactive particle tracer [40]. In addition, Cray supports a commercial version of MPGS (Multi-Purpose Graphics System), a distributed graphics program providing facilities for structured and unstructured data, such as arrows, particle traces, contour lines, and isosurfaces.

Other software. In addition to the general and flexible application builders which can be programmed for flow visualization, such as apE,[19] AVS,[20] Explorer,[21] or Khoros[22]—other packages exist that are useful for displaying scalar and vector data. For example,

VISUAL3,[23] displays the data in multiple windows containing correlated cursors—one window represents the volumetric data and two other windows

19. TaraVisual Corporation, Inc.

20. Stardent Computer, Inc.

21. Silicon Graphics, Inc.

22. Available by anonymous ftp at pprg.eece.unm.edu in the U.S. and ftp.uni-erlangen.de in Germany.

23. Massachussets Institute of Technology.

display 2-D and 1-D cuts. Specific facilities include streamribbons, streamtubes, and X-Rays for rendering of scalar data [62, 78].

VISAGE[24]—an object-oriented visualization system for structured or unstructured grids—provides facilities such as isosurfaces, streamtubes, streamribbons, arrows and cutting planes [79].

The Data Visualizer[25] handles structured and unstructured grids, and different versions exist for a large variety of hardware configurations. Facilities include 2-D and 3-D graphics, arrows, cutting planes, streamlines, volume rendering, and streamribbons.

FIELDVIEW,[26] which runs on a variety of UNIX workstations, provides cutting planes, isosurfaces, arrows, contour lines, streamlines, as well as a calculator module for field operations [80]. Finally,

PV-WAVE[27] is a visualization package intended for the display and analysis of large multidimensional data sets. It is not specifically intended for flow visualization but may be used to display scalar and vector data.

5.6 ACKNOWLEDGEMENTS

The authors are grateful to J. Helman, M. Briscolini, P. Santangelo, J. Hultquist, W. Schroeder, C. Volpe, and W. Lorensen for contributing images that greatly enhanced the scope of this chapter. Valuable comments on earlier versions of this chapter were given by Paul Ning, Mark Peercy and Tomiko Yoda. Paul Ning implemented the Marching Cubes algorithm on which our isosurface extraction algorithm is based. Yuval Levy computed the data represented in Figures 5.22 and 5.24, Rogers et al.[81] computed the data in Figure 5.8, and Ying et al.[82] computed the data in Figures 5.4, 5.5 5.11, 5.16, 5.17 and 5.18. Cantwell and Coles [83] measured the data displayed in Figures 5.14 and 5.15. Extensive use of FAST Beta version 2.1 greatly facilitated this work. The authors are supported by NASA under contract NCA-781 which includes support from the NASA Ames Numerical Aerodynamics Simulation Program and the NASA Ames Fluid Dynamics Division, and also by NSF under grant ECS8815815.

5.7 REFERENCES

[1] B. H. McCormick, T. A. DeFanti, and M. D. Brown, "Visualization in scientific computing: a synopsis," IEEE Computer Graphics and Applications, vol. 7, no. 4, pp. 61–70, 1987.

[2] R. B. Haber, "Visualization techniques for engineering mechanics," Computing Systems in Engineering, vol. 1, no. 1, pp. 37–50, 1990.

[3] R. B. Haber and D. A. McNabb, "Visualization idioms: a conceptual model for scientific visualization systems," in Visualization in Scientific Computing (G. M. Nielson and B. Shriver, eds.), pp. 74–93, CS Press, Los Alamitos, CA, 1990.

24. General Electric Corporate Research and Development.

25. Wavefront Technologies, Inc.

26. Intelligent Light, Inc.

27. Precision Visuals, Inc.

[4] P. Ning and L. Hesselink, "Fast volume rendering of compressed data," in Proc. IEEE Visualization '93, CS Press, Los Alamitos, CA., 1993.

[5] A. I. Borisenko and I. E. Tarapov, Vector and Tensor Analysis with Applications. Dover Publications, New York, 1979.

[6] W. E. Lorensen and H. E. Cline, "Marching cubes: A high resolution 3-D surface construction algorithm," Computer Graphics, vol. 21, no. 4, pp. 163–169, 1987.

[7] M. Levoy, "Display of surfaces from volume data," IEEE Computer Graphics and Applications, vol. 8, no. 3, pp. 29–37, 1988.

[8] R. A. Drebin, L. Carpenter, and P. Hanrahan, "Volume rendering," Computer Graphics, vol. 22, no. 4, pp. 110–119, 1988.

[9] T. Delmarcelle and L. Hesselink, "Visualizing second-order tensor fields with hyperstreamlines," IEEE Computer Graphics and Applications, vol. 13, no. 4, pp. 25–33, 1993. Special issue on scientific visualization.

[10] T. Delmarcelle and L. Hesselink, "Visualization of second order tensor fields and matrix data," in Proc. IEEE Visualization '92, pp. 316–323, CS Press, Los Alamitos, CA., 1992.

[11] C. Upson, R. Wolff, R. Weinberg, and D. Kerlick, Two and Three Dimensional Visualization Workshop. ACM SIGGRAPH, 1989. SIGGRAPH 1989 course notes 13.

[12] M. M. Blattner, R. M. Greenberg, and M. Kamegai, "Listening to turbulence: an example of scientific audiolization," in Multimedia Interface Design (M. M. Blattner and R. B. Dannenberg, eds.), ch. 6, ACM Press, Addison-Wesley, New York, 1992.

[13] N. J. Zabusky, "Computational synergetics," Physics Today, no. 7, pp. 36–46, 1984.

[14] K.-H. A. Winkler and M. L. Norman, "Munacolor: understanding high-resolution gas dynamical simulations through color graphics," in Astrophysical Radiation Hydrodynamics (K.-H. A. Winkler and M. L. Norman, eds.), pp. 223–243, D. Reidel Publishing Company, Dordrecht, Holland, 1986.

[15] J. C. Agui and L. Hesselink, "Flow visualization and numerical analysis of a coflowing jet: a three-dimensional approach," Journal of Fluid Mechanics, vol. 191, pp. 19–45, 1988.

[16] R. Crawfis and N. Max, "Direct volume visualization of three-dimensional vector fields," in Proc. 1992 Workshop on Volume Visualization, pp. 55–60, ACM SIGGRAPH, Oct. 1992.

[17] N. Max, R. Crawfis, and D. Williams, "Visualization for climate modeling," IEEE Computer Graphics and Applications, vol. 13, no. 4, pp. 34–41, 1993. Special issue on scientific visualization.

[18] R. D. Bergeron and G. G. Grinstein, "A reference model for the visualization of multi-dimensional data," in EUROGRAPHICS '89 (W. Hansmann, F. Hopgood, and W. Strasser, eds.), pp. 393–399, Elsevier Science Publishers B.V. (North-Holland), 1989.

[19] G. D. Kerlick, "Moving iconic objects in scientific visualization," in Proc. IEEE Visualization '90, pp. 124–130, CS Press, Los Alamitos, CA., 1990.

[20] F. de Saussure, "Course in general linguistics," in Critical theory since 1965 (H. Adams and L. Searle, eds.), Florida State University Press, 1986.

[21] C. S. Peirce, Philosophical Writings of Peirce, selected and edited with an introduction by Julius Buchtler. Dover Publications, New York, 1955.

[22] Y. L. Kergosien, "Generic sign systems in medical imaging," IEEE Computer Graphics and Applications, vol. 11, no. 5, pp. 46–65, 1991.

[23] V. Tejera, Semiotics from Peirce to Barthes: a conceptual introduction to the study of communication, interpretation, and expression. E. J. Brill, Leiden, The Netherlands, 1988.

[24] J. Bertin, Semiology of Graphics. The University of Wisconsin Press, 1983. Translation of Sémiologie Graphique, Editions Gauthier-Villars, Paris, 1967.

[25] J. Bertin, Graphics and Graphic Information Processing. Walter de Gruyter, 1981. Translation of La Graphique et le Traitement Graphique de l'Information, Flammarion, Paris, 1977.

[26] P. K. Robertson, "A methodology for choosing data representations," IEEE Computer Graphics and Applications, vol. 11, no. 3, pp. 56–67, 1991. Special issue on visualization.

[27] M. Briscolini and P. Santangelo, "Animation of computer simulations of two-dimensional turbulence and three-dimensional flows," IBM Journal of Research and Development, vol. 35, no. 1, pp. 119–139, 1991. Special issue on visual interpretation of complex data.

[28] F. J. Bitz and N. J. Zabusky, "David and Visiometrics: visualizing and quantifying evolving amorphous objects," Computer in Physics, no. 6, pp. 603–613, 1990.

[29] M. V. Melander and N. J. Zabusky, "Interaction and apparent reconnection of 3-D vortex tubes via direct numerical simulations," Fluid Dynamics Research, vol. 3, pp. 247–250, 1988.

[30] N. J. Zabusky and M. V. Melander, "Three-dimensional vortex tube reconnections: morphology for orthogonally-offset tubes," Physica D, vol. 37, pp. 555–562, 1989.

[31] D. Silver and N. J. Zabusky, "3-D visualization and quantification of evolving amorphous objects," in Extracting Meaning from Complex Data: Processing, Display, Interaction II (Proc. SPIE), vol. 1459, pp. 97–108, SPIE, Bellingham, WA., 1991.

[32] D. Silver, M. Gao, and N. Zabusky, "Visualizing causal effects in 4-D space-time vector fields," in Proc. IEEE Visualization '91, pp. 12–16, CS Press, Los Alamitos, CA., 1991.

[33] W. Merzkirch, Flow Visualization. Academic Press, London, second ed., 1987.

[34] K. A. Kroos, "Computer graphics techniques for three-dimensional flow visualization," in Frontiers in Computer Graphics (Proc. Computer Graphics Tokyo'84) (T. L. Kunii, ed.), Springer-Verlag, 1985.

[35] G. D. Kerlick, "Isolev: a level surface cutting plane program for fluid flow data," in Extracting Meaning from Complex Data: Processing, Display, Interaction (Proc. SPIE), vol. 1259, pp. 2–13, SPIE, Bellingham, WA., 1990.

[36] L. Yaeger, C. Upson, and R. Myers, "Combining physical and visual simulation—creation of the planet jupiter for the film '2010'," Computer Graphics, vol. 20, no. 4, pp. 85–93, 1986.

[37] G. K. Batchelor, "The effect of homogeneous turbulence on material lines and surfaces," Proceedings of the Royal Society of London Ser. A, vol. 213, pp. 349–366, 1952.

[38] P. G. Buning, "Sources of error in the graphical analysis of CFD results," Journal of Scientific Computing, vol. 3, no. 2, pp. 149–164, 1988.

[39] P. Yeung and S. Pope, "An algorithm for tracking fluid particles in numerical simulations of homogeneous turbulence," Journal of Computational Physics, vol. 79, pp. 373–416, 1988.

[40] S. E. Rogers, P. G. Buning, and F. J. Merritt, "Distributed interactive graphics. Applications in computational fluid dynamics," The International Journal of Supercomputer Applications, vol. 1, no. 4, pp. 96–105, 1987.

[41] S. Bryson and C. Levit, "The virtual wind tunnel," IEEE Computer Graphics and Applications, vol. 12, no. 4, pp. 25–34, 1992. Special issue on visualization.

[42] J. J. van Wijk, "A raster graphics approach to flow visualization," in EUROGRAPHICS '90 (W. Hansmann, F. Hopgood, and W. Strasser, eds.), pp. 251–259, Elsevier Science Publishers B.V. (North-Holland), 1990.

[43] D. N. Kenwright and G. D. Mallinson, "A 3-D streamline tracking algorithm using dual stream functions," in Proc. IEEE Visualization '92, pp. 62–68, CS Press, Los Alamitos, CA., 1992.

[44] J. J. van Wijk, "Spot noise. Texture synthesis for data visualization," Computer Graphics, vol. 25, no. 4, pp. 309–318, 1991.

[45] B. Cabral and L. C. Leedom, "Imaging vector fields using line integral convolution," Computer Graphics, (*SIGGRAPH '93 Proceedings*), Aug. 1993, J. T. Kajiya, Ed., Vol. 27, pp. 263–272

[46] K. Perlin, "Hypertexture," Computer Graphics, vol. 23, no. 3, pp. 253–262, 1989.

[47] J. P. M. Hultquist, "Constructing stream surfaces in steady 3-D vector fields," in Proc. IEEE Visualization '92, pp. 171–178, CS Press, Los Alamitos, CA., 1992.

[48] J. L. Helman and L. Hesselink, "Visualization of vector field topology in fluid flows," IEEE Computer Graphics and Applications, vol. 11, no. 3, pp. 36–46, 1991. Special issue on visualization.

[49] J. L. Helman and L. Hesselink, "Surface representations of two- and three-dimensional fluid flow topology," in Proc. IEEE Visualization '90, pp. 6–13, CS Press, Los Alamitos, CA., 1990.

[50] J. J. van Wijk, "Flow visualization with surface particles," IEEE Computer Graphics and Applications, vol. 13, no. 4, pp. 18–24, 1993. Special issue on scientific visualization.

[51] W. Kaplan, Ordinary Differential Equations. Addison-Wesley, New York, 1958.

[52] L. S. Pontryagin, Ordinary Differential Equations. Addison-Wesley, New York, 1962.

[53] A. Perry and B. Fairlie, "Critical points in flow patterns," Advances in Geophysics B, vol. 18, pp. 299–315, 1974.

[54] A. Perry and M. Chong, "A description of eddying motions and flow patterns using critical point concepts," Annual Review of Fluid Mechanics, vol. 19, pp. 125–155, 1987.

[55] M. S. Chong, A. E. Perry, and B. J. Cantwell, "A general classification of three-dimensional flow fields," Physics of Fluids A, vol. 2, no. 5, pp. 765–777, 1990.

[56] A. Globus, C. Levit, and T. Lasinski, "A tool for visualizing the topology of three-dimensional vector fields," in Proc. IEEE Visualization '91, pp. 33–40, CS Press, Los Alamitos, CA., 1991.

[57] H. Vollmers, "The recovering of flow features from large numerical databases," in Computer Graphics and Flow Visualization in Computational Fluid Dynamics (von Karman Lecture Series 1991-07), von Karman Institute for Fluid Dynamics, Rhode Saint Genese, Belgium, Sept. 1991.

[58] R. R. Dickinson, "Interactive analysis of the topology of 4-D vector fields," IBM Journal of Research and Development, vol. 35, no. 1, pp. 59–66, 1991. Special issue on visual interpretation of complex data.

[59] G. Belie, "Flow visualization in the space shuttle's main engine," Mechanical Engineering, vol. 107, no. 9, pp. 27–33, 1985.

[60] G. Volpe, "Streamlines and streamribbons in aerodynamics," in AIAA 27th Aerospace Sciences Meeting, Jan. 1989. AIAA paper 89-0140.

[61] W. J. Schroeder, C. R. Volpe, and W. E. Lorensen, "The stream polygon: a technique for 3-D

vector field visualization," in Proc. IEEE Visualization '91, pp. 126–132, CS Press, Los Alamitos, CA., 1991.

[62] R. Haimes, M. Giles, and D. Darmofal, "Visual3—a software environment for flow visualization," in Computer Graphics and Flow Visualization in Computational Fluid Dynamics (von Karman Lecture Series 1991-007), von Karman Institute for Fluid Dynamics, Rhode Saint Genese, Belgium, Sept. 1991.

[63] L. Hesselink, "Digital image processing in flow visualization," Annual Review of Fluid Mechanics, vol. 20, pp. 421–485, 1988.

[64] M. J. Lighthill, "Introduction. Boundary layer theory," in Laminar Boundary Layers (L. Rosenhead, ed.), pp. 46–113, Oxford University Press, 1963.

[65] J. L. Helman and L. Hesselink, "Representation and display of vector field topology in fluid flow data sets," Computer, vol. 22, no. 8, pp. 27–36, 1989. Special issue on scientific visualization.

[66] M. Tobak and D. J. Peake, "Topology of three-dimensional separated flows," Annual Review of Fluid Mechanics, vol. 14, pp. 61–85, 1982.

[67] G. T. Chapman and L. A. Yates, "Topology of flow separation on three-dimensional bodies," Applied Mechanics Reviews, vol. 44, pp. 329–345, July 1991.

[68] G. K. Batchelor, "Axial flow in trailing line vortices," Journal of Fluid Mechanics, vol. 20, no. 4, pp. 645–658, 1964.

[69] L. A. Yates and G. T. Chapman, "Streamlines, vorticity lines, and vortices around three-dimensional bodies," AIAA Journal, vol. 30, no. 7, pp. 1819–1826, 1992.

[70] H. K. Moffat, "The degree of knottedness of tangled vortex lines," Journal of Fluid Mechanics, vol. 35, no. 1, pp. 117–129, 1969.

[71] Y. Levy, D. Degani, and A. Seginer, "Graphical visualization of vortical flows by means of helicity," AIAA Journal, vol. 28, pp. 1347–1352, Aug. 1990.

[72] R. R. Dickinson, "A unified approach to the design of visualization software for the analysis of field problems," in 3D Visualization and Display Technologies (Proc. SPIE), vol. 1083, pp. 173–180, SPIE, Bellingham, WA., 1989.

[73] E. A. Earnshaw and N. Wisenan, An Introductory Guide to Scientific Visualization. Springer-Verlag, Berlin, 1992.

[74] K. W. Brodlie, L. Carpenter, R. Earnshaw, J. Gallop, R. Hubbold, A. Mumford, C. Osland, and P. Quarendon, eds., Scientific Visualization, ch. 7. Springer-Verlag, Berlin, 1992.

[75] G. V. Bancroft, F. J. Merritt, T. C. Plessel, P. G. Kelaita, R. K. McCabe, and A. Globus, "FAST: a multi-processed environment for visualization of computational fluid dynamics," in Proc. IEEE Visualization '90, pp. 14–27, CS Press, Los Alamitos, CA., 1990.

[76] D. Tristam, P. Walatka, and E. Raible, "Panel library programmers manual, version 9.5," Tech. Rep. RNR-90-006, NASA Ames Research Center, 1990.

[77] P. P. Walatka, J. Clucas, R. K. McCabe, and T. Plessel, "FAST user guide. Beta 2.1," tech. rep., NASA Ames Research Center, Apr. 1992.

[78] R. Haimes and D. Darmofal, "Visualization in computational fluid dynamics: A case study," in Proc. IEEE Visualization '91, pp. 392–397, CS Press, Los Alamitos, CA., 1991.

[79] W. J. Schroeder, W. E. Lorensen, G. Montanaro, and C. Volpe, "Visage: an object-oriented scientific visualization system," in Proc. IEEE Visualization '92, pp. 219–226, CS Press, Los Alamitos, CA., 1992.

[80] S. M. Legensky, "Interactive investigation of fluid mechanics data sets," in Proc. IEEE Visualization '90, pp. 435–438, CS Press, Los Alamitos, CA., 1990.

[81] S. Rogers, D. Kwak, and U. Kaul, "A numerical study of three-dimensional incompressible flow around multiple posts," in AIAA Aerospace Sciences Conference, (Reno, NV), Jan. 1986. AIAA Paper 86-0353.

[82] S. X. Ying, L. B. Schiff, and J. L. Steger, "A numerical study of 3-D separated flow past a hemisphere cylinder," in Proc. AIAA 19th Fluid Dynamics, Plasma Dynamics and Lasers Conference, June 1987. AIAA Paper 87-1207.

[83] B. Cantwell and D. Coles, "An experimental study of entrainment and transport in the turbulent near wake of a circular cylinder," Journal of Fluid Mechanics, vol. 136, pp. 321–374, 1983.

[84] T. Delmarcelle and L. Hesselink, "The topology of second-order tensor fields," in Proc. IEEE Visualization '94, CS Press, Los Alamitos, CA, 1994.

C H A P T E R

Continuum Volume Display

ARIE E. KAUFMAN AND
LISA M. SOBIERAJSKI

THIS CHAPTER presents the terminology, important concepts, and methods
for visualizing volume data. Volume data are obtained by sampling (such as
Computed Tomography), simulation (such as those running on a supercomputer), or modeling (such as computer-aided design using synthetic
geometric objects). Although volumetric representations and visualization
techniques seem more natural for sampled and computed data sets, their
advantages are also attracting traditional modeling applications.

Surface rendering algorithms for volume data are briefly described, in
which an intermediate geometric representation of the data is used to generate an image of a surface contained within the data. The main focus of the
chapter, however, is on volume rendering techniques that attempt to represent
the entire three-dimensional data in a two-dimensional image. Three-
dimensional object order, two-dimensional image order, and hybrid volume
rendering techniques are described. Volume rendering images convey more
information than surface rendering images, but at the cost of increased algorithm complexity, and consequently increased rendering times. To improve
interactivity in volume rendering, many methods of optimization have been
developed. The basic approaches of several of these techniques are described
in this chapter.

6.1
INTRODUCTION

As technology advances and methods for obtaining data are developed and
improved, volume visualization of three-dimensional data is becoming an
integral part of many scientific, engineering, and medical fields [14].
Volume data are obtained by sampling, simulation, or modeling techniques. For
example, a sequence of 2-D slices obtained from Magnetic Resonance Imaging
(MRI) or Computed Tomography (CT) is 3-D reconstructed into a volume model,
and visualized for medical diagnostic purposes and for planning of treatment or

0-8493-9050-8/95/$0.00+$.50

surgery. Similarly, confocal microscopes produce data which is visualized to study the morphology of biological structures. The same technology is often used with industrial CT for non-destructive inspection of composite materials or mechanical parts. In many computational fields, such as in computational fluid dynamics and design of new materials, the results of simulation typically running on a supercomputer are often visualized as volume data for analysis and verification. Recently, many traditional computer graphics applications, such as CAD and flight simulation, have been exploiting the advantages of volume techniques for modeling and visualization.

Many techniques have been developed over the years to visualize three-dimensional data. Since methods for displaying geometric primitives were already well-established, most of the early methods involve approximating a surface contained within the data using geometric primitives. When volumetric data is visualized using a surface rendering technique, a dimension of information is essentially thrown away. In response to this, volume rendering techniques were developed that attempt to represent the entire three-dimensional data in a two-dimensional image. Volume rendering images convey more information than surface rendering images, but at the cost of increased algorithm complexity, and consequently increased rendering times. To improve interactivity in volume rendering, many methods of optimization have been developed.

This chapter begins with an introduction to volume rendering terminology used throughout the chapter. In Section 6.3, some surface rendering techniques for volumetric data are briefly described. Section 6.4 covers many volume rendering techniques, including image-order, object-order, and hybrid methods. Optimization methods for volume rendering are discussed in Section 6.5.

6.2
VOLUME RENDERING TERMINOLOGY

Volume rendering is a name given to the process of creating a two-dimensional image directly from three-dimensional volumetric data. The data is typically a set S of samples (x, y, z, v), representing the value v of some property of the data, at a three-dimensional location (x, y, z). If the value is simply a 0 or a 1, with a value of 0 indicating background and a value of 1 indicating the object, then the data is referred to as binary data. The data may instead be multivalued, with the value representing some measurable property of the data, including, for example, color, density, heat or pressure. The value v may even be a vector, representing, for example, velocity at each location.

In general, the samples may be taken at purely random locations in space, but in this chapter we will consider only sets which contain samples taken at regularly spaced intervals along three orthogonal axes. The spacing between samples along each axis is a constant, but there may be three different spacing constants for the three axes. If a set of samples does not have this property, such as in irregular grids [3, 8, 23, 30, 31], a preprocessing step of resampling can be employed to create a new set which can be used with the algorithms described in this chapter. Since the set of samples is defined on a regular grid, a three-dimensional array (called also *volume buffer, cubic frame buffer, 3-D raster*) is typically used to store the values, with the element location indicating position of the sample on the grid. For this reason, the set S will be referred to as the array of values $S(x, y, z)$, which is defined only at grid locations.

The array S only defines the value of some measured property of the data at discrete locations in space. A function $f(x, y, z)$ may be defined over R^3 in order to describe the value at any continuous location. The function $f(x, y, z) = S(x, y, z)$ if (x, y, z) is a grid location, otherwise $f(x, y, z)$ approximates the sample value at a location (x, y, z) by applying some interpolation function to S. There are many possible interpolation functions. The simplest interpolation function is known as zero-order interpolation, which is actually just a nearest-neighbor function. The value at any location in R^3 is simply the value of the closest sample to that location. With this interpolation method there is a region of constant value around each sample in S. Since the samples in S are regularly spaced, each region has uniform size and shape. This requires a slight modification to the standard nearest-neighbor function, since that would produce regions of infinite size around the borders of the sample set. This is done simply by letting $f(x, y, z) = 0$ if (x, y, z) lies outside of some bounding box placed around the sample array S. An example of zero-order interpolation is given in Figure 6.1. The region of constant value that surrounds each sample is known as a voxel (short for *volume element* or *volume cell*), with each voxel having six faces, twelve edges, and eight corners.

Higher-order interpolation functions can also be used to define $f(x, y, z)$ between sample points. Figure 6.2 illustrates the basic concept of a higher-order

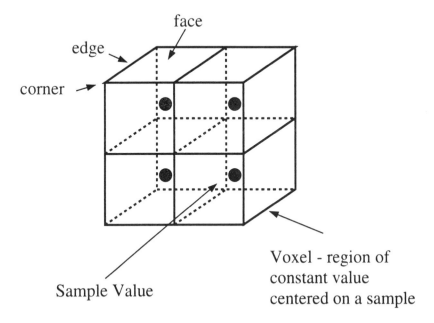

Figure 6.1: Zero-order interpolation

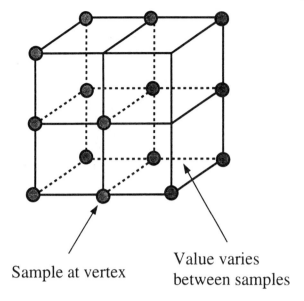

Sample at vertex   Value varies
                          between samples

Figure 6.2: Higher-order interpolation

interpolation function. One common interpolation function is a piecewise function known as trilinear interpolation. With this interpolation function, the value is assumed to vary linearly along directions parallel to one of the major axes. Figure 6.3 illustrates a simplified version of trilinear interpolation. The point P lies at location (x_p, y_p, z_p) within the regular hexahedron, known as a *cell*, defined by samples A through H. For simplicity, the distance between samples in all three directions is 1, with sample A at $(0, 0, 0)$ with a value of V_A, and sample H at $(1, 1, 1)$ with a value of V_H. The value V_P, according to trilinear interpolation, is then:

$$V_P = V_A(1-x_p)(1-y_p)(1-z_p) + V_E(1-x_p)(1-y_p)(z_p) + \qquad [6.1]$$
$$V_B(x_p)(1-y_p)(1-z_p) + V_F(x_p)(1-y_p)(z_p) +$$
$$V_C(1-x_p)(y_p)(1-z_p) + V_G(1-x_p)(y_p)(z_p) +$$
$$V_D(x_p)(y_p)(1-z_p) + V_H(x_p)(y_p)(z_p)$$

In general, A will be at some location (x_A, y_A, z_A), and H will be at (x_H, y_H, z_H). In this case, x_p in Equation 8.1 would be replaced by $(x_p - x_A)/(x_H - x_A)$, with similar substitutions made for y_p and z_p.

6.3
SURFACE RENDERING TECHNIQUES

Several surface rendering techniques have been developed which approximate a surface contained within volumetric data using geometric primitives, which can be rendered using conventional graphics hardware. A surface can be defined

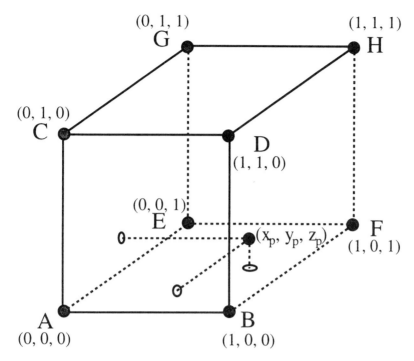

Figure 6.3: Trilinear interpolation

by applying a binary segmentation function $B(v)$ to the volumetric data. $B(v)$ evaluates to 1 if the value v is considered part of the object, and evaluates to 0 if the value v is part of the background. The surface is then the region where $B(v)$ changes from 0 to 1. If a zero-order interpolation function is being used, then the surface is simply the set of faces which are shared by voxels with differing values of $B(v)$. If a higher-order interpolation function is being used, then the surface passes between sample points according to the interpolation function.

For zero-order interpolation functions, the natural choice for a geometric primitive is the 3-D rectangular cuboid, since the surface is a set of faces, and each face is a rectangle. An early algorithm for displaying human organs from computed tomograms uses the square face as the geometric primitive [10]. This algorithm was developed before graphics hardware was generally available, so, in order to simplify the projection calculation and decrease rendering times, the assumption is made that the sample spacing in all three directions is the same. A software Z-buffer algorithm is then used to project the shaded squares onto the image plane to create the final image.

With continuous interpolation functions, a surface, known as an *iso-valued surface* or an *iso-surface,* may be defined by a single value. Several methods for rendering iso-surfaces are briefly described here. The subject is considered in greater detail in Chapter 4 of this book.

The Marching Cubes algorithm was developed to approximate an iso-valued surface with a triangle mesh [19]. The algorithm breaks down the ways in which a surface can pass through a cell into 256 cases, and reduces by symmetry to 15 topologies. For each of these 15 cases, a generic set of triangles representing the surface is stored in a look-up table. Each cell through which a surface passes maps to one of the 15 cases, with the actual triangle vertex locations being determined using linear interpolation on the cell vertices. A normal value is estimated for each triangle vertex, and standard graphics hardware can be utilized to project the triangles, resulting in a smooth shaded image of the iso-valued surface.

When rendering a sufficiently large data set with the Marching Cubes algorithm, many of the triangles map to a single pixel when projected onto the image plane. This fact led to the development of surface rendering algorithms that use 3-D points as the geometric primitive. One such algorithm is Dividing Cubes, which subdivides each cell through which a surface passes into subcells [5]. The number of divisions is selected such that the subcells project onto a single pixel on the image plane. Another algorithm which uses 3-D points as the geometric primitive is the Trimmed Voxel Lists method [22]. Instead of subdividing, this method uses only one 3-D point per visible surface cell, projecting that point on up to three pixels of the image plane to insure coverage in the image.

6.4
VOLUME RENDERING TECHNIQUES

Although representing a surface contained within a volumetric data set using geometric primitives can be useful in many applications, there are several main drawbacks to this approach. First, geometric primitives can only approximate the surface contained within the original data. Adequate approximations may require an excessive amount of geometric primitives. Therefore, a trade-off must be made between accuracy and space requirements. Second, since only a surface representation is used, much of the information contained within the data is lost during the rendering process. For example, in CT scanned data useful information is contained not only on the surfaces, but within the data as well. Also, amorphous phenomena, such as clouds, fog, and fire cannot be adequately represented using surfaces, and therefore must have a volumetric representation, and must be displayed using volume rendering techniques.

In the next subsections we will explore various volume rendering techniques. Although several of the methods described in these subsections render surfaces contained within volumetric data, these methods operate on the actual data samples, without the intermediate geometric primitive representations used by the algorithms in Section 6.3.

Volume rendering can be achieved using an *object-order* technique, an *image-order* technique, or a hybrid technique which combines the two approaches. Object-order volume rendering techniques use a *forward mapping* scheme where the volume data is mapped onto the image plane. In image-order algorithms, a *backward mapping* scheme is used where rays are cast from each pixel in the image plane through the volume data to determine the pixel value. Some volume rendering algorithms consist of several steps where, for example, first an object-order technique is applied, followed by an image-order technique which produces the final pixel values. These techniques are classified as hybrid volume rendering algorithms.

6.4.1 Object-Order Techniques

Object-order techniques involve mapping the data samples to the image plane. One way to accomplish a projection of a surface contained within the volume is to loop through the data samples, projecting each sample which is part of the object onto the image plane. An algorithm of this type was developed by Frieder, Gordon, and Reynolds [7]. For this algorithm, the data samples are binary voxels, with a value of 0 indicating background and a value of 1 indicating the object. Also, the data samples are on a grid with uniform spacing in all three directions.

If an image is produced by projecting all voxels with a value of 1 to the image plane in an arbitrary order, we are not guaranteed a correct image. If two voxels project to the same pixel on the image plane, the one that was projected later will prevail, even if it is farther from the image plane than the earlier projected voxel. This problem can be solved by traversing the data samples in a back-to-front order. A strictly back-to-front algorithm would require that if we process n voxels in the order $v_1, v_2, \cdots v_n$, then the distance from the image plane to v_i is greater than or equal to the distance from the image plane to v_{i+1}, for all $1 < i < n - 1$. For this algorithm, the definition of back-to-front can be relaxed to require that if v_i and v_j project to the same pixel on the image plane, and $i < j$, then v_i must be farther away from the image plane than v_j. This can be accomplished by traversing the data plane-by-plane, and row-by-row inside each plane. If, for example, the image plane is placed such that the origin of the data is farthest from the image plane, then the data samples can be traversed in a back-to-front manner by considering the elements in the order of increasing x, y, and z. For arbitrary orientations of the data in relation to the image plane, we may traverse some axes in an increasing order, while others may be considered in a decreasing order. The traversal can be accomplished with three nested loops, indexing on x, y, and z. Although the relative orientations of the data and the image plane specify whether each axis should be traversed in an increasing or decreasing manner, the ordering of the axes in the traversal (and therefore the nesting of the loops) is arbitrary.

An alternative to back-to-front projection is a front-to-back method in which the voxels are traversed in the order of increasing distance from the image plane. Although a back-to-front method is easier to implement, a front-to-back method has the advantage that once a voxel is projected onto a pixel, we need not process any more voxels which project to the same pixel, since they would be hidden by the first voxel. Another advantage of front-to-back projection methods is that if the axis which is most parallel to the viewing direction is chosen to be the outermost loop of the data traversal, meaningful partial image results can be displayed to the user. Partial image results can be displayed to the user during a back-to-front method also, but the value of a pixel may change many times during image generation. With a front-to-back method, once a pixel value is set, its value remains unchanged. The partial image when only half the voxels have been traversed is often a close approximation of the final image. This also allows the user to terminate the image generation if, for example, an incorrect view direction was selected.

Clipping planes orthogonal to the three major axes, and clipping planes parallel to the view plane are easy to implement using either a back-to-front or a front-to-back algorithm. For orthogonal clipping planes, we need only limit our traversal of the data to a smaller rectangular region within the full data set. To implement clipping planes parallel to the image plane, we would ignore data samples whose distance to the image plane is less than the distance between the cut plane and the image plane. This ability to explore the whole data set is a major difference between volume rendering techniques and the surface rendering techniques described in Section 6.3. In surface rendering techniques, we may need to modify our geometric primitive representation of the object in order to implement cut planes, which could be a time-consuming process. In this back-to-front method, cut planes can be achieved by simply modifying the bounds of our data traversal, and utilizing a condition when placing depth values in the image plane pixels.

For each voxel, we could store its distance to the image plane in the pixel to which it maps. If we traverse the data in the method described above, at the end of this traversal we will have a two-dimensional array of depth values, called a *Z-buffer*, where the value at each pixel in the Z-buffer is the distance to the closest voxel. A two-dimensional discrete shading technique can then be applied to the image, resulting in a shaded image suitable for display. The two-dimensional discrete shading techniques described here take as input a two-dimensional array of depth values, and produce as output a two-dimensional image of intensity values. The simplest 2-D discrete shading method is known as depth shading, or *depth-only shading,* where the intensity value stored in each pixel of the output image is inversely proportional to the depth of the corresponding input pixel [11, 28]. This produces images where features far from the image plane appear dark, while close feature are bright. Since surface orientation is not considered in this shading method, most details such as surface discontinuities and object boundaries are lost.

A more accurately shaded image can be obtained by passing the 2-D depth image to a gradient-shader that can take into account the object surface orientation and the distance from the light at each pixel to produce a shaded image [9]. This method evaluates the gradient at each (x, y) pixel location in the input image by

$$\nabla z = \left(\frac{\delta z}{\delta x}, \frac{\delta z}{\delta y}, 1 \right) \qquad [6.2]$$

where $z = D(x, y)$ is the depth associated with pixel (x, y). The estimated gradient vector at each pixel is then used as a normal vector for shading purposes.

The value $\delta z / \delta x$ can be approximated using a backward difference $D(x, y) - D(x - 1, y)$, a forward difference $D(x + 1, y) - D(x, y)$, or a central difference

$$\frac{1}{2}\big(D(x + 1, y) - D(x - 1, y)\big).$$

Similar equations exist for approximating $\delta z / \delta y$. In general, the central difference is a better approximation of the derivative, but along object edges where, for example, pixels (x, y) and $(x + 1, y)$ belong to two different objects, a backward difference would provide a better approximation. A context sensitive normal estimation method was developed to provide more accurate normal estimations by detecting image discontinuities [37]. In this method, two pixels are considered to be in the same "context" if their depth values, and the first derivative of the depth at these locations do not greatly differ. Similar depth values indicate C^0 continuity, and similar first derivatives indicate C^1 continuity. The gradient vector at some pixel p is then estimated by considering only those pixels which lie within a user-defined neighborhood, and belong to the same context as p. This ensures that sharp object edges, and slope changes are not smoothed out in the final image.

The previous rendering methods consider only binary data samples where a value of 1 indicates the object and a value of 0 indicates the background. Many forms of data acquisition (e.g., CT) produce data samples with 8, 12, or even more bits of data per sample. If we consider these data samples to represent the values at some sample points, and let the value vary according to some convolution applied to the data samples which will reconstruct the original three-dimensional signal, we then have a scalar field that approximates the original three-dimensional signal.

One way to reconstruct the original signal is, as described previously, to define a function $f(x, y, z)$ that determines the value at any location in space based on an interpolation function applied to the nearest data samples. This is the technique typically employed by backward-mapping (image-order) algorithms. In forward mapping algorithms, the original signal is reconstructed by spreading the value at a data sample into space. Westover describes a splatting algorithm for object-ordered volume rendering in which the value of the data samples represents a density [29]. Each data sample $s = (x_s, y_s, z_s, \rho(s))$, $s \in S$, has a function defining its contribution to every point (x, y, z) in the space:

$$\text{contribution}_s(x, y, z) = h_v(x - x_s, y - y_s, z - z_s)\rho(s) \qquad [6.3]$$

where $h_v()$ is the volume reconstruction kernel and $\rho(s)$ is the density of sample s which is located at (x_s, y_s, z_s). The contribution of a sample s to an image plane pixel (x, y) can then be computed by integration:

$$\text{contribution}_s(x, y) = \rho(s) \int_{-\infty}^{\infty} h_v(x - x_s, y - y_s, w)dw \qquad [6.4]$$

where the w coordinate axis is parallel to the view ray. Since this integral is independent of the sample's density, and depends only on its (x, y) projected location, a footprint function can be defined as follows:

$$\text{footprint}(x, y) = \int_{-\infty}^{\infty} h_v(x, y, w)dw \qquad [6.5]$$

where (x, y) is the displacement of an image sample from the center of the sample's image plane projection. The weight at each pixel can then be expressed as:

$$\text{weight}(x,y)_s = \text{footprint}(x - x_s, y - y_s) \qquad [6.6]$$

where (x, y) is the pixel's location, and (x_s, y_s) is the image plane location of the sample s.

A footprint table can be generated by evaluating the integral in Equation 6.5 on a grid with a resolution much higher than the image plane resolution. An example of a footprint table is given in Figure 6.4, with the table value represented by a gray-scale value, where white has zero weight, and black has highest weight. The extent of the footprint table is shown with a dashed circle. All table values lying outside of the footprint table extent have zero weight and therefore need not be considered when generating an image. If we have a footprint table for a

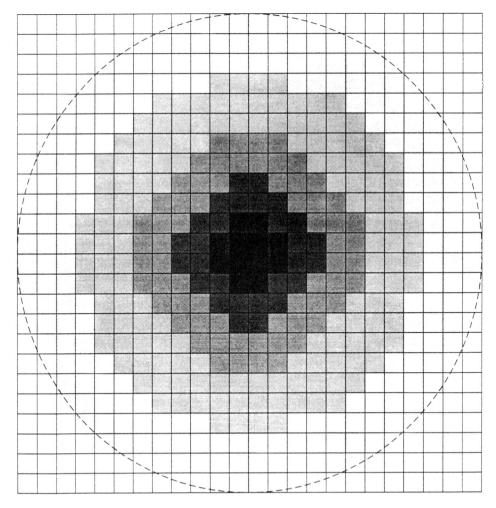

Figure 6.4: A footprint table

data sample *s,* we can center this table on the projected image plane location of *s,* and sample it in order to determine the weight of the contribution of *s* to each pixel on the image plane. Multiplying this weight by $\rho(s)$ then gives us the contribution of *s* to each pixel.

Computing a footprint table can be difficult due to the integration required. Discrete integration methods can be used to approximate the continuous integral, but generating a footprint table is still a costly operation. Luckily, for orthographic projections, the footprint of each sample is the same except for an image plane offset. Therefore we need only calculate one footprint table per view. Since this still would require too much computation time, only one generic footprint table is built for the kernel. For each view, a view-transformed footprint table is created from the generic footprint table. The generic footprint table can be precomputed, therefore it does not matter how long the computation takes.

Generating a view-transformed footprint table from the generic footprint table can be accomplished in three steps. First, the image plane extent of the projection of the reconstruction kernel is determined. Next, a mapping is computed between this extent and the extent that surrounds the generic footprint table. Finally, the value for each entry in the view-transformed footprint table is determined by mapping the location of the entry to the generic footprint table, and sampling. The extent of the reconstruction kernel is either a sphere, or is bounded by a sphere, so the extent of the generic footprint table is always a circle. If the grid spacing of the data samples is uniform along all three axes, then the reconstruction kernel is a sphere, and the image plane extent of the reconstruction kernel will be a circle. The mapping from this extent to the extent of the generic footprint table is simply a scaling operation. If the grid spacing differs along the three axes, then the reconstruction kernel is an ellipsoid and the image plane extent of the reconstruction kernel will be an ellipse. In this case, a mapping from this ellipse to the circular extent of the generic footprint table must be computed. The extents and mapping for both spherical and elliptical kernels are shown in Figures 6.5 and 6.6.

There are three modifiable parameters in this algorithm that can greatly affect image quality. First, the size of the footprint table can be varied. Small footprint tables will produce blocky images, while large footprint tables may smooth out details and require more space. Second, different sampling methods can be used when generating the view-transformed footprint table from the generic footprint table. Using a nearest-neighbor approach is fast, but may produce aliasing artifacts. On the other hand, using bilinear interpolation will produce smoother images at the expense of longer rendering times. The third parameter which can be modified is the reconstruction kernel itself. The choice of, for example, a cone function, Gaussian function, sync function or bilinear function affects the final image.

6.4.2 Image-Order Techniques

Image-order volume rendering techniques are fundamentally different from object-order rendering techniques. Instead of determining how a data sample affects the pixels on the image plane, in an image-order technique we determine for each pixel on the image plane which data samples contribute to it.

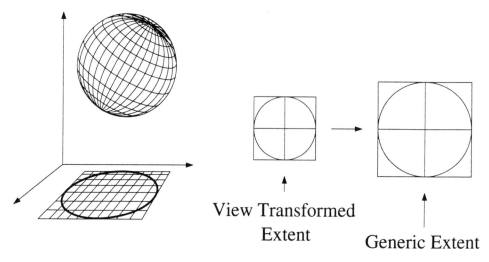

View Transformed
Extent

Generic Extent

Figure 6.5: Extent and mapping for a spherical reconstruction kernel

One of the first image-order volume rendering techniques, which may be called *binary ray casting*, was developed by Tuy and Tuy [26]. It was developed to generate images of surfaces contained within binary volumetric data without the need to explicitly perform boundary detection and hidden-surface removal. In order to provide all possible views, the data is kept in a fixed position and the image plane is allowed to move. The image plane is defined initially with the center located at C_0. A new image plane with its center at C can then be defined by C_0 and three angular parameters α, β, and γ which specify three rotations R_α, R_β, and R_γ about the X, Y, and Z axes, respectively. Applying these three rotations to the initial image with center C_0 produces the new image plane location with center

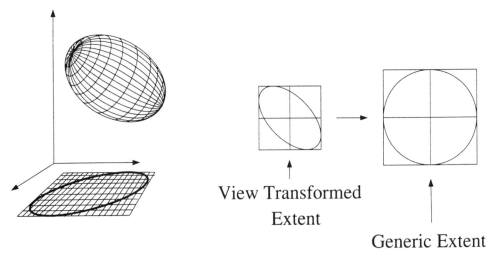

View Transformed
Extent

Generic Extent

Figure 6.6: Extent and mapping for an elliptical reconstruction kernel

C. If the view vector for the initial image is $V_0 = (0, 0, 1)$, the view vector V for the current image plane can be computed by applying R_α, R_β, and R_γ to V.

For each pixel on the image plane, we send a ray from that pixel and determine if it intersects the surface contained within the data. For parallel projections, all rays are parallel to the view direction, where, for perspective projections, rays are cast from the eye point according to the view direction and the field of view. A two-dimensional example of both parallel and perspective projections is shown in Figure 6.7. If an intersection does occur, shading is performed at the intersection, and the resulting color is placed in the pixel. To determine the first intersection along the ray a stepping technique is used where the value is determined at regular intervals along the ray until the object is intersected. Data samples with a value of 0 are considered to be the background while those with a value of

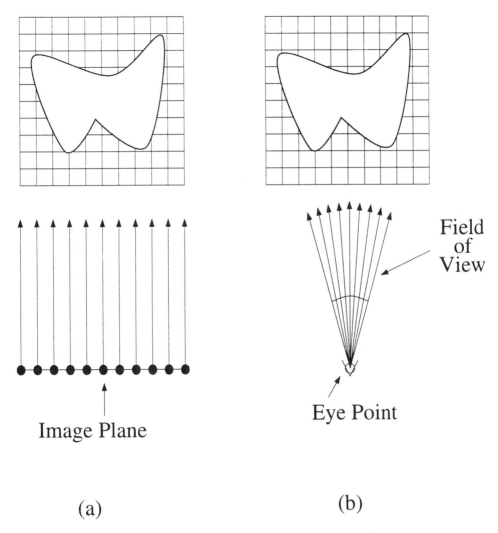

(a)   (b)

Figure 6.7: (a) Parallel projection, (b) Perspective projection

1 are considered to be part of the object. A zero-order interpolation technique is used, so the value at a location along the ray is 0 if that location is outside of the bounding box of the data, otherwise it is the value of the closest data sample. For a step size d, the ith point sample p_i would be taken at a distance $i \times d$ along the ray. For a given ray, either all point samples along the ray have a value of 0 (the ray missed the object entirely), or there is some sample p_i taken at a distance $i \times d$ along the ray, such that all samples p_j, $j < i$, have a value of 0, and sample p_i has a value of 1. Point sample p_i is then considered to be the first intersection along the ray. A 2-D example of this stepping technique is given in Figure 6.8, where the value of p_0 through p_5 is 0, and the value of p_6 is 1.

In this algorithm, the step size d must be chosen carefully. If d is too large, small features in the data may not be detected. On the other hand, if d is small, the intersection point is more accurately estimated at the cost of higher computation time.

There are two optimizations which can be made to this algorithm. First, we can reduce the number of steps which must be made along each ray if we traverse

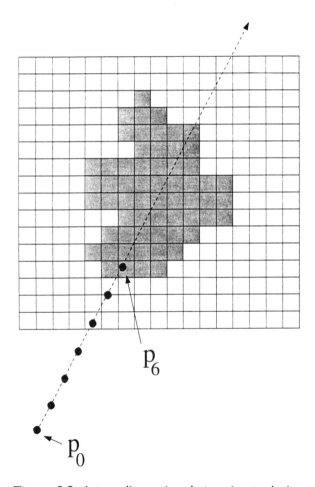

Figure 6.8: A two-dimensional stepping technique

only the part of the ray contained within the bounding box of the data. If P_0 is the location of the pixel on the image plane, then any location P along the view ray V through that pixel can be expressed as $P = P_0 + kV$. We can then find the two values k_1 and k_2 such that if $k_1 < k < k_2$, P lies within the bounding box of the data. Once we know these two values, we can skip over the steps which would be made along the ray between the pixel and where the ray enters the bounding box, and we can terminate our search when the ray exits the bounding box. An illustration of this is given in Figure 6.9.

The second optimization involves the representation of the data in memory. This algorithm was originally developed on a machine with only 32K of RAM, so data compression was a critical issue. Instead of simply storing the data as a binary array of 1s and 0s, a scan-line representation can be used. Since the data is binary, each scan-line can be thought of as a sequence of alternating-valued segments. For each scan-line in the data, a list of end points can be stored which represent the segments belonging to the object. This representation is compact, yet does not add too much time to the intersection calculation. A 2-D example of this compression technique for one scan line of a two-dimensional slice of data is shown in Figure 6.10.

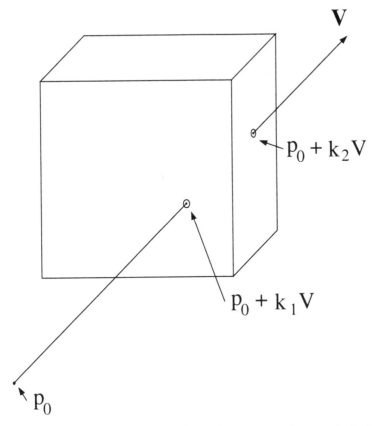

Figure 6.9 Reducing the number of point samples needed along a ray

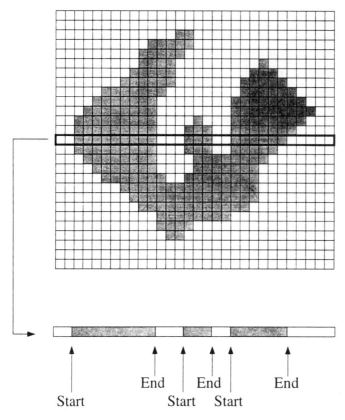

Figure 6.10: Compression technique for binary data

The previous algorithm deals with the display of surfaces within binary data. A more general algorithm can be used to generate surface and composite projections of multivalued data. Instead of traversing a continuous ray and determining the closest data sample for each step with a zero-order interpolation function, we could traverse a discrete representation of the ray generated using a 3D Bresenham-like algorithm, called a 3-D line scan-conversion or *voxelization* algorithm [13, 14].

As in the previous algorithms, we need to determine for each pixel in the image plane which data samples contribute to it. This can be done by casting a ray from each pixel in the direction of the viewing ray. This ray will be discretized, and the contribution from each voxel along the path is considered when producing the final pixel value. This technique is referred to as discrete ray casting.

In order to generate a 3-D discrete ray using a voxelization algorithm, the 3-D discrete topology of 3-D paths has to be understood. There are three types of connected paths: 6-connected, 18-connected, and 26-connected, which are based upon three adjacency relationships between consecutive voxels along the path. Assuming a voxel is represented as a box centered at the grid point, two voxels are said to be 6-connected if they share a face, they are 18-connected if they share a face or an edge, and they are 26-connected if they share a face, an edge or a vertex. A 6-connected path is a sequence of voxels, $v_1, v_2, \cdots v_N$, where for each pair of voxels v_i, v_{i+1} $(1 \leq i < N)$, v_i and v_{i+1} are 6-connected. Similar definitions exist for 18- and 26- connected paths. An example of these three types of connected paths is given in Figure 6.11.

In discrete ray casting, a ray is discretized into a 6-, 18-, or 26-connected path, and only the voxels along this path are considered when determining the final pixel value. If a surface projection is required, we traverse the path until we encounter the first voxel which is part of the object. We then shade at this voxel and store the resulting color value in the pixel. 6-connected paths contain almost twice as many voxels as 26-connected paths, so an image created using 26-connected paths would require less computation, but a 26-connected path may miss an intersection that would be otherwise detected using a 6-connected path.

To produce a shaded image we could store at each pixel in the image the distance to the closest intersection, then pass this image to a two-dimensional discrete shader, such as those described previously. However, better results can be obtained by performing a three-dimensional discrete shading operation at the intersection point. One three-dimensional discrete shading method, known as *normal-based contextual shading* can be used to estimate the normal when zero-order interpolation is used [4]. The normal for a face of a voxel that is on the surface of the object is determined by examining the orientation of that face, and the orientation of the four faces on the surface that are edge connected to that face. Since a face of a voxel can have only six possible orientations, the error in the approximated normal can be significant. More accurate results can be obtained using a

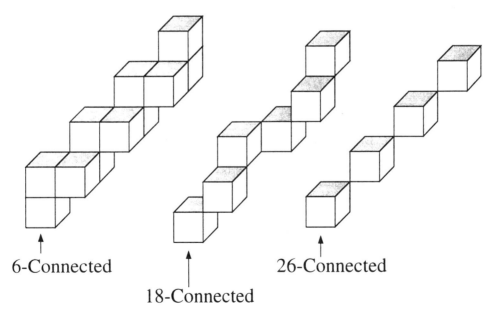

6-Connected   18-Connected   26-Connected

Figure 6.11 6-, 18-, and 26-connected paths

technique known as *gray-level* shading [2, 5, 12, 24, 25]. If the intersection occurs at location (*x, y, z*) in the data, then the gray-level gradient at that location can be approximated with a central difference:

$$G_x = \frac{f(x+1,y,z)-f(x-1,y,z)}{2S_x},$$ [6.7]

$$G_y = \frac{f(x,y+1,z)-f(x,y-1,z)}{2S_y},$$

$$G_z = \frac{f(x,y,z+1)-f(x,y,z-1)}{2S_z},$$

where (G_x, G_x, G_z) is the gradient vector, and S_x, S_y, and S_z are the distances between neighboring samples in the *x, y,* and *z* directions, respectively. The gradient vector is used as a normal vector for shading calculation, and the intensity value obtained from shading is stored in the image. A normal estimation can be performed at the surface point, and this information, along with the light direction, and the distance can be used for shading.

Actually, stopping at the first opaque voxel and shading there is only one of many operations which can be performed on the voxels along a discrete path or continuous ray. Instead, we can traverse the whole ray, storing in the image plane pixel the maximum value encountered along the ray. Figure 6.12(a) is a first opaque, or surface, projection of a bullfrog sympathetic ganglion cell, that was reconstructed from confocal microscope data, while Figure 6.12(b) is a maximum projection of the same cell. Figure 6.12 was generated using the PARC algorithm, described in Section 6.5. As opposed to a surface projection, a maximum projection is capable of revealing internal features of the data. For example, the high intensity regions of Figure 6.12(b) are boutons, which lie below the surface of the

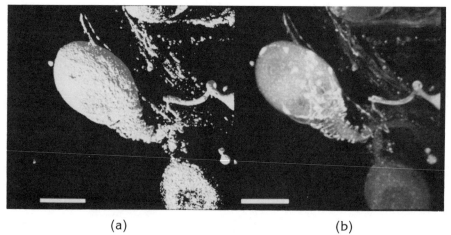

(a)   (b)

Figure 6.12: (a) A surface projection of a nerve cell. (b) A maximum projection of a nerve cell (See color section, plate 6.12)

cell and are therefore not visible in Figure 6.12(a). Another option is to store the sum (simulating X-rays) or average of all values along the ray. More complex techniques exist, which may involve defining an opacity and color for each scalar value, then accumulating intensity along the ray according to some compositing function.

The two previous rendering techniques, binary ray casting and discrete ray casting, use zero-order interpolation in order to define the scalar value at any location in R^3. One advantage to using zero-order interpolation is simplicity and speed, since many of the calculations required can be done using integer arithmetic. One disadvantage, though, is the aliasing effects in the image. Higher-order interpolation functions can be used to create a more accurate image, but generally at the cost of algorithm complexity and computation time. The next three algorithms described in this section all use higher-order interpolation functions.

When creating a composite projection of a data set, there are two important parameters, the color at a location, and the opacity at that location. An image-order volume rendering algorithm developed by Levoy states that given an array of data samples S, we can use preprocessing techniques to generate two new arrays S_c and S_α, which define the color and opacity at each grid location [18]. We then define the interpolation functions $f(x, y, z)$, $f_c(x, y, z)$, and $f_\alpha(x, y, z)$, which define the sample value, color, and opacity at any location in R^3.

Generating the array S_c of color values involves performing a shading operation, such as gray-level shading, at each data sample in the original array S. For this purpose, the Phong illumination model could be used. The normal at each data sample is the unit gradient vector at that location. The gradient vector at any location can be computed by partially differentiating the interpolation function with respect to x, y, and z to get each component of the gradient. If the interpolation function is not first derivative continuous, aliasing artifacts will occur in the image due to the discontinuous normal vector. A smoother set of gradient vectors can be obtained using a central differencing method similar to the one described previously in this section.

Calculating the array S_α is essentially a surface classification operation. There are various different ways to classify surfaces within a scalar field, and each way requires a new mapping from $S(x, y, z)$ to $S_\alpha(x, y, z)$. If we wish to view an iso-surface at some constant value v with an opacity α_v, we could simply assign $S_\alpha(x, y, z)$ to α_v if $S(x, y, z)$ is v, otherwise $S_\alpha(x, y, z) = 0$. This will produce aliasing artifacts, which can be reduced by setting $S_\alpha(x, y, z)$ close to α_v if $S(x, y, z)$ is close to v. The best results are obtained when the thickness of the transition region is constant throughout the volume. This can be approximated by having the opacity fall off at a rate inversely proportional to the magnitude of the local gradient vector.

Multiple iso-surfaces can be displayed in a single image by separately applying the classification mappings, then combining the opacities. For example, if N iso-value surfaces are to be displayed with values v_n and opacities α_{v_n}, $1 \leq n \leq N$, we would define N opacity mappings, and compute the total opacity by:

$$\alpha_{\text{total}}(x, y, z) = 1 - \prod_{n=1}^{N}\left(1 - \alpha_n(x, y, z)\right)$$ [6.8]

Once we have the $S_c(x, y, z)$ and $S_\alpha(x, y, z)$ arrays, we then cast rays from the pixels, through these two arrays, sampling at evenly spaced locations. To determine the value at a location, the trilinear interpolation functions $f_c()$ and $f_\alpha()$ are used. Once we have these point samples along the ray, we add in a fully opaque background, and then composite the values in a back-to-front order to produce a single color that is placed in the pixel.

Two rendering techniques for displaying volumetric data, known as the V-Buffer method, were developed by Upson and Keeler [27]. One of the methods for visualizing the scalar field is an image-order ray-casting technique. The other method is a hybrid technique, and will therefore be described in Section 6.4.3.

In the ray-casting V-Buffer method, rays are cast from each pixel on the image plane into the volume. For each cell in the volume along the path of this ray, the scalar value is determined at the point where the ray first intersects the cell. The ray is then stepped along until it traverses the entire cell, with calculations for scalar values, shading, opacity, texture mapping, and depth cuing performed at each stepping point. This process is repeated for each cell along the ray, accumulating color and opacity, until the ray exits the volume, or the accumulated opacity reaches unity. At this point, the accumulated color and opacity for that pixel are stored, and the next ray is cast.

The goal of this method is not to produce a realistic image, but rather to provide a representation of the volumetric data which can be interpreted by a scientist, or an engineer. For this purpose, the user is given the ability to modify certain parameters in the shading equations which will lead to an informative, rather than physically accurate shaded image. A simplified shading equation is used where the perceived intensity as a function of wavelength, $I(\lambda)$ is defined as:

$$I(\lambda) = K_a(\lambda)I_a + K_d(\lambda)\sum_j\left[(N \cdot L_j)I_j\right] \qquad [6.9]$$

In this equation, K_a is the ambient coefficient, I_a is the ambient intensity, K_d is the diffuse coefficient, N is the normal approximated by the local gradient, L_j is the vector to the jth light source, and I_j is the intensity of the jth light source. In order to highlight certain features in the final image, the diffuse coefficient can be defined as a function of not only wavelength, but also scalar value and solid texture:

$$K_d(\lambda, S, M) = K(\lambda)T_d\left(\lambda, S(x, y, z)M(\lambda, x, y, z)\right) \qquad [6.10]$$

where K is the actual diffuse coefficient, T_d is the color transfer function, S is the sample array, and M is the solid texture map. The color transfer function is defined for r, g, and b, and maps scalar value to intensity. When we accumulate along the ray in this method, we are approximating the following intensity integral:

$$I(\lambda) = \qquad [6.11]$$

$$\int_w \left[att(d)O(S)\left[K_a(\lambda)I_a + K_d(\lambda, S, M)\sum\left[(N \cdot L_j)I_j\right]\right] + \left(1 - att(d)bg(\lambda)\right)\right]dw$$

where $att(d)$ represents normalized atmospheric attenuation as a function of distance d, O is the opacity transfer function, bg is the background color, and w is a vector in the direction of the view ray. The opacity transfer function is similar to the color transfer function in that it defines opacity as a function of scalar value. Different color and opacity transfer functions can be defined to highlight different features in the volume. For example, the transfer functions defined in Figure 6.13 will highlight three surfaces in the volume, one in red, one in green, and one in blue.

In order to simulate light coming from translucent objects, volumetric data with data samples representing density values can be considered as a field of density emitters (as proposed by Sabella [20]). A density emitter is a tiny particle that both emits and scatters light. The amount of density emitters in any small region within the volume is proportional to the scalar value in that region. These density emitters are used to correctly model the occlusion of deeper parts of the volume by closer parts, but both shadowing and color variation due to differences in scattering at different wavelengths are ignored. These effects are ignored because it is believed that they would complicate the image, detracting from the perception of density variation. Similar to the V-Buffer method, rays are cast from the eye point through each pixel on the image plane, and into the volume. The intensity I of light for a given pixel is calculated according to:

$$I = \int_{t_1}^{t_2} e^{-\tau \int_{t_1}^{t} \rho^\gamma(\lambda)d\lambda} \, \rho^\gamma(t) \, dt \qquad [6.12]$$

In this equation, the ray is traversed from t_1 to t_2, accumulating at each location t the density $\rho^\gamma(t)$ at that location attenuated by the probability

$$e^{-\tau \int_{t_1}^{t} \rho^\gamma(\lambda)d\lambda}$$

that this light will be scattered before reaching the eye. The parameter τ is modifiable, and controls the attenuation, with higher values of τ specifying a medium which darkens more rapidly. The parameter γ is also modifiable, and can be used to control the spread of density values. Low γ values produce a diffuse cloud appearance, while higher γ values highlight dense portions of the data.

For each ray, three values in addition to I are computed. The value M is the

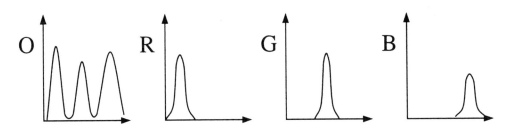

Figure 6.13: Transfer functions for red, green, blue, and opacity as a function of scalar value

maximum value encountered along the ray with D being the distance at which that maximum occurred. The value C is the center of gravity of density emitters along the ray. By mapping these four values to different color parameters, interesting effects can be achieved. For example, M may be mapped to hue, D to saturation, and I to value, to highlight certain characteristics of the volume data.

Krueger showed that the various existing volume rendering models can be described as special cases of an underlying transport theory model of the transfer of particles in inhomogeneous media [16]. The basic idea is that a beam of "virtual" particles is sent through the volume, with the user selecting the particle properties and the laws of interaction between the particles and the data. The image plane then contains the "scattered" virtual particles, and information about the data is obtained from the scattering pattern. If, for example, the virtual particles are chosen to have the properties of photons, and the laws of interaction are governed by optical laws, then this model essentially becomes a generalized ray tracer. Other virtual particles and interaction laws can be used, for example, to identify periodicities and similar hidden symmetries of the data.

Using Krueger's transport theory model, the intensity of light I at a pixel can be described as a path integral along the view ray:

$$I = \int_{S_{near}}^{S_{far}} Q(S)e^{-\int_{S_{near}}^{S} \sigma_a(S') + \sigma_{sc}(S')dS'} dS \qquad [6.13]$$

The emission at each point S along the ray is scaled by the optical depth to the eye to produce the final intensity value for a pixel. The optical depth is a function of the total extinction coefficient, which is composed of the absorption coefficient σ_a, and the scattering coefficient σ_{sc}. The generalized source $Q(S)$ is defined as:

$$Q(S) = q(S) + \sigma_{sc}(S)\int \rho_{sc}(\vec{\omega}' \to \vec{\omega})I(S, \vec{\omega}')d\vec{\omega}' \qquad [6.14]$$

This generalized source consists of the emission at a given point $q(S)$, and the incoming intensity along all direction scaled by the scattering phase ρ_{sc}. Typically, a low albedo approximation is used to simplify the calculations, reducing the integral in Equation 6.14 to a sum over all light sources.

The algorithms described so far in this section are concerned primarily with conveying useful information in the final image, rather than generating photorealistic images. A 3-D raster ray tracing (RRT) method, developed by Yagel, Cohen and Kaufman produces realistic images of volumetric data using a global illumination model [32, 34]. The RRT algorithm is a discrete ray-tracing algorithm similar to the discrete ray-casting algorithm described earlier in this section. Discrete primary rays are cast from the image plane, through the data to determine pixel values. Secondary rays are recursively spawned when a ray encounters a voxel belonging to an object in the data. To save time, the view-independent parts of the illumination equation can be precomputed and added to the voxel's color, thereby avoiding the calculation of this quantity during the ray tracing. Also, two bits per light source per voxel can be precomputed, indicating whether the light is definitely visible, possibly visible, or definitely not visible from that voxel.

Shadow rays need only be cast during the ray tracing if the bits indicate that the light is possibly visible through a translucent object. Actually, all view-independent attributes (including normal, texture, and antialiasing) can be precomputed and stored with each voxel.

There are several advantages to using RRT instead of conventional ray tracing. One such advantage is that sampled or computed data, possibly intermixed with voxelized geometric data, can be ray traced directly without having to approximate the sampled data using geometric primitives. Another advantage is that there is only one primitive to deal with—the voxel, which greatly simplifies ray-object intersection calculations. Unlike conventional ray tracing that computes expensive continuous ray-object intersections, RRT traverses discrete rays through discrete data and therefore it is basically insensitive to scene complexity and object complexity. RRT is also very effective for ray tracing voxelized geometric models, such as constructive solid geometry (CSG) models. This is an example for the emerging field of volume graphics in which geometric scenes are modeled using voxelized objects and efficiently rendered using a volume rendering algorithm such as RRT [15]. Volume graphics has the potential to supersede surface graphics for handling and visualizing volumes, as well as for modeling and rendering synthetic scenes composed of surfaces.

6.4.3 Hybrid Techniques

Some volume rendering techniques are not completely image-order or object-order methods, but actually are a combination of both. Two of these techniques are described in this subsection.

As mentioned in Section 6.4.2, Upson and Keeler developed two volume rendering techniques for displaying scalar fields, known as the V-Buffer method [27]. The image-order technique was described in the Section 6.4.2. The other method for visualizing the scalar field is a cell-by-cell processing technique, where within each cell an image-order ray-casting technique is used, thus making this a hybrid technique.

In this method, each cell in the volume is processed in a front-to-back order. Processing begins on the plane closest to the viewpoint, and progresses in a plane-by-plane manner. Within each plane, processing begins with the cell closest to the viewpoint, then continues in order of increasing distance from the viewpoint. Figure 6.14 illustrates this ordering for one plane of the data. Note that cells with the same number can be processed concurrently, since no two cells with the same number in a plane can affect the same pixel in the image plane. Each cell is processed by first determining, for each scan-line in the image plane, which pixels are affected by the cell. Then, for each pixel an integration volume is determined as shown in Figure 6.15. Within the bounds of the integration volume, an intensity calculation similar to Equation 6.11 is performed according to:

$$I(\lambda) = \int_x \int_y \int_z \left[att(d)O(S)\left[K_a(\lambda)I_a + K_d(\lambda, S, M)\Sigma\left[(N \cdot L_j)I_j\right]\right] + \left(1 - att(d)bg(\lambda)\right)\right] dx\,dy\,dz \quad [6.15]$$

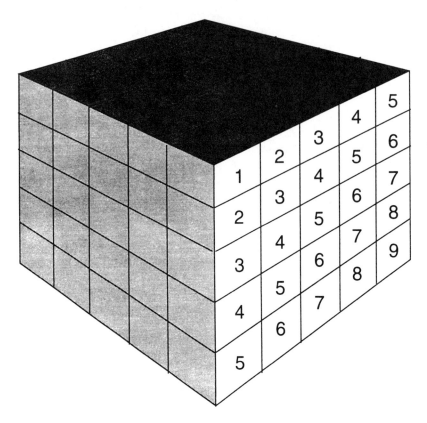

Figure 6.14: Cell ordering for V-Buffer volume rendering

This process continues in a front-to-back order, until all cells have been processed, with intensity accumulated into pixel values. Once a pixel's opacity reaches unity, a flag is set and this pixel is not processed further. Due to the front-to-back nature of this algorithm, incremental display of the image is possible.

Drebin, Carpenter, and Hanrahan developed a technique for rendering volumes that contain mixtures of materials, such as CT data containing bone, muscle and flesh [6]. In this method, various assumptions about the volume data are made. First, it is assumed that the scalar field was sampled above the Nyquist frequency, or a low-pass filter was used to remove high frequencies before sampling. The volume contains either several scalar fields, or one scalar field representing the composition of several materials. If the latter is the case, it is assumed that material can be differentiated either by the scalar value at each point, or by additional information about the composition of each volume element.

The first step in this rendering algorithm is to create new scalar fields, known as material percentage volumes, from the input data. Each material percentage volume is a scalar field representing only one material. Color and opacity are then associated with each material, with composite color and opacity obtained by linearly combining the color and opacity for each material percentage volume. A

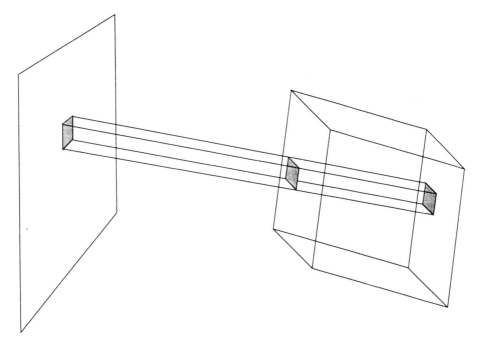

Figure 6.15: Integration volume for V-Buffer volume rendering

matte volume, that is, a scalar field on the volume with values ranging between 0 and 1, is used to slice the volume, or to perform other spatial set operations. Actual rendering of the final composite scalar field is obtained by transforming the volume so that one axis is perpendicular to the image plane. The data is then projected plane by plane in a back-to-front manner and composited to form the final image.

6.5
VOLUME RENDERING OPTIMIZATIONS

Volume rendering can produce informative images that can be useful in data analysis, but a major drawback of many of the techniques described in this chapter is the time required to generate a high-quality image. In this section, several volume rendering optimizations are described that decrease rendering times, and therefore increase interactivity and productivity. Other optimizations have been briefly discussed earlier in the chapter, along with the original algorithm.

Object-order volume rendering typically loops through the data, calculating the contribution of each volume sample to pixels on the image plane. This is a costly operation for moderate to large sized data sets (e.g., 128M bytes for a 512^3 sample data set, with one byte per sample), leading to rendering times that are not interactive. Viewing the intermediate results in the image plane may be useful, but these partial image results are not always representative of the final image. For the purpose of interaction, it is useful to be able to generate a lower quality image in a shorter amount of time. For a data set with binary sample values, we could pack the bits into bytes such that each byte represents a $2 \times 2 \times 2$ portion of the data [26]. We would process the data bit by bit to generate the full resolution image, but we could generate a lower resolution image by processing the data byte by byte. If more than four bits of the byte are set, the byte is considered to represent an element of the object, otherwise it represents the background. This will produce an image with one-half the linear resolution in approximately one-eighth the time.

A more general method for decreasing data resolution is to build a pyramid data structure, which for an original data set of N^3 data samples, consists of a sequence of $\log N$ volumes. The first volume is the original data set, while the second volume is created by averaging each $2 \times 2 \times 2$ group of samples of the original data set to create a volume of one-eight the resolution. The third volume is created from the second volume in a similar fashion, with this process continuing until all $\log N$ volumes have been created. An efficient implementation of the splatting algorithm, called hierarchical splatting, uses such a pyramid data structure [17]. According to the desired image quality, this algorithm scans the appropriate level of the pyramid in a back-to-front order. Each element is splatted onto the image plane using the appropriate sized splat. The splats themselves are approximated by polygons which can efficiently be rendered by graphics hardware.

Image-order volume rendering involves casting rays from the image plane into the data, and sampling along the ray in order to determine pixel values. In discrete ray casting, the ray is discretized, and the contribution from each voxel along the path is considered when producing the final pixel value. It would be quite computationally expensive to discretize every ray cast from the image plane. Fortunately, this is unnecessary for parallel projections. Since all the rays are parallel, one ray can be discretized and used as a "template" for all other rays. This technique, developed by Yagel and Kaufman, is called *template-based volume viewing* [35]. A 26-connected template $v_1, v_2, \cdots v_N$ is created such that removing any v_i, $(1 < i < N)$, would destroy the connectivity of the path. If this template were used to cast a ray from each pixel in the image plane, some voxels in the data may contribute to the image twice while others may not be considered at all. A two-dimensional example of this problem is shown in Figure 6.16(a). (A 26-connected ray in three dimensions is analogous to an 8-connected ray in two dimensions.) To solve this problem, the rays are cast instead from a base plane, that is, the plane of the volume buffer most parallel to the image plane. This ensures that each data sample can contribute, at most, once to the final image, and all data samples could potentially contribute. But when we extend these rays back to the image plane, we notice that we have not cast the rays exactly from the pixels. Once all the rays have been cast, we need a simple final step of resampling which uses bilinear interpolation to determine the pixel values from the ray values we have calculated. Figure 6.16(b) shows this process for a two-dimensional data set with a one-dimensional image line.

An extension can be made to this template-based ray casting to allow higher-

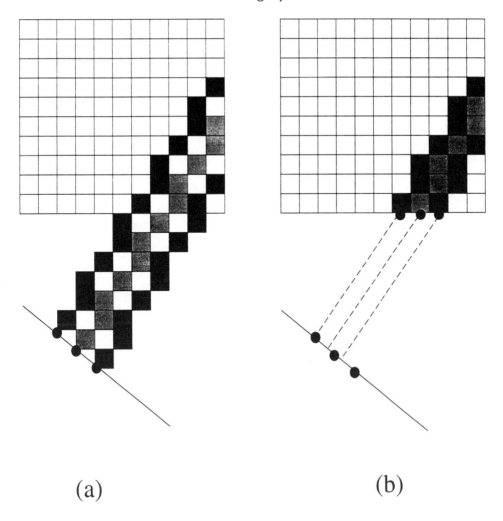

(a)   (b)

Figure 6.16: Discrete rays cast from the image plane (a) and base plane (b)

order interpolation [36]. The template for higher-order interpolation consists of connected cells, as opposed to the connected voxel template used for zero-order interpolation. Since the value varies within a cell, it is desirable to take multiple samples along the continuous ray inside of each cell. Since these samples are taken at regular intervals, and the same template is used for every ray, there is only a finite number of 3-D locations (relative to a cell) at which sampling occurs. This fact allows us to precompute part of the interpolation function and store it in a table, allowing for faster rendering times.

Another extension to template-based ray casting allows for screen space super-sampling to improve image quality [33]. This is accomplished by allowing rays to originate at sub-pixel locations. A finite number of sub-pixel locations from which a ray can originate is selected, and a template is created for each. When a ray is cast, its sub-pixel location determines which template is used. For example, to accomplish a 2×2 uniform supersampling, four rays would be cast per pixel, and therefore four sub-pixel locations are possible. Stochastic supersampling can also be supported by limiting the possible ray origins to a finite number of sub-pixel locations, and precomputing a template for each.

One obvious optimization for both discrete and continuous ray casting which has already been discussed is to limit the sampling to the segment of the ray that intersects the data, since samples outside of the data evaluate to 0 and do not contribute to the pixel value. If the data itself contains many zero-valued data samples, or a segmentation function is applied to the data that evaluates to 0 for many samples, the efficiency of ray casting can be greatly enhanced by further limiting the segment of the ray in which samples are taken. One algorithm of this sort is known as *polygon assisted ray casting,* or PARC [1]. This algorithm approximates objects contained within a volume using a crude polyhedral representation. The polyhedral representation is created so that it completely contains the objects. Using conventional graphics hardware, the polygons are projected twice to create two Z-buffers. The first Z-buffer is the standard closest-distance Z-buffer, while the second is a farthest-distance Z-buffer. Since the object is completely contained within the representation, the two Z-buffer values for a given image plane pixel can be used as the starting and ending points of a ray segment on which samples are taken. A comparative illustration of brute-force ray casting and PARC for rendering a surface contained within a volume are shown in Figure 6.17, with the closest distance Z-buffer values shown as a solid line, and the farthest distance Z-buffer values shown as a dashed line.

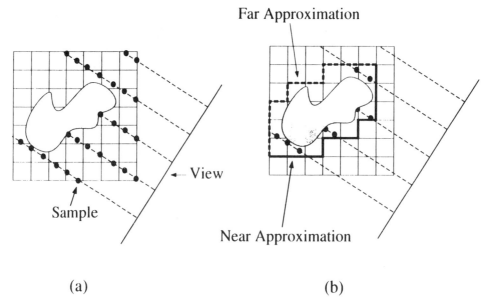

Figure 6.17: (a) Brute-force ray casting (b) Polygon assisted ray casting (PARC)

The PARC algorithm is part of the VolVis volume visualization system that provides a multi-algorithm progressive refinement approach for interactivity [1]. With available graphics hardware, the user is given the ability to manipulate in real-time the polyhedral representation of the data. When the user is satisfied with the placement of the data, light sources, and view, the Z-buffer information is passed to the PARC algorithm, which produces a ray-cast image. In a final step, this image is further refined by continuing to follow the PARC rays which intersected the data according to a volumetric ray tracing algorithm in order to generate shadows, reflections, and transparency [21]. The ray-tracing algorithm uses various optimization techniques, including uniform space subdivision and bounding boxes, to increase the efficiency of the secondary rays. Surface rendering, as well as transparency with color and opacity transfer functions, are incorporated within a global illumination model.

Figures 6.18 and 6.19 illustrate a typical sequence of images in this progressive refinement. The scene shown consists of three volumetric data sets and one geometric object. The leftmost object is a quantum mechanics simulation of a high potential iron protein, the middle object is a bullfrog sympathetic ganglion cell acquired with a laser-scanning confocal microscope, and the right object is a human head obtained from Magnetic Resonance Imaging. Below these three objects, a geometric polygon was placed. Figure 6.18 (a) is the polyhedral representation of the scene used for interactive navigation and to create the Z-buffers for the PARC algorithm. Figure 6.18 (b) is the PARC rendering, and Figure 6.19 is the volumetric ray-traced version of the scene.

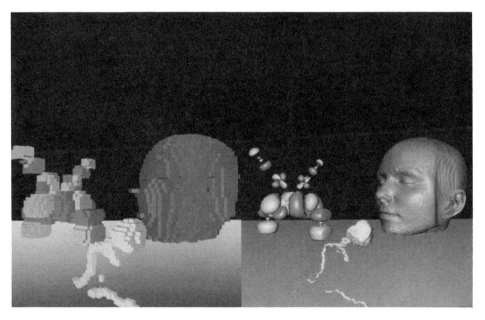

Figure 6.18: (a) VolVis polyhedral representation of a complex scene. (b) VolVis PARC rendering of the scene. (See color section plate 6.18.)

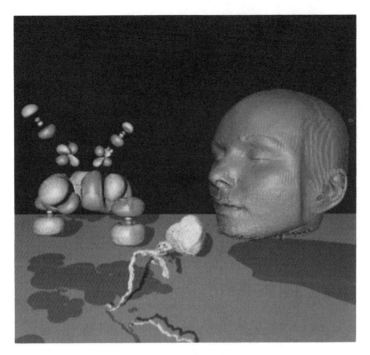

Figure 6.19: VolVis ray-traced rendering of a complex scene

6.6
CONCLUSIONS

This chapter has presented many of the important concepts and methods of volume visualization. We described surface rendering algorithms for volume data in which an intermediate representation of the data is used to generate an image of a surface contained within the data. Object order, image order, and hybrid volume rendering techniques for generating images of surfaces within the data were presented, as well as volume rendered images that attempt to represent all three dimensions of information in the two-dimensional image. Several optimization techniques that aim to decrease the rendering time for volume visualization were also described in this chapter.

Although volumetric representations and visualization techniques seem more natural for sampled or computed data sets, their advantages are also attracting traditional surface-based applications. This trend implies an expanding role for volume visualization, and it has the potential to revolutionize the field of computer graphics, by providing a better alternative to surface graphics.

Various methods for volume rendering have been discussed, yet many more techniques exist than could fit in one chapter. As the volume visualization field expands, old rendering methods are improved, and new techniques for visualization are developed. Each new development brings us closer to the ultimate goal of accurate, real-time volume visualization.

6.7
REFERENCES

1. Avila, R. S., Sobierajski, L. M. and Kaufman, A. E., "Towards a Comprehensive Volume Visualization System," Visualization '92 Proceedings, October 1992, 13–20.
2. Barillot, C., Gibaud, B., Luo, L. M. and Scarabin, I. M., "3D Representation of Anatomic Structures From CT Examinations," Proceedings SPIE, 602, (1985), 307–314.
3. Challinger, J., "Parallel Volume Rendering for Curvilinear Volumes," IEEE Computer Society Proceedings Scalable High Performance Computing Conference, April 1992, 14–21.
4. Chen, L. S., Herman, G. T., Reynolds, R. A. and Udupa, J. K., "Surface Shading in the Cuberille Environment," IEEE Computer Graphics & Applications, 5, 12 (December 1985), 33–43.
5. Cline, H. E., Lorensen, W. E., Ludke, S., Crawford, C. R. and Teeter, B. C., "Two Algorithms for the Three-Dimensional Construction of Tomograms," Medical Physics, 15, 3 (May/June 1988), 320–327.
6. Drebin, R. A., Carpenter, L. and Hanrahan, P., "Volume Rendering," Computer Graphics, 22, 4 (August 1988), 64–75.
7. Frieder, G., Gordon, D. and Reynolds, R. A., "Back-to-Front Display of Voxel-Based Objects," IEEE Computer Graphics and Applications, 5, 1 (January 1985), 52–59.
8. Giersten, C., "Volume Visualization of Sparse Irregular Meshes," IEEE Computer Graphics and Applications, 12, 2 (March 1992), 40–48.
9. Gordon, D. and Reynolds, R. A., "Image Space Shading of 3-Dimensional Objects," Computer Graphics and Image Processing, 29, 3 (March 1985), 361–376.
10. Herman, G. T. and Liu, H. K., "Three-Dimensional Display of Human Organs from Computed Tomograms," Computer Graphics and Image Processing, 9, 1 (January 1979), 1–21.
11. Herman, G. T. and Udupa, J. K., "Display of Three Dimensional Discrete Surfaces," Proceedings SPIE, 1981, 90–97.
12. Hoehne, K. H. and Bernstein, R., "Shading 3-D Images from CT Using Gray-Level Gradients," IEEE Transactions on Medical Imaging, MI-5, (March 1986), 45–47.
13. Kaufman, A. and Shimony, E., "3D Scan-Conversion Algorithms for Voxel-Based Graphics," Proceedings ACM Workshop Interactive 3D Graphics, 1986, 45–76.
14. Kaufman, A., Volume Visualization, IEEE Computer Society Press Tutorial, Los Alamitos, CA, 1991.
15. Kaufman, A., Yagel, R. and Cohen, D., "Volume Graphics," IEEE Computer, 26, 7 (July 1993), 51–64.
16. Krueger, W., "The Application of Transport Theory to Visualization of 3D Scalar Data Fields," Computers in Physics, July/August 1991, 397–406.
17. Laur, D. and Hanrahan, P., "Hierarchical Splatting: A Progressing Refinement Algorithm for Volume Rendering," Computer Graphics (Proc. SIGGRAPH), 25, 4 (July 1991), 285–288.
18. Levoy, M., "Display of Surfaces from Volume Data," IEEE Computer Graphics and Applications, 8, 5 (May 1988), 29–37.
19. Lorensen, W. E. and Cline, H. E., "Marching Cubes: A High Resolution 3D Surface Construction Algorithm," Computer Graphics (Proc. SIGGRAPH), 21, 4 (July 1987), 163–169.
20. Sabella, P., "A Rendering Algorithm for Visualizing 3D Scalar Fields," Computer Graphics (Proc. SIGGRAPH), 22, 4 (August 1988), 160–165.
21. Sobierajski, L. M. and Kaufman, A., "Volumetric Ray Tracing." Technical Report 94.03.31, Computer Science, SUNY Stony Brook, March 1994.
22. Sobierajski, L., Cohen, D., Kaufman, A., Yagel, R. and Acker, D., "A Fast Display Method for Volumetric Data," The Visual Computer, 10, 2 (1993), 116–124.
23. Speray, D. and Kennon, S., "Volume Probes: Interactive Data Exploration on Arbitrary Grids," San Diego Workshop on Volume Visualization, Computer Graphics, 24, 5 (December 1990), 5–12.
24. Tiede, U., Hoehne, K. H. and Riemer, M., "Comparison of Surface Rendering Techniques for 3D Tomographics Objects," in Computer Assisted Radiology, U. Lemke (ed.), Springer, Berlin Heidelberg New York, 1987, 599–610.
25. Tiede, U., Riemer, M., Bomans, M. and Hoehne, K. H., "Display Techniques for 3-D Tomographic Volume Data," Proceedings NCGA '88 Conference, 3, (March 1988), 188–197.
26. Tuy, H. K. and Tuy, L. T., "Direct 2-D Display of 3-D Objects," IEEE Computer Graphics and Applications, 4, 10 (October 1984), 29–33.
27. Upson, C. and Keeler, M., "V-BUFFER: Visible Volume Rendering," Computer Graphics (Proc. SIGGRAPH), 22, 4 (August 1988), 59–64.
28. Vannier, M. W., Marsh, J. L. and Warren, J. O., "Three Dimensional Computer Graphics for Craniofacial Surgical Planning and Evaluation," Computer Graphics (Proc. SIGGRAPH), 17, 3 (July 1983), 263–273.

29. Westover, L., "Footprint Evaluation for Volume Rendering," Computer Graphics (Proc. SIG-GRAPH), 24, 4 (August 1990), 367–376.
30. Wilhelms, J., Challinger, J., Alper, N., Ramamoorthy, S. and Vaziri, A., "Direct Volume Rendering of Curvilinear Volumes," San Diego Workshop on Volume Visualization, Computer Graphics, 24, 5 (December 1990), 41–47.
31. Williams, P. L., "Issues in Interactive Direct Projection Volume Rendering of Nonrectilinear Meshed Data Sets." Work in Progress Report, San Diego Workshop on Volume Visualization, December 1990.
32. Yagel, R., Kaufman, A. and Zhang, Q., "Realistic Volume Imaging," IEEE Visualization '90 Proceedings, San Diego, CA, October 1991, 226–231.
33. Yagel, R., "Efficient Methods for Volumetric Graphics," PhD Dissertation, SUNY at Stony Brook, December 1991.
34. Yagel, R., Cohen, D. and Kaufman, A., "Discrete Ray Tracing," IEEE Computer Graphics and Applications, 12, 5 (September 1992), 19–28.
35. Yagel, R. and Kaufman, A., "Template-Based Volume Viewing," Proceedings Eurographics '92, Cambridge, UK, September 1992, 153–167.
36. Yagel, R., "High Quality Template-Based Volume Viewing," OSU-CISRC-10/92-TR28, Department of Computer and Information Science, The Ohio State University, October 1992.
37. Yagel, R., Cohen, D. and Kaufman, A., "Normal estimation in 3D discrete Space," The Visual Computer, 8, (1992), 278–291.

CHAPTER

Animation and the Examination of Behavior Over Time

ERIC PEPKE

ANIMATION PROVIDES THE important ability to visualize behavior as it changes in time and space. This chapter discusses the technical issues of animation in visualization, including the representation of motion, object and observer behavior in animation, and computer graphics issues in generating animated sequences.

Many of the practical issues in producing animated sequences of behavior are examined, including presentation and timing issues, online and offline frame capture methods, and interfacing with film, video and multimedia.

7.1
INTRODUCTION

Animation is the presentation of a series of images to give the impression of motion. When the individual images, called *frames*, change quickly enough, the human visual system integrates them into continuous motion.

Traditional animation was developed by artists beginning centuries ago to give the illusion of life. In this century, along with the development of filmmaking, animation has become a highly refined art form. In recent years, the emerging technology of computer graphics has blended with traditional animation techniques to provide a new form of animation, in which an artist controls the motion of 3-D shapes over time, and the computer renders the shapes into images.

Scientific animation has borrowed much of its vocabulary, techniques and algorithms from traditional animation. Nevertheless, scientific animation is very much its own field. Scientific animation should be true to the underlying data, although this is not required in animation for entertainment. Scientific fidelity may require a more straightforward design approach than traditional animation to avoid distractions from the data.

7.1.1 Animation as an Educational and Analysis Tool

The most obvious use of animation is as an educational tool, to convey the results of research which is already well understood. Less obvious, but even more important, is the use of animation as an integral part of the research and development process to enhance understanding every step of the way. The requirements of these two uses may be very different. An animation for education might consume weeks or months of a large collaboration to produce a polished product, but the speed and ease of producing animations on an everyday basis are more important when animations are produced for research.

There are many benefits in using animation as an integral part of the analysis process, beginning at the earliest stage as possible. Animation can be used as a debugging tool for analysis software. There is a large class of program errors which are subtle yet instantly obvious in an animation. Animation can also be used to test design assumptions. Conflict in the motion of parts, for example, may be much easier seen in an animation of the motion than in static visualizations. Animation can help spark the creative process as well. Improvements often come to mind while watching an animation of a design.

This chapter concentrates primarily on animation as an analysis tool, although the information can be applied easily to animation as an educational tool as well. It is divided into two basic sections. *Designing animations* describes the basics of animations and some of the numerical methods and algorithms involved, and includes concepts that can be used for many hardware configurations and software packages. *Producing animations* describes the mechanics of online or offline animation production, and contains information specific to certain kinds of equipment.

7.2
DESIGNING ANIMATIONS

Design is the first step in creating an animation. The basic decisions include how to use the progression of time to show varying quantities in the data, how to control this variation through software, and how to blend a series of sequences into a complete animation.

7.2.1 Animation Control

There are two basic strategies for animation control: algorithmic and key frame. In the first, *algorithmic control,* animation is done by a procedure developed specifically for the purpose. In *key frame control,* the software is shown the state of the animation at various times and is instructed to interpolate between the states.

Key frame animation can be understood as a special case of algorithmic control, in which a sequence of key frames and interpolation methods is the input to the algorithm. The line between key frame and algorithmic control is not sharp, and some blending may be desirable. Hybrid approaches are becoming more common, for example, when a primarily key frame animation requires an algorithm to animate a certain parameter.

7.2.1.1 Algorithmic animation control

Algorithmic control refers to any control of animation by a programmed procedure. The most basic form of algorithmic control is simply a dedicated computer program which changes parameters to produce a given animation. Some visualization toolkits allow modules to be written and built into the visualization process. A special purpose animation module can be written to control all the parameters of the animation. The module must be able to discover which frame is being recorded. Except for arbitrary limits imposed by toolkits, algorithmic animation is completely flexible: any quantity which can be changed within a procedure can be used for animation. However, algorithmic control is awkward to use for any but the simplest sequences, and it is difficult to build into the system the kind of global knowledge needed for smooth complex motions. Algorithmic control systems and modules can be difficult to reuse unless great care is taken in their design.

7.2.1.2 Key frame animation control

In traditional hand-drawn animation, the animator produces *key frames*, which are drawings spaced up to several seconds apart. The assistant animator produces the in-between drawings (sometimes known as *in-betweens or tweens*), which complete the smooth motion from one key frame to the next [12, 23]. Key frame computer animation uses a similar approach, except that the computer produces the in-betweens automatically. This process, called *tweening,* is critical in producing a good animation.

In traditional computer animation for entertainment, key frames are used to control visual aspects of the animation, such as object positions, lighting, and color [25]. To be useful for scientific animation, key frames should control arbitrarily selected parameters of the visualization or data as well.

Key frames are produced by setting parameters for points in time; in effect, showing the program the state of the visualization at time of each key frame. Typically, this is done through an editor which shows an animation sequence as a complete document. A sample animation control panel from the SciAn animation package appears in Figure 7.1 [27].

The animation sequence is shown as a group of lines in a scrollable window. Time goes from left to right. Each line shows an object or a set of parameters in an object and is labeled on the left. A shaded rectangle indicates a key frame which affects a set of parameters. Lines between the key frames indicate continuity, and the color of the lines indicates whether the value changes between the key frames and what kind of interpolation is used. At the top of the window is a time cursor

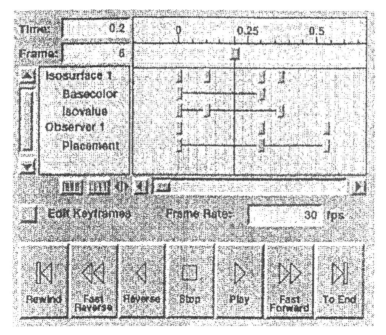

Figure 7.1. A key frame animation editor. The key frames in the animation are displayed symbolically in an editable window. Individual animated quantities are shown as time lines which trace behavior over time from left to right. The layout provides easy access to any point in the animation for editing.

that indicates the current time in the animation. This can be moved back and forth to select different times for editing or playback.

The animation is edited by moving the time cursor to various key frames, and showing the program how each key frame is to be set up by moving other controls. When the "Edit Key Frames" check box is on, any operation on any control that affects the visualization will edit a key frame at the current location of the cursor, automatically creating one if necessary. Key frames can also be selected and moved from within the control panel, and modified or deleted using menu items.

At the bottom is a series of controls which allow the animation sequence to be recorded on an offline device or played back on the screen. When the animation is recorded, the key frames and interpolation information are used to produce the sequence.

7.2.2 Parameters to Animate

The first step in designing an animation is to decide which parameters of the visualization to animate and how to animate them. Parameters to animate fall into three basic categories: animating the data, animating visualization techniques, and animating the view.

7.2.2.1 Animating the data

Animating the data includes animating any quantity which affects the datasets directly, before visualization is done. In general, any set of data quantities which can be reduced to single scalar or vector values can be animated, subject to software limitations.

Time-dependent datasets

In time-dependent datasets, the current time may be varied to show how the dataset changes through time. The mapping from real time to animation time need not be one-to-one or even linear. It is sometimes useful to show an animation at several different time rates to show different patterns in the data. It is a good idea to include a visible clock in the image to give an impression of how quickly time is going by, especially when more than one time rate is used in an animation. Other time-like parameters may be animated as well. For example, the sequential steps in a computation or the temperature of a simulated annealing process can be animated.

Filter parameters

Some datasets need to be filtered before visualization, and it may be useful to animate the parameters of these filters. For example, the slice value of an orthographic slicer which selects a single 2-D slice can be varied. If a dataset has missing data, the interpretation of the missing data can be changed to show the effect of different assumptions. Various functions can be applied to the data, including linear scale exaggeration and log or exponential mapping, and these can be animated as well.

For example, if one axis of a computation must be exaggerated to show fine surface details, the exaggeration can be animated to show the audience what is being done to the data, and thus avoid confusion that the exaggerated scale is physically accurate.

Deforming grids

When a dataset consists of data samples defined over a grid, both the data and the grid can be animated. For example, a finite element problem can use an unstructured grid to hold values for stress, temperature, etc. The values at each grid vertex or face may vary, and the location of the grid vertices themselves may change, as well.

In these cases, think of the grid as being defined by another time-dependent vector dataset. The vector at each index gives the location of each grid vertex. Conceptually, the problem then reduces to one of varying and interpolating several datasets at once.

It is usually best to interpolate the data and grid separately rather than try to do spatial interpolation on some derived result. This is true even if the data will be resampled to another grid at a later stage in the process. For example, consider the case of a moving projectile, where the projectile carries its own grid showing local pressure, and this is to be resampled with a larger fixed grid showing global pressure. If the projectile moves a significant distance between key frames, interpolating the grids and scalar values separately before combining displays fluid motion, while interpolating after the field has been resampled will result in the appearance of the pressure pattern fading out at the old location while fading in at the new.

Interpolation Methods

There are a number of different philosophies about performing interpolation. Traditional computer graphics philosophy generally holds that smoother is better. In engineering analysis, it is important to remain true to the data, and it is valuable to see the grid over which the computation was done, both temporally as well as spatially. For many problems, a compromise is best; smoothing is done, but care is taken to avoid artifacts which are not consistent with the data as a result of that interpolation. Linear interpolation works well in many cases, and has the strength that is unlikely to produce wild data values. However, in some cases, linear interpolation may produce a throbbing appearance to the animation, because the motion changes sharply at each key frame.

For more complex motions, especially in multiple dimensions, *spline curves* can be used. Spline curves are parametric polynomial curves defined by a series of control points and sometimes tangent vectors. Splines differ in their shape, smoothness, and computational complexity. Reference [4] gives a comprehensive information about various splines.

One important feature of a spline is whether it is guaranteed to pass through any of its control points. If so, a series of splines can be arranged to provide smooth interpolation between time steps, guaranteeing that each time step is accurately shown, simply by allowing certain control points to coincide with the time steps. The *Bezier* form as described by Foley et. al., for example, is guaranteed to pass through two of its four control points [14]. The other two control points are used to determine control point tangents and the smoothness of the curve. The *Hermite* form is guaranteed to pass through its two control points along tangent vectors defined at those control points.

Another important feature of a spline is its behavior between control points. The spline curve should not stray beyond a reasonable interpolation of the data. In particular, the curve should not overshoot local minima or maxima, because that would give a false impression of the range of the data. Consider the two splines of a series of scalar data points shown in Figure 7.2. At the left is the strict linear interpolation between the data points. At the center is an acceptable spline. At the right is an unacceptable spline that passes through the control points yet exceeds the range of the data between control points. For scalar data, a good spline can be ensured by requiring that the tangent vectors point in the direction of no change in the scalar value, or horizontal on a value/key frame plot. This is shown by the arrows in Figure 7.2. Depending on the spline, there may also be some constraints on the magnitude of the tangent vector to ensure uniformity and avoid retrograde motion and looping. The Bezier form, for example, works well when the tangent vectors are matched between subsequent spline patches to compromise on approximately one-third the distance between key frames [36].

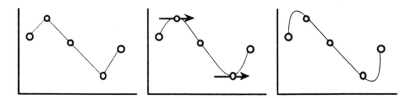

Figure 7.2. A comparison of linear interpolation and two splines for interpolating between data points. The spline on the right is unacceptable because it overshoots local minima and maxima. This can be avoided by ensuring that the tangent vectors at local minima and maxima are horizontal, as in the spline in the center.

It is easiest to interpolate the scalar data points that make up the dataset separately. When something about the problem domain is known by the interpolation routines, this information can be used to constrain the interpolation of several quantities. One example arises in computational fluid dynamics, where the values at the vertices of a cell are known at the key frames, and the values in-between must be interpolated. The individual values could be interpolated separately, but using knowledge of the conservation of mass to constrain the interpolated values can produce better results.

Another example arises in finite element calculations, where the grid is deformed. Naive Cartesian interpolation of each of the grid points, separately, works for small changes, but when the changes are large undesirable effects can result. Figure 7.3 shows two frames in the animation of a deformed multiple grid on an airfoil computation performed by T. Reu and S. Ying. The curvilinear grid wrapped around the airfoil is connected to an unstructured grid surrounding it. As the computation and animation progress, the grid around the airfoil rotates without changing its shape, deforming the unstructured grid around it. Knowledge about the stiffness of the curvilinear grid results in correct behavior, while naive Cartesian interpolation would give the grid a squashed appearance during interpolation. Figure 7.4 shows two frames of animation of the color density on the two grids.

Psychological factors

As more parameters are allowed to vary in an animation at once, it becomes more difficult to interpret the results visually. In most cases, simple animations avoid distracting the audience from the information presented [7].

Periodic motion requires special care in timing. If it is presented too slowly, it may not be recognized as periodic. If it is presented too quickly, it may be perceived as annoying visual noise. This is particularly noticeable in CFD problems with turbulence. Some experimentation may be needed to "tune" the rate of the visualization to the perception of the audience.

7.2.2.2 Animating visualization techniques

Parameters relating to the creation of the visualization itself can be animated to present more information about a visualization than can be expressed with a static image. For example, the isovalue of an isosurface can be changed to sweep

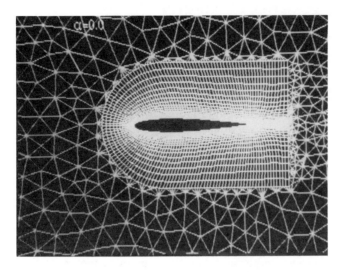

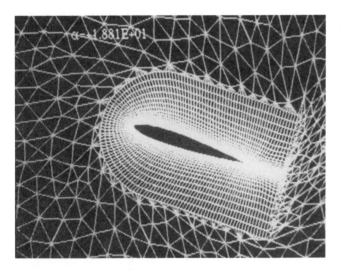

Figure 7.3. Example of an animated deformed grid. Two frames in the animation of a deformed grid. Note that the curvilinear portion rotates, while the unstructured portion is deformed. This information must be built into the animation to avoid unwanted deformation of the curvilinear portion. (Visualization by Taekyu Reu at the Supercomputer Computations Research Institute.) (See color section plate 7.3)

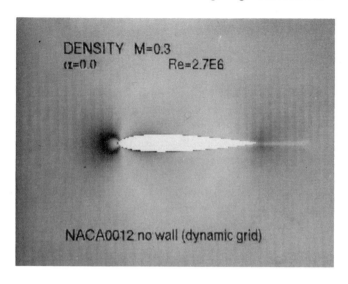

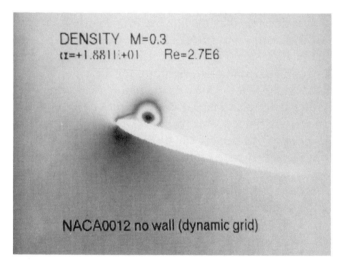

Figure 7.4. Data over an animated deformed grid. The same grid shown in Figure 7.3 is used to display density from a CFD calculation by Taekyu Reu and Susan Ying. (See color section, plate 7.4)

out the range of values, or the position of a color slice can be changed to sweep through a volume. Techniques used on several visualization objects can be combined, such as sweeping a color slice through a volume while cutting away an isosurface or volume visualization like an onion, exposing the layers inside.

Geometric parameters can be animated as well. To emphasize one portion of the visualization, all but that portion can be darkened or faded to transparency. The colors of a visualization can be cycled to give the appearance of motion, as described later in Section 7.3.1.5 on color table animation.

7.2.2.3 Animating the view

Once the 3-D geometry for the visualization is produced, it must be viewed to produce an image. Animating the view refers to all motions of the observer and, to a lesser extent, motions of the visualization objects within the field of view. This section describes the basics of observer motions and models and how they are interpolated.

Overview of camera moves

The basic camera moves were developed by the film industry. Figure 7.5 shows a few traditional camera moves. *Panning* and *tilting* refer to rotating the camera around its axis, which results in a change of the apparent position of the subject without parallax. The camera can be panned left, right, up, or down, and it can be tilted around its forward axis right or left. *Dollying* or *craning* refer to moving the camera in 3-D space, which results in a change of the apparent position of the subject with parallax. The moves are named after the pieces of equipment traditionally used to generate the motion. The camera can be dollied in or out or right or left, or craned up and down. *Arcing* refers to rotating the camera in a great circle around the subject while keeping the lens fixed on the subject, combining panning and dollying or craning. The camera can be arced right or left, over or under. *Zooming* refers to changing the optics of the camera lens to change the apparent size of the subject [39].

In computer visualization, the *observer* corresponds to a physical camera. It is described mathematically as having a location, an orientation, and a perspective projection. The location and orientation are defined in world space. The observer may also have near and far clipping planes that specify the range of distances over which the observer works.

The basic camera moves have mathematical analogues for observers. Panning and tilting correspond to rotating the observer without changing its location. Dollying and craning correspond to changing the location of the observer without changing its orientation. Arcing corresponds to rotating the observer around a focus point within the subject or rotating the subject itself around the focus point of the observer. Zooming corresponds to changing the angle of view of the perspective projection.

Panning is useful for following a moving subject. Arcing around an object is useful for showing the 3-D structure of an object without changing its apparent size. Zooming and dollying have similar effects; both change the apparent size of the subject. The difference is that dollying results in motion parallax and will give the

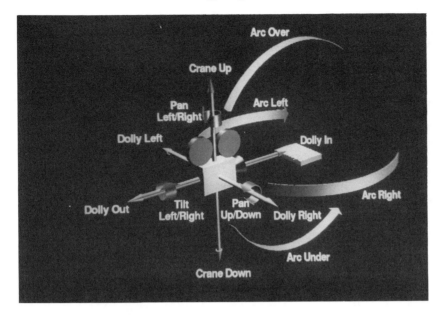

Figure 7.5. Basic Camera Moves. The basic camera moves are panning and tilting, which are rotations of the camera about its axis, dollying and craning, which are linear motions of the camera in space, and arcing, which is motion of the camera in an arc around a subject of interest. Zooming is not a camera move but is rather a change to the camera lens. (See color section plate 7.5)

impression of moving toward the subject. Zooming will give more of an impression of merely focusing attention on a portion of the subject. A narrow zoom produces less foreshortening of objects due to distance than does a wide zoom.

It is useful to think of the observer as carrying around its own local coordinate system, **uvw**. When the image is transformed to viewing coordinates and displayed on a screen, **u** is to the right of the screen, **v** is toward the top of the screen, and **w** is out of the center of the screen toward the person looking at the image. This provides a right-handed coordinate system which is easy to use. The lens or front of the observer actually points in the −**w** direction.

The world, as shown in Figure 7.6, is a 3-D Cartesian coordinate space **xyz** that contains both the visualization and the observer. Modeling transformations place the visualizations within the world space. The placement of the observer eventually reduces to viewing transformations, but for convenience in interpolation it is usually kept in some other form. When it is necessary to determine the viewing parameters for a frame, this information can be converted back into a transformation matrix and used to produce a viewing matrix.

Observer placement

The location and orientation of the observer, taken together, are called the observer *placement*. Placement is defined relative to a reference placement, usually at the origin of world space with the principal axes of the observer aligned with

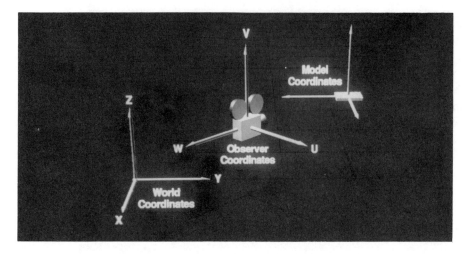

Figure 7.6. The World Coordinate System. The world is a 3-D Cartesian coordinate system in which the visualizations and the observer reside.

the principal axes of the world space (u||x, v||y, w||z). Observer placement may be thought of as translation and rotation from the reference placement, so any methods of doing translation and rotation are candidates for defining placement. Observer placement may also be viewed as a point in world space and a series of unit vectors defining the principal axes of the observer in world coordinates.

There are many mathematical models for placement. For the most part they convey the same information but differ in convenience and behavior during interpolation. In general, the orientation component of placement is much more sensitive to artifacts of interpolation than is location. Some common placement models exhibit gimbal lock, where some degrees of freedom are lost for certain orientations [36]. This can result in division by zero or erratic behavior around critical orientations. Other models can exhibit nonuniform rotation from uniformly separated key frames or nonuniform rotation away from certain privileged axes.

Transformation matrices

Transformation matrices are the most common way of specifying rotations and translations in computer graphics. A 4 by 4 transformation matrix for homogeneous coordinates can specify observer placement completely. The matrix can be multiplied with modeling and perspective matrices to provide a viewing matrix, or it can be multiplied with homogeneous points or vectors to produce transformed points and vectors. An observer matrix looks like Formula 7.1.

$$M = \begin{bmatrix} r_{11} & r_{12} & r_{13} & 0 \\ r_{21} & r_{22} & r_{23} & 0 \\ r_{31} & r_{32} & r_{33} & 0 \\ t_x & t_y & t_z & 1 \end{bmatrix}$$

[7.1]

An observer transformation matrix

Limiting the matrix to rotation and translation with no scaling or skewing simplifies working with the matrix. The 3 by 3 matrix R in the upper left corner gives the rotation of the observer, and the 3-vector T at the bottom left gives the location of the observer in world coordinates.

One interesting property of matrices containing only rotation and translation is that the directions of the principal axes of the observer in world coordinates can be read directly off the matrix. When the observer axis vectors **u**, **v**, and **w**, expressed as row vectors in world coordinates, are stacked on top of each other, they result in the rotation portion of the observer matrix. This is shown in Formula 7.2. This can be seen easily by premultiplying the principal unit vectors in observer coordinates by the matrix.

$$\begin{bmatrix} u_x & u_y & u_z & 0 \\ v_x & v_y & v_z & 0 \\ w_x & w_y & w_z & 0 \\ t_x & t_y & t_z & 1 \end{bmatrix} = \begin{bmatrix} r_{11} & r_{12} & r_{13} & 0 \\ r_{21} & r_{22} & r_{23} & 0 \\ r_{31} & r_{32} & r_{33} & 0 \\ t_x & t_y & t_z & 1 \end{bmatrix}$$

[7.2]
The principal observer axes
and the observer matrix

The transformation matrix itself is not inherently well suited for animation, because there is no obvious way to interpolate in matrix form to produce natural rotation, except by decomposing into separate rotation and translation portions and interpolating separately.

Lookfrom/lookat/up

In the *lookfrom/lookat/up* model, the placement of the camera is specified by two points and one unit vector in world coordinates. The *lookfrom* point is the location, in world coordinates, of the origin of the observer's coordinate system. The *lookat* point is the point in world coordinates at which the observer is looking. The *up* vector is a unit vector pointing in the observer's up direction.

The transformation matrix can be derived from this model by deriving the **u**, **v**, and **w** unit vectors in world coordinates and then stacking them to form the rotation portion. The **w** unit vector is determined by normalizing the vector from the *lookat* to the *lookfrom* point. The **v** unit vector is the same as the up vector, which is expected to be orthogonal to the **w** vector. The **u** unit vector is determined by taking the cross product $\mathbf{u} = \mathbf{v} \times \mathbf{w}$. This completely describes the observer's principal axes in world coordinates and it can be used to create the rotation portion of a transformation matrix. The algorithm can be made more robust with respect to slight deviations from orthogonality and unit vectors by normalizing at every step and calculating $\mathbf{w} = \mathbf{u} \times \mathbf{v}$ as a final step. The translation portion of the matrix is the coordinates of the *lookfrom* point.

The *lookat* point gives additional information which does not affect an ordinary viewing transformation but is handy for other purposes. For example, the distance to the focus point can be used in calculations for stereo viewing. One simple way of interpolating this observer model is interpolating the *lookat* and *lookfrom* points separately, using Cartesian cubic splines. The **up** vector can be interpolated in Cartesian space or as a point on the surface of a sphere constrained to be orthogonal to the forward vector. This gives good results when the *lookat* point is at a feature of interest.

This model is free from interpolation singularities and gimbal lock, and its components are easy to understand. However, when rotation is done with key frames that are far apart, a nonuniform rate of rotation will result.

Lookfrom/lookat/twist

In the *lookfrom/lookat/twist* model, the placement of the camera is specified by two points in world space and one scalar value. *Lookfrom* and *lookat* are defined as in the lookfrom/lookat/up model. The *twist* scalar value is the angle of twist of the observer around its forward vector, relative to a reference orientation.

The **w** unit vector is determined the same way as *lookfrom/lookat/up*. To find the **v** unit vector, imagine a radial disc perpendicular to the **w** vector. The **v** unit vector must be a unit vector lying on this disc, perpendicular to the **w** unit vector. The *twist* angle selects the appropriate vector relative to a reference unit vector in world coordinates, most commonly the **z** unit vector. The **z** unit vector is projected onto the disc, is normalized, and is rotated by the twist angle around the **w** axis, giving the **v** unit vector.

The *lookfrom* and *lookat* points can be interpolated separately using Cartesian splines. The angle of twist is even easier to interpolate than the **up** vector, because it is a single scalar. This method works reasonably well as long as the observer is nearly horizontal. However, when the **w** axis is parallel to the reference vector, the projection of the reference vector onto the axial disc is zero, resulting in a situation where the projected vector has no magnitude, and it is not clear what the angle of twist means. Perturbing the reference vector can avoid mathematical singularities, but interpolation near the area may be subject to erratic and unpredictable motion.

Euler angles

Euler angles refer to a family of methods by which an object is rotated successively three times around three fixed axes to produce a composite rotation. Some other method, such as a *lookfrom* point, must be used to provide the location of the placement. There are many possible rotation conventions which have been called Euler angles. The most familiar to computer graphics is *yaw/pitch/roll.* An observer starts out in its reference orientation. First it is rotated by an angle ϕ around its **v** axis, giving a yaw. Then it is rotated by an angle θ around its recently rotated **u** axis, giving a pitch. Positive rotations are usually defined to tip the front of the observer up. Finally, the observer is rotated through an angle ψ around its recently rotated **w** axis, giving a roll.

Euler angles are familiar and easy to apply, requiring only three scalar numbers to specify them, and they can produce all possible orientations. However, Euler angles do not provide an appropriate space for interpolation without counterintuitive motion and gimbal lock [36]. Like *lookat/lookfrom/twist,* Euler angles work reasonably well for nearly horizontal observers.

Quaternions were invented in 1843 by Sir William Rowan Hamilton as a successor to complex numbers [17]. They provide an effective and convenient means for representing the orientation of an observer with good behavior during interpolation.

A quaternion is made of two parts: a scalar s and a 3-vector V, or $Q = [s, V]$, where $V = [v_1 \ v_2 \ v_3]$. Rotations are defined by unit quaternions, where $s^2 + v_1^2 + v_2^2 + v_3^2 = 1$. These quaternions can be thought of as points on the surface of a unit sphere in 4-dimensional space, known as a 4-sphere. A quaternion can be decoded into a single rotation θ around a unit axis A. The vector portion V points along A with magnitude $|V| = \sin(\theta/2)$. The scalar portion s is equal to $\cos(\theta/2)$. To take the inverse of a rotation quaternion, reverse the sign of either s or V, but not both. This reverses the direction of the rotation.

Reversing the sign of both s and V results in another quaternion specifying the same rotation. Because there are two quaternions for each rotation, there are always two choices for each subsequent quaternion during interpolation. One easy way to choose between them is to select every subsequent quaternion in a sequence to be the closer of the two to the previous quaternion when each is represented as a point in 4-dimensional space.

Multiplication of quaternions is defined as in Formula 7.3. Like transformation matrices, a series of rotation quaternions can be multiplied together to produce a composite rotation.

$$Q_1 Q_2 = [s_1, V_1][s_2, V_2] = [(s_1 s_2 - V_1 \cdot V_2), (s_1 V_2 + s_2 V_1 + V_1 \times V_2)] \qquad [7.3]$$

Quaternion multiplication

To rotate a vector V by a quaternion Q, the vector is first represented as a quaternion with the vector equal to V and the scalar equal to 0, or $W = [0, V]$. This vector quaternion is premultiplied with the inverse of the rotation quaternion and postmultiplied with the rotation quaternion to provide the rotated vector, $R = Q^{-1} W Q$.

A series of quaternions can be interpolated smoothly with no gimbal lock, singularities, or privileged axes, and they maintain perceptually smooth and consistent motion at all times. Most of the techniques exploit the fact that rotation quaternions can be viewed as points on a unit 4-sphere and seek to find spline curves on the 4-sphere. Shoemake describes a simple but effective method of doing interpolations using Bezier curves [36]. Barr et. al. and Gabriel and Kajiya describe more complex methods [3, 15].

Psychological factors

In the design of observer motions, it is important to remember that the observer represents the eyes of the audience. Some people are sensitive to motion sickness, which may be triggered by excessively wild motion. The motions with which people are familiar are based on everyday experiences such as walking, turning around to see a panorama, moving close to look at a feature, walking around an object, and driving a car. Motion pictures expand this to include the experiences of arcing over and under, and smoothly dollying and craning. The use of kinds of motion unfamiliar to the audience may distract from the contents of the animation.

Unfortunately, the Cartesian splines that are most common in computer animation can produce varying acceleration in haphazard directions, causing a bouncy or mushy feel to the motion. This can be a useful stylistic technique in art animation, but the mushy feel can distract from the contents of the visualization in scientific animation. The haphazard motion may also result in artifacts in which parts of the visualization appear to change size or speed. Simple sequences of observer motions which stop before changing may be less confusing than smooth motion.

7.2.3 Assembling a Complete Animation

When the engineers working on the analysis problem are the only ones who will view the animation, it may be sufficient to generate a single sequence showing the visualization of interest. However, if the animation is to be viewed by another audience, additional care in designing an effective complete presentation is important.

An effective animation requires careful design, always keeping the audience in mind. An animation should be just the right length, neither too short nor too long, and it should provide enough information to get the point across without confusing the audience with "information overload." [7]

7.2.3.1 Frame rate

One important factor in animation is the frame rate, or the rate at which images are presented during playback. Every recording medium has a natural playback rate: 30 or 25 frames per second for video, 24 frames per second for film. To animate "on ones" is to use every available frame to show a different image, thus maximizing the frame rate. To animate "on twos" is to use every other frame, "on threes" is to use every third frame, etc. Good commercial film animation is usually animated on twos or on ones. Saturday morning cartoons are often animated on threes or worse. The frame rate is a tradeoff. The greater the frame rate, the smoother the animation will appear, but because there will be more frames, more work will be required to produce the animation. It is best to aim high when choosing a frame rate. Between 20 and 25 frames per second is a threshold below which many people will perceive flicker [22].

7.2.3.2 Sequences and transitions

Animations are made of a number of sequences, each of which shows a group of smoothly changing images. A *transition* between sequences occurs whenever a major element leaves or enters the scene or the scene completely changes. There are a number of ways of doing transitions [28]. The simplest transition is a *cut*, where sequences change instantly from one to the other. Cuts works well when the scene changes completely between sequences. *Dissolves* involve fading out one sequence and fading in another. Dissolves can be implemented as weighted sums of the pixels in resulting images or by fading individual objects in the visualization. Dissolves work well when elements appear in or disappear from existing scenes. There are more elaborate ways of doing transitions, such as *wipes,* but, as with every aspect of scientific visualization, the means of presentation should not distract from what is being presented.

7.2.3.3 Titles and text

Titles and other text can be used to present information in addition to what can be seen directly in the visualization. Descriptive titles, formulas, and parameters explain to the audience what is being viewed. Numbered scales, running digital clocks, and numerical readouts of parameters give valuable quantitative information about the computation.

It is easy to overestimate the amount of text that can be used when designing an animation on a high-resolution screen. One must keep in mind how the animation will be used when adding text. There are severe limitations on the size of legible text, described later, if an animation is to be recorded onto video. Furthermore, animations may be presented to audiences at less than ideal conditions, as in large auditoriums with dim projectors. A useful test of the legibility of text on a frame is to look at the screen from several meters' distance.

Some pieces of text, such as a clock readout or a numbered scale, only require a glance. However, longer pieces of text must be read by the audience to be useful. Titles should be kept on the screen for twice the amount of time necessary to read them aloud at moderate speed [28].

7.2.3.4 Narration

For any piece of symbolic information that must be conveyed, there are two basic choices: text on the screen or narration. Narration has several advantages over on-screen text. It is easier to understand the spoken word, and hearing does not distract the eye away from the visualization. Narration does not depend on variable reading speeds and viewing conditions, although it does require a clear sound system.

One disadvantage of narration is that only one piece of information can be delivered at a time. When several pieces of information must be conveyed, they must be spoken in turn. This is actually a blessing in disguise, because requiring the important topics to be separated results in an improved presentation. Narration does not inherently indicate a place on the screen, but it can be combined with an on-screen cue, such as an arrow, dot, or temporarily brightened geometric item, to show the area of the visualization to which the narration refers.

Narration is usually dubbed onto tape after a complete animation has been prepared [30]. A pleasant voice should be recorded in a soundproof environment. In some situations, it may be acceptable to record the voice of a person who is demonstrating an interactive real-time animation. This will add a more immediate and less polished feel to the result. Interactive narration is difficult to record near noisy workstations. One solution is to move the monitor and keyboard to a room separate from the workstation itself to reduce background noise.

7.2.3.5 Sonification

Sonification refers to the expression of scientific data through sound, much as visualization refers to the expression of data through vision. The soundtrack represents a parameter of the visualization, such as a tone which varies in pitch according to a scalar quantity, a series of clicks which represent individual events, or a click track to indicate the progression of time.

Sonification is still in its infancy, but some good applications have already been made. Sonification must be done at the time the images are generated, which is problematic for some single-frame recording techniques. A possible solution is to generate the sonification track separately and dub it onto the final animation. Another solution is to store digital information for pitch, volume, and timbre on the recording device and use a computer program to play back the animation, and convert the digital information into waveforms in real time. Some optical disc recorders, for example, have the ability to associate a small amount of arbitrary digital information with frames on the disc [38].

7.2.3.6 Music

A musical soundtrack can enhance the polish of an animation. In most cases it is illegal to use commercially produced music on an animation unless a fee is paid to the publisher. Companies which sell music for use in advertisements exist, and collections of themes can be purchased with no additional fees for unlimited use [28]. Another source is sequenced classical music, which can be played through a synthesizer and recorded. An advantage of sequenced music is that the speed of the piece can be adjusted to match the length of an animation.

7.3
PRODUCING ANIMATIONS

Once an animation has been designed, it must be produced in a form that can be viewed. The two basic ways of producing animations are *online* and *offline*. Online animations are produced directly on the workstation and viewed in real time as they progress. Offline animations are recorded and stored on video or film equipment for later playback.

7.3.1 Animating Online

Some animations can be displayed in real time directly on a workstation or frame buffer. Although animations made this way tend to be slow or limited in length and complexity, they are nevertheless useful for many applications. Online animations can be viewed quickly after the analysis results are complete and can be videotaped in real time using inexpensive equipment. This section describes a variety of techniques to do online animation.

7.3.1.1 Direct display

Depending on the time it takes to draw the visualization, it may be practical to animate by drawing each frame in sequence on the workstation screen. This technique generally works best for simple visualizations made of lines and solid polygons, without lighting or shading calculations which tend to slow down rendering. For direct display to work, it must be possible to draw each frame quickly.

When the time needed to draw each frame varies widely from frame to frame, the perception of the passage of time in the animation will not be uniform. There are two general approaches to solving this problem. One approach involves placing an artificial delay after each frame to make each frame appear for the same amount of time. For example, to display four frames per second, if a frame takes 0.1 seconds to draw, delay another 0.15 seconds after drawing it before drawing the next. This approach has the advantage that every frame will be displayed, but it is limited by the fact that every frame must be slowed down to the speed of the slowest frame. The second approach involves running the animation clock at a variable rate depending on how much time it takes to draw each individual frame. If a frame takes 0.1 seconds to draw, advance the animation clock by 0.1 seconds for the next frame. This approach requires the animation to display real-valued time steps and is not guaranteed to show every frame.

Animating using direct display requires a double buffer, which breaks up the graphics screen into two buffers. Only the front buffer is used to display the image on the screen. Each new image is drawn into the back buffer; then the buffers are swapped, resulting in the instantaneous disappearance of the old graphics and appearance of the new. The double buffer eliminates flashing caused by redrawing the image [14].

7.3.1.2 Display list animation

Some workstations have *display lists,* sometimes called *display objects* or *graphical objects* [26]. A display list keeps a group of graphics commands (sometimes called primitives) together in memory for easy access. It corresponds roughly to the software concept known as a *segment* [14], and segments are often implemented as display lists. Typically, a display list is produced by opening a new display list, issuing a series of graphics calls, and then closing the display list. Instead of drawing on the screen, the graphics calls result in commands stored in the display list. Later, the display list can be referred to through a pointer or integer and can be drawn with a single call. To use display lists for animation, each frame in the animation is drawn into its own display list, and the display lists are drawn in sequence.

Display lists are provided by the software and hardware of the workstation and are usually designed closely to the hardware characteristics. For this reason, display lists tend to be faster than drawing the graphical objects separately.

Because display lists contain 3-D graphical commands which are rendered to 2-D images when they are drawn, it is possible to change the observer placement while the animation is running. The chief disadvantage of display lists is that the complete geometry of each frame must be stored; this can consume quite a lot of memory.

7.3.1.3 Pencil tests

A *pencil test* is a traditional animation technique in which the pencil drawings of animators are shown in sequence to indicate how they will move [23]. In scientific visualization, a pencil test can be any case where an animation is artificially simplified to the point at which it can be animated online using direct display or display lists.

The most common form of a pencil test is a wire frame display, where only the outlines of the objects in the visualization are shown. Because many workstations can draw lines much faster than polygons, even highly complex visualizations can sometimes be displayed quickly. Other techniques involve displaying smooth-shaded polygons as flat-shaded or decomposing visualizations into fewer and simpler polygons. The fastest forms of simplification depend on the hardware in use.

7.3.1.4 Image animation

It is becoming more common for workstations and personal computers to be able to play full color images at video or near-video rates. This can be used to do online animation by generating a series of frames and displaying them within a window on the screen. The amount of memory required and the display speed depend on the image size. One advantage of image animation over direct display and display list animation is that the display speed of each frame is not related to the complexity of the geometry in each frame, although it may be related to the complexity of the image. Disadvantages include large memory requirements and the inability to change the viewpoint during playback.

There are a number of established mechanisms for saving image animations into files, such as QuickTime [11], MPEG [8], AVI, and VfW [33]. Animations saved into files can be played online on a variety of workstations and personal computers. Some formats even allow soundtracks to accompany the video, which are played back through the computer. Animation files tend to be large, in spite of aggressive internal compression.

7.3.1.5 Color table animation

Each pixel on the screen of a raster graphics system is made up of a number of bits. Frame buffers are often organized into *bit planes,* each of which contributes one bit to every pixel on the screen. On graphics systems with *color tables,* the bits for each pixel are combined into an integer and used as an index into a color table. The color table, sometimes called a *color lookup table, color map,* or *palette,* maps the values in the frame buffer onto colors, usually given as RGB triplets [14]. The color table is usually implemented in hardware, and it is much faster to change the entire color table than it is to change the image on the screen. This feature of frame buffers can be used to do animation [37].

There are two online animation techniques that take advantage of color tables.

In both cases, the entire sequence of images is placed into the frame buffer before the animation occurs. Then the color table is changed to play the animation. Because the images are placed first in the frame buffer, and subsequent animation only changes the color table, the speed of animation does not depend in any way on the complexity of the images.

Color table animation techniques are limited in the complexity and subtlety of the visualizations, due to the limited number of colors and tradeoffs between colors and animation length. In spite of these shortcoming, the techniques are still useful for many applications, especially for short animations of 2-D visualizations.

Color cycling

Color cycling involves mapping a sequence of moving events onto a range of color indices. Once the image has been drawn, a series of colors is placed into the appropriate entries in the color table. When it is time to advance to the next frame, the color range is changed, usually by shifting the range of colors up or down in a cycle.

As a simple example, consider a visualization with a rectangle that must flash alternately black and red as a warning signal. The rectangle is drawn with a certain color index. When it is time to flash the rectangle on and off, red (255, 0, 0) and black (0, 0, 0) are alternately placed into this entry in the color table. Although the actual image in the bit planes will not change, the rectangle will appear to flash on and off.

Color cycling is particularly useful on particle traces to display a vector field, such as fluid flow within a chamber or as airflow around a wing. For example, take a computation which calculates airflow around a blunt body, advecting particles for 10 time steps to be visualized on a workstation with 16 color table entries. Six entries (0 through 5) can be used to draw the static portion of the image: the blunt body, annotations, and everything else which does not change from frame to frame. One of these colors must be a neutral background behind the particles. The remaining colors (6 through 15) are used to draw the time steps of the visualization. The first time step is drawn using color 6, the second using color 7, and successively to the tenth time step.

When it is time to run the animation, colors 6 through 15 are cleared to the background color. No particles will appear. The animation is advanced to the first time step by setting color 6 to white and the remaining colors to the background. The next time step is shown by setting color 7 to white and the remaining colors to the background. When the colors are cycled quickly enough, the particles will appear to move.

One advantage of this technique is that all the time steps can be shown at once as motion tracks by placing a range of colors, such as a rainbow sequence, in color indices 6 through 15. The two techniques can be combined by placing a rainbow of colors in the indices and cycling the range up and down. All time steps will be visible, and the cycling of colors will also show animated motion.

The greatest limitation of this technique is that it can only be used when all time steps will fit on the screen without obscuring each other. Particles work well if they are small, constantly moving, and sparse. Solid graphical objects can be used when there is no retrograde motion, such as diffusion of gas into a chamber or a 2-D simulation of molten plastic flowing into a mold.

Color table partitioning

Color table partitioning is more general but costlier in terms of bit planes and image colors. This technique involves dividing the bit planes in the frame buffer into separate groups and using each group to store a separate image. The total number of bits in all the images must not exceed the total number of bit planes in the frame buffer. A frame buffer with 12 bit planes which normally index 4096 colors can be used to store 2 images with 6 bits (64 colors) each, 3 images with 4 bits (16 colors) each, 4 images with 3 bits (8 colors) each, 6 images with 2 bits (4 colors) each, or 12 images with 1 bit (2 colors) each.

To demonstrate this technique, take a simple case, where 2 separate images are to be shown on a system with 4 bit planes, or 64 color entries. Each image can use 2 bit planes, or four colors. Assume the desired colors are in Table 7.1.

The four bits in the color table are divided into two groups of two bits each. Bits 0 and 1 are used for the first image, and bits 2 and 3 are used for the second. The first image is drawn only into bits 0 and 1, leaving bits 2 and 3 alone. The second image is drawn only into bits 2 and 3, leaving bits 0 and 1. The result is two separate images in the frame buffer at once, each using two bits for four colors each.

To display only the first frame in the sequence, go through all 16 (2^4) entries in the color table. Set all entries for which bits 0 and 1 are both 0 to black, regardless of the values of the other bits. Set all entries for which bits 0 and 1 match the pattern 01 to red, all entries that match 10 to green, and all entries that match 11 to white. The resulting color table will appear like the "Frame 1 Color" column in Table 7.2. The colors displayed depend only on the bottom two bits and not on the top two bits. The end result is that only the image in the bottom two bits will be displayed.

To display the second frame in the sequence, go through all of the color table entries setting the colors according to the pattern in bits 3 and 4, resulting in a color table like the Frame 2 Color column. Only the image in bits 3 and 4 will be displayed. Flip the color table back and forth between the two states, and the two images will alternately appear.

Color table partitioning is flexible, depending only on the number of desired images and the number of bits in the color table. This technique can be combined

TABLE 7.1: Four colors for a partitioned color table

Color Index	Bit Pattern	Color
0	00	Black
1	01	Red
2	10	Green
3	11	White

TABLE 7.2: A partitioned color table.
Two images with two bits each are stored in a color table with four bit planes. One image is stored in bits 0 and 1 and the other in bits 2 and 3. When the color table is switched between the states in the Frame 1 Color and Frame 2 Color columns, the images appear to alternate.

Color Index	Bit Pattern	Frame 1 Color	Frame 2 Color
0	0000	Black	Black
1	0001	Red	Black
2	0010	Green	Black
3	0011	White	Black
4	0100	Black	Red
5	0101	Red	Red
6	0110	Green	Red
7	0111	White	Red
8	1000	Black	Green
9	1001	Red	Green
10	1010	Green	Green
11	1011	White	Green
12	1100	Black	White
13	1101	Red	White
14	1110	Green	White
15	1111	White	White

with double buffering to double the number of frames by going through all the possibilities in one buffer, swapping the buffers, and repeating the process. In this way, it is possible to get an animation of up to 24 1-bit images on a system with 12 double-buffered color table bit planes.

To use color table partitioning, one must draw only into a certain set of bit planes. Some frame buffers can mask out certain bits while drawing graphics objects. For those that cannot, it is necessary to generate the images separately and then form a single composite image as a separate step.

7.3.2 Animating Offline

Animating offline describes all techniques for generating and storing an animation to be played later in real time. Because it is not necessary to generate images as fast as they will be displayed, the quality of the images and the smoothness of playback can be significantly improved over online animation.

7.3.2.1 Video recording

Analog video systems are based on the technology of *cathode ray tubes (CRTs)*. A CRT is a conical vacuum tube with a steerable electron beam that shoots from the back into an array of phosphors located on the inside of the screen. Electrons hitting the phosphors cause them to light up, producing an image on the screen. Color is produced by using multiple electron beams to shoot through a shadow mask, which is a sheet of metal with small holes placed just behind the phosphors.

The phosphors are laid down in a pattern of colors to correspond to the placement of the holes, and the angle of the electron beam through the holes causes only phosphors of a certain color to illuminate.

The electron beam travels quickly from left to right. When it reaches the right side of the screen, it snaps back to the left side. This is called the *horizontal retrace*. After each line has been traced, the next line is slightly lower on the screen. Eventually, the beam gets to the bottom of the screen and snaps back to the top, during the *vertical retrace*. The beam is blanked during the retraces. This is shown in Figure 7.7.

One complete image on the screen is called a frame. When the beam has moved once from the top to the bottom of the screen, it has traced out one field. On non-interlaced systems, such as most workstation monitors, one field fills a complete frame. On interlaced systems, such as standard video transmission, a frame is made up of two fields. The first field fills in every other line, and the second field returns and fills in the lines missed during the first field [18].

A video signal contains an analog sequence of levels which vary as the beam sweeps out across the screen. All video requires a sync signal that contains pulses at the horizontal and vertical retraces which synchronize the monitor to the video signal. In component video, the several color and sync components of the color video signal are transmitted separately. There are many kinds of component video including RGB, S-VHS, and Betacam. The horizontal and vertical sync signals may be transmitted on separate lines, on a single composite sync line, or on one of the components, such as the Green channel of RGB. In composite video, which is used for all broadcast and most video recording, all of the information necessary to make the entire color video image is compressed into a single signal.

Video signals are usually transmitted over 75-ohm coaxial cable in an analog signal normalized to 1V or 0.7V peak-to-peak [6]. Some workstations and personal computers use a digital output at 5V, which must be converted to the correct analog signal before it can be used.

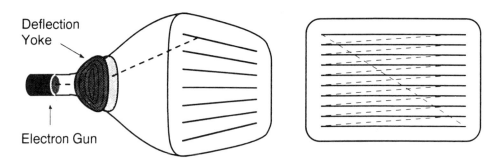

Figure 7.7. A Cathode Ray Tube. An electron shoots a beam that is deflected by a magnetic yoke to strike a phosphorous screen. The beam traces horizontally from left to right and then retraces horizontally to the left again for the next line. When it arrives at the bottom, it retraces vertically to the top. The illustration at the right is simplified for clarity. In reality, the vertical retrace takes several horizontal retrace times.

Overview of video standards

NTSC, PAL, and SECAM are the three major video standards in the world today. There are also several efforts to develop new high definition television standards, or HDTV. Producing animations that look acceptable on video requires understanding of and designing around the inherent limitations of a target video standard.

NTSC

The NTSC video system, used in North America, parts of South America, and parts of Asia including Japan, was developed by the second National Television System Committee, from which it gets its name [5]. In 1953, the NTSC was given an enormously difficult task: to develop a full color television system which required no more bandwidth than the existing black-and-white broadcast system (in essence, requiring 3 to 1 data compression) and was fully compatible with existing television sets. The engineering involved to solve this problem with 1953 consumer technology was brilliant. Unfortunately, many of the decisions that were made then get in our way today [35].

The NTSC system is based on an interlaced timing standard with 525 lines per frame at 29.97 frames per second, or 59.94 fields per second. These numbers differ slightly from 30 and 60 because of a decision made to improve compatibility with existing black and white sets made at the time. This timing standard is referred to as RS-170A [35].

NTSC builds upon this timing to produce a composite video signal with no more bandwidth than a black and white signal at the same video rate. This is achieved by dividing the signal into one luminance channel and two chromaticity channels. The bandwidth of the luminance channel is reduced, and the bandwidth of the two chromaticity channels is reduced even more. The chroma values are stored as phase information in such a way that they are decoded into color information on color sets and appear as fine bands on black and white sets, resulting in a gray image [24, 13].

Because of the different bandwidths, it is not really meaningful to ask how many pixels are on a line. The pixel density varies according to the color and luminance transitions being done. In a sense, it could be said that there are more light and dark pixels per line than colored pixels, and there are more green and yellow pixels than there are red and blue pixels. Violating the bandwidth limitations by using fine details of the wrong colors will cause blurred images, bleeding from the luminance to the chroma channels or vice versa, or *chroma crawl,* where herringbone patterns crawl up the screen at sharp color transitions. Depending on the color patterns and equipment used, pixel densities can be anywhere from approximately 200 to 600 pixels per line.

PAL

The PAL (Phased Alternation Line) system is standard in most of western Europe, most of Africa, Australia, New Zealand, and parts of Asia and South America [5]. The system displays 625 interlaced lines at 25 frames per second. PAL was developed in Europe after NTSC had already been developed in America [24]. PAL has better color than NTSC and higher picture resolution. It still suffers from bandwidth and chroma/luminance bleeding problems, although not as badly as NTSC. The 50 Hz. refresh rate is closer to the perceptual flicker threshold than the 60 Hz. rate of NTSC.

SECAM

The SECAM (Sequentiel Couleur avec Mémoire) system is standard in France, Russia, eastern Europe, and parts of Africa [31] [5]. The frame rate and resolution is identical to PAL. The only difference is how the color information is encoded onto composite video [24]. Conversion between SECAM and PAL is easily done with inexpensive equipment, and many videotape units can accommodate both standards.

HDTV

HDTV, or High-Definition Television, refers to efforts to replace existing video standards with much higher resolution. There are two HDTV production standards endorsed in the United States by the Society of Motion Picture and Television Engineers (SMPTE), both of which specify 1125 lines at 60 fields per second. Current work involves engineering ways to transmit a high-definition video signal using bandwidth no greater than existing NTSC signals. Whatever broadcast standard is ultimately chosen, it is likely that there will be converters to convert between the SMPTE standard and the broadcast standard, at the expense of much of the information in the video [35] [5].

Converting images to video

There are two basic ways to convert computer output to composite video: *composite video encoders* which encode component video without changing resolution, and *scan converters* or *format converters,* which can change resolution as well [25].

NTSC composite video encoders only work on workstations or frame buffers which can produce signals with RS-170A timing. The RGB and Sync signals from the workstation or frame buffer go to the NTSC encoder, which produces a single composite video output. PAL and SECAM encoders work in a similar manner.

For workstations that have RS-170A output, NTSC encoders provide an inexpensive method of generating video. However, there are drawbacks. The output of the workstation may not conform exactly to RS-170A timings, resulting in bad colors and an inability to sync properly. Typically, only a portion of the workstation frame buffer screen is used for the video portion, and everything must be drawn into this area. The horizontal pixel density of the video screen is too high for the video bandwidth on all color combinations, so great care must be taken in the choice of colors and transitions. NTSC encoders vary widely in quality, especially in their suitability for the images typical of scientific visualization.

Scan converters take RGB input at a variety of resolutions and frame rates and produce composite NTSC, PAL, SECAM, or HDTV output. Scan converters resample the image and may allow panning and zooming over the entire workstation screen. The reduction of the full screen image gives an extra benefit of blurring and averaging the image, which reduces aliasing and the effects of bandwidth problems. Like NTSC encoders, scan converters vary widely in quality and capabilities.

Many encoders and scan converters have filters, such as comb and notch filters, which can improve the quality of an image and minimize bandwidth problems [24]. Filters provide only heuristic improvements and should be used in conjunction with good image design.

Most NTSC encoders and scan converters are automatically able to sync onto the video signals they receive. A method called Genlock allows a single reference signal from a sync generator to drive all pieces of equipment in the system: workstation, converter or encoder, and video recorder. This method requires that all components in the system accept Genlock signals. Genlock can be expensive, but it can significantly improve color encoding and recording [6].

Video animations can be converted between NTSC and PAL formats using scan conversion. Dedicated units for format conversion tend to be less expensive than fully general scan converters. For low-volume work, it may be more economical to have tapes converted outside the lab. Video and camera shops provide format conversion for a fee. Some international shops rent videotapes from different countries and can provide format conversion as well.

Design considerations

Achieving adequate results on video requires that the image be designed with video in mind. An image designed to be easily visible on a high-resolution workstation screen is not guaranteed to be visible on video. Unlike workstation screens which show the entire image, most video monitors have overscan, which means that the electron beam travels past the edge of the screen. Anything near the edge, such as a title, may be lost. To be safe, titles and important features should be placed within the *safe title* area, leaving margins of about 15% of the total screen width at the left and right sides and a little less than 15% of the total screen height at the top and bottom [28].

Large, smooth, solid objects are the least likely to produce problems with video. Single-pixel horizontal lines will produce flickering, as single line appears only in one of the two video frames. Single-pixel vertical lines will cause high-frequency transitions in the video signal, which may produce ringing, blurring, loss of color, and chroma crawl. 2- and 3-pixel lines work better. Line anti-aliasing can reduce the problems.

Text is especially difficult with video, because letters contain small details with sharp edges. The best fonts are bold and simple, and avoid narrow lines or serifs. As a general rule, no font in which any character is smaller than $\frac{1}{25}$ the total image height should be used on standard video. With smaller fonts, fine details of the letters will gradually be lost, and there may be problems with composite video artifacts [28].

The luminance and two chroma channels have different bandwidths in NTSC video, so certain color transitions cannot be done sharply, thus constraining the colors that can be used. A sharp horizontal change in luminance is preferable to a sharp change in chromaticity, because luminance has the highest bandwidth. Sharp transitions of the wrong colors will be filtered out by a good scan converter, resulting in a colorless blur at an edge, or will pass through into the video signal, where they can cause luminance problems or chroma crawl [13].

Figure 7.8 shows a sample color test pattern photograph of a typical NTSC monitor. The columns are arranged from left to right with background colors black, red, green, yellow, blue, magenta, cyan, and white. The rows are arranged from bottom to top with foreground colors in the same sequence. The lines within each intersection go from one to four pixels wide. The text is 12 point Helvetica Bold, which produces capital letters about 12 pixels high and fits approximately 60 characters per line on the active area of a video frame. The photographs show a single frame of video. The herringbone patterns that appear around color transitions show as moving croma crawl on the screen. This still image does not show problems with sharp horizontal transitions, which result in annoying flicker.

White or cyan with black are good combinations. White works reasonably well with every other color. Black works reasonably well with magenta, yellow, and green, but not with red and blue. Cyan works well with blue. Most other color combinations are mediocre at best. Green with red or magenta or red with blue are especially unacceptable.

Video animations are usually done on ones, where each frame has a different image. On interlaced systems, fields are played back at twice the frame rate. It is

Figure 7.8. An NTSC test pattern. Columns show background colors from left to right, ordered black, red, green, yellow, blue, magenta, cyan, and white. Rows show foreground colors from bottom to top in the same order. Note the artifacts produced in some horizontal color transitions. (See color section plate 7.8)

possible to get exceptionally smooth motion by recording separate images onto each field, which might be called animating "on halves." This usually requires that two separate fields be combined into one frame which is recorded at once. One disadvantage is that a single frame of an animation produced this way cannot be frozen, because each single frame will display a herringbone motion blur pattern caused by showing two different fields with different images [1]. In practice, the results are seldom worth the effort except for sequences very sensitive to motion smoothness.

An animation for presentation on a video projector requires that the characteristics of the projector be taken into account as well. There are two common types of video projectors. One uses three bright black-and-white CRTs which shine through red, green, and blue filters, focused separately onto the screen. This kind works essentially like a television with similar problems. Another and newer projector uses a light that shines through a liquid crystal shutter and is focused on the screen. Their small size, low cost, and durability have made them more readily available. Because the image is not scanned sequentially, many of the problems associated with video do not appear at all. Ironically, the sharp appearance of images from these projectors can give a false impression of low resolution.

Frame-accurate video recording

The simplest way to record an animation is to run the animation online, hook up a video or film recorder, and record in real time. For all but the simplest animations, however, real-time animation does not produce smooth animations of complex images. The ability to record animations offline frame by frame for later playback at video or film rates is required. Then, it is necessary to use a recording device that can record individual frames. Many such devices exist, including frame-accurate videotape recorders, multiframe buffers, write-once videodisc recorders, and film recorders.

Videotape recorders

Some videotape recording units have the ability to record individual frames, but to understand this process, it is necessary to know a little about videotape recording. Audio tapes simply travel through a tape mechanism, and stationary recording heads pick up or record the signals. The faster the tape runs, the more information can be recorded per unit of time.

There is too much information in a video signal to record this way—the speed of the tape would be prohibitively fast. Instead, videotape uses a technique called *helical scan*. The record and playback heads are mounted on a cylinder (called a flying head) which spins quickly while the tape passes it slowly. With each revolution of the head a helical path is traced onto the tape. The video signal is laid down on the tape in adjacent helical tracks, which appear as diagonal tracks as shown in Figure 7.9 [16].

There are also linear tracks on the tape to record sound and synchronization information, and an interlock mechanism to make sure that the helical tracks do not overwrite the linear tracks. The speed of the flying head is synchronized to

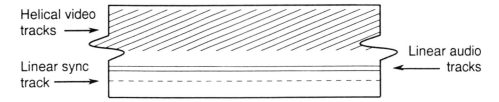

Figure 7.9. A section of video tape. The video is laid down as a series of tracks by a rapidly spinning head at an angle. The spinning head describes a helix in the frame of reference of the tape, and the resulting tracks appear diagonal. There are linear sync and audio tracks. Some tape formats have helical high-fidelity audio tracks as well. This figure is intended to show the basic technique of helical recording, but not to specify any particular tape format.

the video signal. Erase heads are linear in low-quality units. Higher quality units have flying erase heads, which are necessary for frame-accurate recording.

One other factor complicates single-frame recording. When the tape is stationary, the sweeps of the flying head pass the tape at a certain angle. When the tape is moving, this angle changes slightly. Videotape recorders have two basic mechanisms for dealing with the discrepancy. High quality studio units perturb the axis of rotation to warp the stationary angle to be the same as the moving angle. Some lower quality units, which include most of those available for lab use, only record while the tape is rolling. Recording a single frame requires several seconds of roll to allow the tape to reach a stable speed before recording the frame. One drawback of video recorders with roll is that every part of the tape has gone under the recording head several hundred times before the tape has been fully recorded. This tends to wear out the tape prematurely.

The most popular videotape format is the VHS cassette. VHS cassettes typically provide 2, 4, or 6 hours of video on ½″ tape, depending on speed. This format is inexpensive but has low resolution and color quality. Versions of VHS exist for both NTSC and PAL; although the tapes look the same, what is recorded on them is very different [2].

Super VHS or *S-VHS* is an improved version of VHS. VHS stores the composite video signal on the tape, but S-VHS stores luminance and chroma signals separately, resulting in higher quality. One major advantage of S-VHS is that it is sometimes possible, using the right cables and equipment, to go all the way from computer to tape to monitor without going through the composite video stage; much better colors and spatial frequency response result [25]. It is increasingly common to find S-VHS players connected directly to S-VHS monitors at conferences.

Betamax, an early cassette standard that is now difficult to find, was in many ways superior to VHS and was better for frame-accurate recording [2]. *Betacam,* a current standard used in many portable professional videotape recorders, is an improvement over Betamax, and uses a similarly shaped tape. Like S-VHS, it has its own component video format, which produces very nice video [25].

232

The 8mm and HI-8 cassette formats show great promise in doing frame-accurate editing. The editing abilities of these formats are mostly found on home camcorders and home editing units, but the HI-8 format is becoming a reasonable choice for low-cost, high-quality professional editing, as well [21].

The ¾″ cassette format is intended for professional use. The tape is wider than the ½″ provided by VHS and Betacam, and the cassettes are larger. The quality of ¾″ tapes is excellent, but the recorders tend to be expensive. There are a variety of recording technologies, but the U-type technology, so named because the tape is pulled out of the cassette into the form of a U while recording or playing, has become most popular due to its ability to keep a time code for editing and single-frame recording [2]. As a result, ¾″ cassettes are often known as U-type cassettes. Players for ¾″ tapes are appearing at some conferences.

1″ and 2″ reel-to-reel videotape is also used by studios and provides excellent quality. However, the recorders can be very expensive, and the tape is much more difficult to handle than cassette formats [2].

Individual frames are located using a time code laid down on the tape. Before any tape is recorded with single frames, it must be *blackstriped,* rerecorded with a solid black video image. This lays down the time codes and synchronization tracks for later access [2, 25].

Studio units in the United States use the SMPTE time code (named after the *Society of Motion Picture and Television Engineers*). The SMPTE code labels each frame with hours, minutes, seconds, and a frame number within the second. A *drop frame* mechanism handles the difference between ideal 30 frames per second and actual 29.97 frames per second [9]. The ¾″ U-type 2″ and 1″ formats use the SMPTE time code directly. Other videotape formats use *ad hoc* time codes which are specific to the device. Some of these time codes are based on an approximation of SMPTE and use a similar numbering system.

Write-once videodisc recorders

Write-once videodisc recorders use a laser to write frames of video onto a disc. As the name implies, each frame can only be written once, but the frames can be written in any order. Each 2-sided disc can store from 30 to 60 minutes of video, depending on the format. Write-once videodisc recorders can record video in real time or single frames quickly, without any roll. They can play back video in real time, still frames, or at variety of speeds. The disc can also be randomly accessed with a short seek time [38].

Each frame can be written only once, but this is not as great a problem as it may first seem. Although a single mistake can ruin a sequence, requiring that it be completely redone, sequences in scientific animation tend to last only a few minutes, and the rare mistake can be re-recorded with a small amount of effort. In practice, the expense of consuming single-use discs is only a small part of the cost of producing animations.

Write-once videodisc recorders may accept composite video, RGB, or Betacam inputs, depending on the model. They usually have serial or parallel ports for communicating with computers and animation controllers. Component video inputs are usually preferable to composite video input, because videodiscs may store component information on the disc separately for higher quality. One important consideration when choosing a videodisc recorder is the quality of internal conversion of component video to composite video. Another important consideration is the ability to record images without dropouts, which appear as discolored pixels on a solid background.

There is no standardization of discs used by write-once videodisc recorders. The technology is different from commercial mass-produced videodiscs, and the discs are not interchangeable. Some manufacturers, however, offer play-only units at lower cost.

Multiframe buffers

Multiframe buffers, sometimes known as RAMcorders, are devices that use high-speed magnetic disk arrays to store a sequence of video images. Typically, a multiframe buffer can hold a minute or two of animation at 30 frames per second. Multiframe buffers are specifically designed for frame-by-frame recording and can record single frames without any roll time [25].

The major advantage of a multiframe buffer over a videodisc recorder is the ability to overwrite individual frames. Disadvantages include high cost and limitations on the length of a recorded sequence.

Animation controllers

Animation controllers are hardware devices which control frame-accurate videotape and videodisc recorders. They have control panels which directly allow limited sequencing and editing. They also have serial connections which allow a computer to control them.

Most animation controllers provide little or no needed functionality in a system which already contains a computer, although they may be useful for editing by hand after the animation has been recorded. The only practical reason to incorporate an animation controller into a computer recording system is if some other component of the system requires it. Some pieces of software only have drivers for certain animation controllers; the animation controller provides a uniform logical interface no matter what physical recorder is being used. Some video recorders require particular animation controllers to do frame accurate recording.

7.3.2.2 Film

Motion picture film is the highest quality material for recording animations available today. Film is an analog medium, representing images by concentrations of silver atoms and dyes on a strip of plastic.

Film formats

The standard film used in movie theaters is 35mm film. It stores 24 frames per second at high quality [39]. 70mm film is used in some theaters to provide greater sharpness. 16mm film, which stores 24 frames per second at reasonable quality is used for less expensive application. 8mm film was once common; it has all but disappeared, since the proliferation of videotape [28, 39]. Sound can be recorded on film using either an optical or magnetic stripe on the edge of the film [28].

Film recorders

Film recorders are devices which take computer-generated images and imprint them directly onto photographic film. There are two basic kinds of film recorders: analog, which receive a video signal, and digital, which use digital information. Digital film recorders process much higher resolution images than even the best workstation screens—on the order of thousands of lines. Film recorders have the highest quality of any method of producing animations. Even if the final product is to be recorded on video, using film first yields the highest quality, in part because the methods of transferring film to videotape are optical and have been under development for many years.

The resolution of motion picture film is a function of its grain, i.e., the size of the chemical granules on the film. The film with the highest resolution is fine-grained. Fine-grained films usually require more exposure than coarse-grained films. Since film recorders can expose film for as long as is needed, fine-grained film can be used in film recorders, thereby generating very high quality [25].

7.3.2.3 Compact discs

The compact disc, or CD, was developed for sound recording in the 1980s. A CD is an optical disc, approximately 5 inches in diameter, that contains a single spiral optical track that winds from the center of the disc to the outer rim. The track stores digital data which is decoded to provide digital samples for conversion into audio [20].

CD ROM is a method for storing digital data on compact discs. A digital protocol is used to store information in a way similar to what is available on a magnetic computer disk, including file and directory information. As CD ROM technology was developed there were several standardization efforts, but now the ISO-9660 standard appears to dominate and is readable on a wide variety of workstations and personal computers [19].

CD-ROM technology allows a large quantity of computer-readable data, such as a series of images for animation, to be stored on an inexpensive disc. Animations are easily distributed without limitations on their format or resolution. However, the problem of playing the animation remains. If standard animation formats such as QuickTime are used, players are readily available for a variety of systems.

CDV, or CD-Video, is a consumer format for recording video images on compact disc along with sound recording. Very little has been done with the CDV format. CDV discs can be played in some consumer laser disc players.

CDI, or CD-Interactive, is way of storing still images, video, audio, and software on a compact disc. The CDI disc is played in a special CDI player, which has a small microprocessor to execute the software on the disc. The user can interact with the software via a small controller similar to the controllers for home video games, which have a 2-D direction switch like a joystick and a few other buttons. There are a variety of still and motion qualities for the video images on CDI. CDI is a promising technology for low-cost interactive presentations, but it is hampered by low microprocessor and drive speeds of current CDI players [32].

Most CD-ROM and CDI discs are mastered and produced in bulk at a cost of thousands of dollars a run [34]. However, a new kind of CD can be recorded directly off a special CD press connected to a computer. Unlike magnetic disks and write-once optical discs, a CD, produced in this way, must be completed in a single step, from start to finish. If an error occurs, the CD must be thrown away, and the process begun again.

7.3.2.4 Videodiscs

Videodiscs include a variety of formats used to store video and audio on 12-inch and 8-inch optical discs. The formats are variously referred to as LaserDisc, LaserVision, and CD Video LD, and store video and audio as analog and/or digital information. Many modern players can deal with the variety of formats automatically [10] [29].

Videodiscs store frames of information on concentric connected optical tracks in two basic ways: *continuous angular velocity,* or *CAV,* and *continuous linear velocity,* or *CLV.* On a CAV disc, the same number of frames are stored on every track, and the motor driving the disc operates at the same angular velocity for each track. On a CLV disc, the frames are packed more densely on tracks near the edge of the disc, where there is more room. The motor changes speed depending on which track is being read, maintaining an approximately constant linear velocity of the disc surface under the read head. CLV discs pack more video onto a disc than CLV discs, but they have the disadvantage that the need to change the speed of the motor can cause jumps in the image, loss of sync, or short blank areas during playback [20]. Most videodisc players can seek CAV discs more easily and quickly than CLV discs, and some provide more flexibility in playback speeds for CAV discs. Like CDs, videodiscs are mastered and then produced in bulk [10].

7.3.2.5 Multimedia and interaction

Normally, animation is understood as an unchanging linear sequence of images. For educational presentations, the use of interaction invites the audience to explore the visualizations. Interactive multimedia presentations can combine video, still pictures, sound, and interaction. The very nature of multimedia combines different technologies. Candidates for multimedia systems include coupled videodisc players and computers, and computers displaying images and playing sound from CD-ROM, and CDI.

Interactive presentations are most effective when members of the audience explore the presentation individually. Individual access to stations, so they can explore the presentation themselves, is most effective. It is difficult to present an interactive resentation to a large audience, and a fixed presentation is often better.

Designing an interactive presentation is difficult and involves as many factors as designing the user interface to a software package. It is easy to produce a bad interactive presentation. Producing a good one requires a major commitment and takes significant effort. If the resources to fulfill this commitment are not available, a fixed animation may be preferable.

7.4
CONCLUSIONS

Animation is a valuable tool for engineering analysis. It is not limited to showing time-dependent behavior, but can be used to bring out many attributes of the data. Animation has become an integral part of the processes of research, education, and peer review.

A variety of techniques exists for doing animation; these vary in cost, effort, and quality of result. Today, animation is no longer limited to the realm of the professional animator and is now within the reach of the working engineer at reasonable cost and effort.

7.5
REFERENCES

[1]. Amanatides, John, and Mitchell, Don P., "Antialiasing of interlaced video animation," Computer Graphics, 24(4): 77–85, 1990.

[2]. Anderson, Gary, Video Editing and Post-production: A Professional Guide, Knowledge Industry Publications, White Plains, NY, 1988.

[3]. Barr, Alan H., Currin, Bena, Gabriel, Steven, and Hughes, John, "Smooth Inerpolation of Orientations with Angular Velocity Constraints using Quaternions," Computer Graphics, 26(2): 313–320, 1992.

[4]. Bartels, Richard H., Beatty, John C., and Barsky, Brian A., An Introduction to Splines for use in Computer Graphics and Geometric Modeling, Morgan Kaufmann, Los Angeles, 1987.

[5]. Benson, K. Blair, and Fink, Donald G., HDTV Advanced Television for the 1990s, McGraw-Hill, New York, 1991.

[6]. Benson, K. Blair, Rayner, Bruce, Remley, Frederick M., and Roizen, Joseph, "Broadcast Production Equipment, Systems, and Services," Television Engineering Handbook, McGraw Hill, New York, 1992.

[7]. Blinn, James F., The Mechanical Universe: An Integrated View of a Large Scale Animation Project, SIGGRAPH '87 Course Notes, 1987.

[8]. Brown, Eric, "Codec e' Go Go: Who's Squeezing Who?" New Media, 3(3): 40–42, 1993.

[9]. Caldwell, Richard J., "Electronic Editing," Television Engineering Handbook, McGraw Hill, New York, 1992.

[10]. Castrignano, Robert A., "Video Disc Recording and Reproduction," Television Engineering Handbook, McGraw Hill, New York, 1992.

[11]. Cillo, Joseph, "Apple's QuickTime: A True Paradigm Shift," Computer Pictures, 10(1): 28–32, 1992.

[12]. Finch, Christopher, The Art of Walt Disney, Harry N. Abrams Inc., 1973.

[13]. Fisher, Joseph F., and Clapp, Richard G., "Waveforms and Spectra of Composite Video Signals," Television Engineering Handbook, McGraw Hill, New York, 1992.

[14]. Foley, James D., van Dam, Andries, Feiner, Steven K., and Hughes, John F., Computer Graphics Principles and Practice, Addison-Wesley, Reading, Mass., 1990.

[15]. Gabriel, S., and Kajiya, J., "Spline interpolation in curved space," State of the Art Image Synthesis, SIGGRAPH '85 Course Notes, 1985.

[16]. Ginsburg, Charles P., "Video Tape Recording," Television Engineering Handbook, McGraw Hill, New York, 1992.

[17]. Hamilton, William R., Lectures on Quaternions: Containing a Systematic Statement of a New Mathematical Method, Hodges and Smith, Dublin, 53.

[18]. Hedler, R. A., Maninger, L. L., Momberger, R. A., Robbins, J. D., and Say, Donald L., "Monochrome and Color Image-Display Devices," Television Engineering Handbook, McGraw Hill, New York, 1992.

[19]. Helgerson, Linda W., "The CD ROM Industry: Past, Present, and Future," The CD ROM Handbook, Chris Sherman, ed., McGraw Hill, New York, 3–16, 1988.

[20]. Isailovic, Jordan, Videodisc Systems Theory & Applications, Prentice-Hall, Englewood Cliffs, New Jersey, 1987.

[21]. Jones, Andrew P., "My Quest for HI-8 Post," Videography, 17(1): 67–69, 90, 1992.

[22]. Kellogg, Gary V., and Wagner, Charles A., "Effects of Update and Refresh Rates on Flight Sim-

ulation Visual Displays," NASA Technical Memo 00415, Dryden Flight Research Facility, Ames Research Center.

[23]. Levitan, Eli L., Handbook of Animation Techniques, Van Nostrand Reinhold Company, New York, 1979.

[24]. Loughlin, Bernard D., "Monochrome and Color Visual Information Transmission," Television Engineering Handbook, McGraw Hill, New York, 1992.

[25]. MacNicol, Gregory, Desktop Computer Animation, Focal Press, Boston, 1992.

[26]. McLendon, Patricia, Graphics Library Programming Guide, Silicon Graphics Inc., Mountain View, California, 1991.

[27]. Pepke, Eric, and Lyons, Jim, SciAn User's Manual, Supercomputer Computations Research Institute, Tallahassee, Florida, 1994.

[28]. Pincus, Edward, and Ascher, Steven, The Filmmaker's Handbook, NAL Penguin, New York, 1984.

[29]. Pioneer Electronic Corporation, CD CDV LD Player Operating Instructions, 1992.

[30]. Roberts, Kenneth H., and Sharples, Win Jr., A Primer for Film-Making, Pegasus, New York, 1971.

[31]. Robertson, Alan R., and Fisher, Joseph F., "Color Vision, Representation, and Reproduction," Television Engineering Handbook, McGraw Hill, New York, 1992.

[32]. Robinson, Phillip, "The Four Multimedia Gospels," BYTE, 15(2): 203–212, 1990.

[33]. Rosenthal, Steve, "QuickTime vs. Video for Windows," New Media, 3(3): 36–39, 1993.

[34]. Roth, Judith Paris, Essential Guide to CD-ROM, Meckler Publishing, Westport, CT, 1986.

[35]. Schubin, Mark, "Research and Development: A Page of History," ideography, 18(4), 1993.

[36]. Shoemake, Ken, "Animating rotations with quaternion curves," Computer Graphics, 19(3): 245–254, 1985.

[37]. Shoup, R., "Color Table Animation," Computer Graphics, 19(3): 8–13, 1979.

[38]. Sony Corporation, Interface Manual LDM-5000, 1989.

[39]. Spottiswoode, Raymond, The Focal Encyclopedia of Film & Television Techniques, Hastings House, New York, 1969.

Applications Issues and Future Trends

Systems Aspects of Visualization Applications

DAVID PARKER

VISUALIZATION APPLICATIONS INVOLVES much more than algorithms for the display of behavior. Understanding behavior includes numerous implementation issues such as interactivity, database architecture, user interfaces, and systems design.

This chapter provides the background needed to understand the systems aspects of currently available visualization application systems. It explores the relevant issues governing the design and implementation of a visualization system suited for the analysis of data resulting from a numerical computation.

8.1
INTRODUCTION

During the past five years there have been amazing advances in computer technology, in both hardware and software, which has greatly affected the way engineers work as well as the kinds of problems they attempt to solve. One of the most significant advancements has been the introduction of new software systems to visualize the results of numerical computations.

Numerous visualization systems available today from commercial vendors, universities and in the public domain, all of which can be used to visualize finite element analysis data. These systems differ in functionality, complexity and flexibility. If a visualization system lacks certain functionality or flexibility it should not be perceived as useless. The definition of useful is that the system fulfills the user's requirements, which differ greatly. For example, a system which can only display the surface contours of stress components on a finite element mesh may completely satisfy some users.

The purpose of this chapter is to provide the background needed to understand the system aspects of currently available visualization systems, and to explore the relevant issues governing the design and implementation of a visualization system suited for the analysis of engineering data resulting from numerical computation.

8.2
SYSTEM ARCHITECTURE

The architecture of a visualization system describes the components of the system and their relationship to one another. The architecture governs, to some extent, the functionality and usability of a system. The architecture of a generic visualization system is shown in Figure 8.1.

The User Interface component defines the mechanisms by which the user communicates with the visualization system. This can be in the form of a command language or graphical interface, and will be discussed in Section 8.3 in greater detail.

The Data Management component encompasses the mechanisms which import data from external sources into the visualization system and manage the data internally. It includes the access to analysis results files (databases) and internal memory management. This will be discussed in more detail in Section 8.4.

A Visualization Module is a set of software components that realize a specific visualization technique, such as contouring a surface or extracting an isosurface from a volume. The components of a module are shown in Figure 8.2. The simplest example of a module is a FORTRAN subroutine (in C, a function). The inputs are the subroutine arguments, the computation body the executable code of the subroutine, and the outputs are other subroutine arguments.

The Flow Control component defines how the visualization modules are executed and how data flows to modules in the system. The method of Flow Control implementation is one of the main characterizations of a visualization system. We use three classifications: turnkey systems, application builders using a visual programming interface and application builders using a language interface.

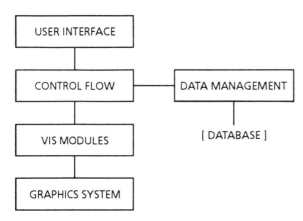

Figure 8.1. Architecture of a generic visualization system.

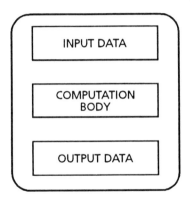

Figure 8.2. Sample
visualization module.

8.2.1 Turnkey Systems

A turnkey or end-user visualization system provides the interface and modules which allow the user to perform visualizations without any programming. These systems are generally easy to use, and allow a novice to quickly visualize his data. Some systems are tailored to a particular application, such as fluid mechanics, with interfaces designed for this purpose.

Turnkey systems can be further classified either as those which provide multiple instances of modules or those that do not. In most systems the Flow Control provides only for the single instance of a given module. Thus, the user is limited to one data set per visualization technique (for example, extracting an isosurface of a scalar field). This architecture is straight-forward to design and implement and, could probably satisfy most users' requirements. It would be very easy to use. To fully understand a problem, however, the user may require the simultaneous visualization of multiple data sets, such as extracting a slice from a volume for both a temperature and pressure field. Examples of this type of system are Field View [11] and PLOT3D [3].

A system with a Flow Control that provides multiple instances of a given module means that a module can execute with any number of different input data sets, producing outputs for each of the inputs. The user can instance multiple visualization techniques, each with a different data set. Thus, for example, you could extract isosurfaces of multiple scalar fields at the same time. This architecture is more difficult to design and implement since the state (the data associated with the module, such as input parameters) of a module must be saved and restored each time it is executed. An example of this type of system is Wavefront's Data Visualizer [2].

Since the functionality of a turnkey system cannot generally be modified by the user (although some systems do allow users to write a custom reader for the importing of data) the design of such a system must provide enough functionality to satisfy the requirements of the majority of its intended users. This fixed functionality is seen as a disadvantage since it is impossible to satisfy the requirements of all users. On the other hand, the ease of use and the ability to customize such systems for a particular discipline may outweigh the disadvantages.

8.2.2 Visual Programming Application Builders

An application builder visualization system provides the user with a set of tools to interactively construct a visualization application. A set of basic visualization modules is generally supplied as well, to support the writing of custom modules.

We can classify application builders by how an application is constructed: using a visual programming interface or a language interface. Most application builders, now available, use a visual programming interface. Some of these systems are apE [6], AVS [11] and Iris Explorer (Silicon Graphics). A visual programming interface allows the user to interactively build an application by interacting with a two dimensional representation of visualization modules. (The use of a visual programming interface for the construction of visualization applications has its foundation in ConMan [4] that used such an interface to construct graphics applications.)

By using an interactive tool to build a directed graph, the user can select a set of modules from a palette, connect the modules together, and create complex visualization applications. Custom modules to perform tasks particular to a user's application can be written and added to this palette. The nodes of the graph are visualization modules, the edges are paths by which data can flow from one module to another, as shown in Figure 8.3. The output of one or more modules can be used as inputs to other modules. A module executes when any of its input data changes.

An example of the power of such an interface can be seen in Figure 8.4. The module "read data" reads a database containing a finite element mesh, a pressure scalar field, a temperature scalar field and a velocity vector field. The module "extract isosurface" then extracts an isosurface from the mesh and pressure field. The extracted isosurface (a set of polygons) is then sent to the "map scalar" and "interpolate vector" modules. The "map scalar" module maps temperature to a color for each vertex of the polygons for the isosurface and is sent to the "graphics" module to be displayed. The "interpolate vector" module creates a set of

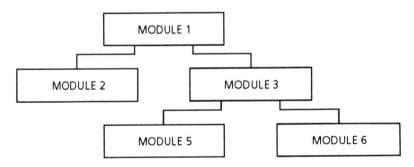

Figure 8.3. In a modular visualization application, specific data flows can be set up between individual modules.

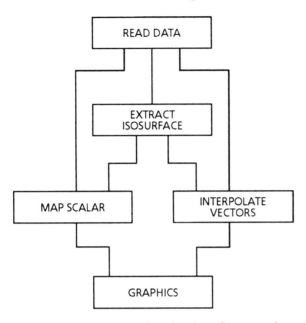

Figure 8.4. An example of a data flow graph
to generate vector data along the isosurfaces
of a finite element model.

arrows to represent the interpolated velocity of each vertex of the polygons for
the isosurface and is sent to the "graphics" module.

Application builders are quite complex to implement. The complexity arises
from the fact that each module can execute as a separate process (in the UNIX
sense of process), and so the visualization system must support some form of inter-
process communication. If a module is a separate process a user can write, compile
and link only the module he is working on without having to re-compile the entire
visualization application. Modules can also execute on remote machines in a heterogeneous computer environment.

There are several methods which can be used (on UNIX systems) to transmit
data between processes. One method used by several visualization systems are
known as sockets. A socket is a communication *application program interface* (API)
which facilitates the transfer of data between two processes. The socket interface
is conceptually similar to file I/O, where you perform open, create, read, write and
close operations. An example of how two processes can establish communication
is shown in Figure 8.5. Detailed information pertaining to sockets can be found
in Stevens [12].

Using sockets to transfer large amounts of data between processes can lead to
memory waste because data is duplicated; both the sender and the receiver have
a copy of the data. It is possible to overcome this problem by using the Unix shared
memory facilities. Shared memory allows two or more processes to share a
memory segment. Most available application builders use a combination of sockets
and shared memory to transfer data between processes (modules). Sockets are used

```
process 1:
  /  create the socket.   /
  socket = create_socket  ()

  /  register the socket name with the operating system.   /
  / when another process wishes to connect to this process /
  / it will use this name.                                 /
  register_socket_name (socket, "process1 socket")

  /  the process is ready to receive connections   /
  /  from other processes.                          /
  receive_connection (socket)

  /  block here until a connection is requested to   /
  /  this process from another process.              /
  msg_fd = wait_for_connection (socket)

  /  read/write data to process2.   /
  forever do
    read (msg_fd, data)
    write (msg_fd, reply)
  end do

process 2:
  /  create the socket.   /
  socket = create_socket  ()

  /  request a connection to the named socket.   /
  connect_to_socket ("process1 socket")

  /  read/write/data to process1.   /
  forever do
    write (socket, data)
    read (socket, reply)
  end do
```

Figure 8.5. Connection of two processes via a socket.

for module synchronization while the actual reading/writing of data is done via shared memory. The description of FAST provides an excellent example of this [1]. Sockets can be used by any visualization system as a means of communication between remote computers. For example, there are several turnkey systems which support visualization computations on remote computers (usually on a super-computer). This will be discussed in Section 8.7.

Application builders are an excellent way to prototype a visualization application. Some systems, like AVS, also allow a module to be an executing finite element analysis program. As the program is executing results can be visualized. Application builders are harder to use than turnkey systems because they require more study by the user, who must acquire two different kinds of knowledge: 1) how to construct the application and 2) how to write a custom module, if needed. These require much more time and resources to use effectively, and are also not tailored to any particular discipline, but are general visualization systems.

8.2.3 Application Builders Using a Language Interface

An application builder can also use a language-based interface to construct applications. The user constructs the visualization application by writing a program within an environment which supports an interpretive language. An interpretive language environment allows programs to be written, tested, and debugged interactively. Debugging aids can be built into the environment and allow the programmer to modify code and check/set variables without recompiling.

An interpretive language may resemble a command language with macros and built-in functions to support a particular application. One example is the Interactive Data Language (Research Systems Inc., Boulder, CO). It supports an array-oriented Pascal-like interpretive language that supports matrix manipulation, graphics and high-level mathematical operations.

If the interpretive language is a true programming language, that is, a language in which general computational constructs can be written, then the application builder will be much more flexible and extensible. An example of such a system is SuperGlue [10]. SuperGlue is centered around a dialect of Lisp called Scheme. High-level flow of control and user interface programming is done in Scheme while compute intensive and graphical functions are written in a compiled language (i.e., C or FORTRAN). Functions not written in Scheme can be modified, compiled and loaded into the system while it is running. SuperGlue also supports an object-oriented programming paradigm, allowing the user to build from pre-defined and constructed custom object classes.

Using such a system as SuperGlue it is easy to envision construction of a solver tightly integrated with the visualization system. Visualization operations could be embedded within the solver code to aid in debugging. For example, we could check the computation of derivatives by displaying them on the mesh in a graphics window. The objects and methods (functions operating on objects) used by the solver would be shared by the visualizer. If a new element were added as an object to the solver then that object (element) and its methods (differentiation, shape function computation, integration, etc.) would immediately be available to the visualizer.

8.3
USER INTERFACES

The User Interface component of a visualization system defines the mechanisms by which the user interacts with the system; specifying actions to be performed, input parameters to visualization modules, setting attributes, among other things. The user interface is extremely important because it is the view of the visualization system presented to the user—its so-called look and feel—and it governs the user's perception of the system. A poorly designed user interface will frustrate the user and will be quickly dismissed as unusable, even though the system may provide excellent functionality. We will discuss two types of user interfaces: command language and graphical.

8.3.1 Command Language Interfaces

A command language interface provides a textual interface to the visualization system. If the command language is concise and the user is experienced and a fast typist, this can be a very efficient method of interaction. Although easy to implement, this type of interface is generally inadequate because of the time necessary for a novice user to learn the command language and the errors created while typing the commands.

A command language is useful, however, when used in conjunction with a graphical interface, where there is a one-to-one relationship between the commands and the graphical interface. When an action is performed using the graphical interface a command can be generated which reflects that action. Such automatic creation of commands is called scripting. Scripting has several uses; the main one is to record a visualization session for playback later. A set of commands can also be stored as a configuration file, creating a user defined environment at the start-up of the visualization system. An example of a script file is shown in Figure 8.6.

```
config data_directory = /usr/vis/fluids/eddy
add technique = "read database"
read_database  name = "simulation_1"
add technique = "mesh to geom"
mesh_to_geom  type = "free edges"
add technique = "isosurface"
isosurface  scalar = "pressure"
            num_surfaces = 6
            map_scalar = "temperature"
geometry  rotate = 45.0 45.0 0.0
```

Figure 8.6. Example of a script file from a visualization session.

248

8.3.2 Graphical Interfaces

A graphical interface provides a visual interface to the visualization system with a mouse. The user interacts with the system via a graphical representation of objects, such as buttons, dials, sliders, menus and icons. Graphical interfaces are easier to learn and less prone to error than command language interfaces. The user does not need to remember the names and syntax of commands, since the operations available to him are displayed.

Icons have been used with success in several CAD packages. They can save space on the computer screen and may be easier to recognize than words. The problem with icons is designing them so that their meaning can be easily recognized and learned. Most visualization systems now use a combination of text and icons, with the icons reserved mostly for graphics operations.

Most of the graphical interfaces used by visualization systems today are based on the X Window System developed by MIT and Digital Equipment Corporation. X facilitates the writing of portable applications that can run on a network of systems from different vendors. Almost all workstation vendors and some personal computer vendors support X. Central to the writing of a graphical interface using X is the idea of a *widget*. A widget is a user interface component such as a button, scrollbar, radio buttons, dial and menu. Widgets are usually implemented as windows or groups of sub-windows. To simplify the complex task of programming a graphical interface and to maintain a common look and feel for applications several libraries of pre-built widgets, called widget sets, have become available. The two most common are OPEN LOOK and Motif.

Even with widget sets the task of programming a graphical interface still requires a great deal of time and resources. *Interface builders* facilitate the layout design and programming of graphical user interfaces by allowing the developer to interactively construct the interface layout. Once the layout is complete, the interface code or library is automatically built and can then be incorporated with the other components of the visualization system. There are several interface builders available today such as XVT-Design (XVT Software, Inc., Boulder, CO), Open Interface (Neuron Data, Palo Alto, CA), Builder Xcessory (Integrated Computer Solutions, Cambridge, MA) and SUIT (University of Virginia, free for non-profit organizations).

The visualization system should be independent of the graphical user interface in order to support different interface standards (such as OPEN LOOK) and window systems. If a user is accustomed to how radio buttons look and operate, using a certain style of interface, then it is beneficial to support that style.

8.4
DATA MANAGEMENT

The Data Management component encompasses the mechanisms which import data from external sources into the visualization system and manage the data internally. This includes access to analysis results files (databases) and internal memory management. Here we will discuss the key issues of efficient data management: databases, data model and data reduction.

8.4.1 Databases

A database is a repository for stored data. Proper data organization is critical to the efficiency and usefulness of the database. There are several types of databases based on the way data is organized: *sequential, relational, hierarchical,* and *object.*

A *sequential* database organizes data as a flat series of data items. The only way to access item n is to first read the $n - 1$ items preceding it. There is no way to access data thus selectively; inefficient storage and slow access time result. Note the example in Figure 8.7a.

A *relational* database organizes data as a table of data items. This type of database has been very successful in the commercial world for many years but cannot support hierarchical data structures, multi-dimensional or time dependent data common to finite element analysis (FEA). In the near future, relational databases may be able to better support FEA because the pure relational organization is being modified to an extended relational model and will accommodate more complex data organizations. A sample relational data structure is shown in Figure 8.7b.

A *hierarchical* database, shown in Figure 8.7c, organizes data as a tree. It is a natural way to model data with hierarchical relationships like finite element meshes. One drawback of this type of database is the difficulty of processing symmetric database operations; for example, "get the element sets of material steel" and "get the materials for all element sets."

An *object* database organizes data as objects, where an object is a complex abstract or real-world entity with relationships to other objects. The relationships and structure of an object is defined by the user. Objects may also have a behavior associated with them. There are several types of databases which manage objects: object-oriented, functional, semantic and extended relational. Such databases may be the most natural choice for FEA since information encompassing the entire design cycle can be integrated and stored in a single database. Large data objects, such as analysis results for distinct regions of the model can be stored as BLOBs (Binary Large OBjects) for efficient storing and retrieval [4].

If analyses are performed in a heterogeneous computer environment—the numerical simulation is performed on a supercomputer and the visualization is performed on a graphics workstation—then access to databases stored on a remote machine becomes an issue. In general, databases written on machines from different vendors cannot be directly shared. One solution to this problem is to write the database in a machine independent format, such as in IEEE format. This would allow the access of the database through the standard networking mechanisms such as NFS, available in the computer environment. One such data format is the Hierarchical Data Format developed at the National Center for Supercomputer Applications, University of Illinois, Urbana-Champaign.

If a device independent database is not supported then the database must be accessed in a distributed fashion. Some commercial DBMS support distributed

a. Sequential

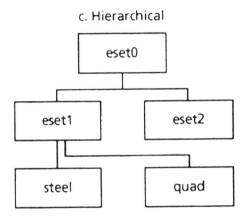

eset0		
MATERIAL 3		
TYPE brick		

eset n		

b. Relational

NAME	MATERIAL	TYPE
eset0	steel	brick
eset1	steel	quad
eset2	rubber	tet

c. Hierarchical

Figure 8.7. Types of database architecture.

database access, allowing a database to be shared across multiple platforms. Distributed databases are also discussed in Section 8.7.

The issues concerning databases must be addressed in the integration of an analysis package (which creates the database) with the visualization system (which uses and perhaps updates the database). For the analysis package the most convenient method for storing data may be in a sequential file but this is not suitable for visualization.

8.4.2 Data Model

The data model for a visualization system refers to the internal organization of analysis data. It encompasses the analysis mesh, initial/boundary conditions and analysis results. The design of the data model is extremely important to the usability of a visualization system. The design should closely reflect the type and structure of data used in analysis. The factors driving the design are: storage efficiency, execution efficiency and complete support for analysis. As computer and analysis technology has advanced, so too have the types of problems being solved, becoming larger (including more than a million elements, and hundreds, if not thousands, of time steps) and more complex (involving contact fluid-solid interaction problems and adaptive meshing, among others). We will present here a hierarchical data model that will satisfy such expanding needs of analysis.

A diagram of the data model is shown in Figure 8.8. A "problem," which encompasses the entire mesh with results data, has a set of time steps defined for it. Each time step corresponds to a physical time step in an analysis. A time step may also be sub-divided into a set of *increments*. An increment is a numerical step in a series of successive approximations to the converged solution for a given time step. Usually only the data for the converged time step is visualized (the last increment) but visualizing the data for increments is useful for solver development.

Under each time step a set of meshes may be stored. For those problems which do not perform adaptive meshing (i.e., meshes which change over time) there will be meshes under the initial time step only. For those problems which do perform adaptive meshing, the new or modified meshes can appear under any time step.

A mesh entity groups element sets for the purpose of modeling. For example, a mesh could contain the elements for a fluid region, a specific piece of geometry of the model (such as the intake for an engine) or an interface between two other meshes (such as the interface between fluid mesh and a solid mesh in a fluid/solid

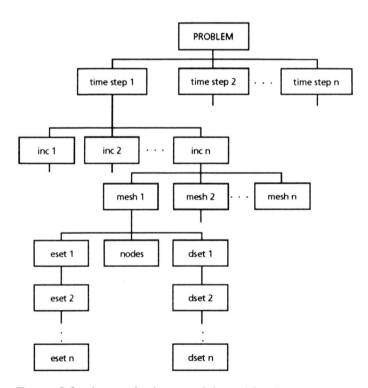

Figure 8.8. A sample data model used for the internal organization of visualization data.

interaction, or area of contact in a contact problem). Each mesh has its own set of nodes separate from other meshes. Grouping of element sets under a mesh allows the user to selectively visualize a region of elements, for example, just the interface between two regions.

Under each mesh entity are stored one or more element sets (eset) and data sets (dset). Elements are grouped into element sets by topology type (quadrilateral, tetrahedron, brick, etc.) and material model. Grouping by topology saves space by sharing attributes (such as number of nodes per element and topology type) and allows computations to be performed on the entire element set in a canonical fashion. For example, when extracting an isosurface from a set of elements the entire set of elements can be efficiently processed. Grouping by material model allows for a more correct visualization of projected values (such as stress) across regions of different materials—the stress should be discontinuous across the region interfaces. These groupings allow the user to selectively visualize element sets and to easily display element set attributes, such as color coding element sets by material or topology.

The data sets under a mesh store the numerical analysis results for the element sets under the mesh. These data sets can either be defined as nodal data (such as displacements and velocities), projected nodal data (such as stresses and vorticity) or element data (such as results at element quadrature points).

8.4.3 Internal Data Management

Internal data management refers to the mechanisms used to manage the data structures used by the visualization system. The efficiency of memory management utilities (such as *malloc* on Unix systems) can vary from platform to platform. For this reason it may be more efficient to manage objects specific to the visualization system. An object is a data structure which stores a particular set of information, such as a mesh, element set or data set. Rather than just freeing the space used by an object the data management system could keep a free list of objects for re-use. The point is that the designer knows the data usage behavior of the visualization system and so can manage the data in a more efficient manner than a general memory management system such as malloc.

8.4.4 Data Reduction

Visualization of large data sets on workstations can be very time consuming and sometimes almost impossible, even on machines with a lot of memory and processing power. By "large" we mean that the size of the data to be visualized is much greater than the capacity (in terms of both memory and compute power) of the machine on which the visualization is being performed. Large on a low-end workstation may be 20,000 elements, for a superworkstation it may be 500,000 elements. Some computational fluid dynamics (CFD) problems have meshes with element counts of over one million and several hundred time steps. Visualizing such meshes on even superworkstations could be difficult.

Reducing the computation for a visualization can be accomplished by defining element sub-sets by specifying an area of interest within the mesh, such as a box. Only the elements within the box are used in the visualization computation. To reduce the amount of data used by the visualization system the data for only those elements within the box could be read in from the database. For example, the user could outline an area surrounding the boundary layer of a wing, extract the data for that area only and contour it.

Another method of reducing the amount of data required to produce a visualization, called *extracts,* is described by Globus [7]. An extract is a sub-set of a results data set intermediate between a graphic object (such as a polygon) and the results data. The extract stores the geometry of a graphics object together with results data for the vertices of the geometry, possibly for multiple time steps. For example, if you wished to visualize a slice from a pressure field of a finite element mesh for 100 time steps, we could create a set of extracts which contained the geometry of the polygons making up the slice and the pressure at each vertex for the polygons at each of the time steps. The slices could then be animated in time by just mapping the pressures at the appropriate time step to colors, and rendering the polygons of the slice. Only a fraction of the storage required for the entire data set is used by the extracts.

8.5 Graphics Systems

The Graphics System component encompasses the mechanisms which display and manipulate the geometric primitives output from a visualization module. These geometric primitives can be markers, text, points, lines or polygons. There are four main components of a typical Graphics System: graphics database manager, view manager, user interface and graphics applications programming interface (API).

8.5.1 Graphics Database Manager

When a set of geometric primitives such as a set of polygons representing an isosurface within a volume of finite elements, is created by a visualization module, they must be stored for display on the computer screen. The graphics database manager is used to organize and manage the storage of graphics objects, such as geometric primitives and their attributes (color, rendering style, visibility, etc.). It should provide a hierarchical structure with attribute inheritance; that is, the children of an object in the hierarchy inherit their parent's attributes. A hierarchical structure supports the grouping of related objects and allows common operations to be performed on all objects within a group.

The graphics database manager also performs the searching operations of the database, such as the location of a geometric primitive closest to a given point (for picking operations) and the determination of the objects within a given area (for selective updates of the screen).

8.5.2 View Manager

The view manager determines where and when objects are displayed. We would like the ability to have multiple graphics windows to display different regions of a model or even different problems in each window. In addition, we would like to have multiple viewports in each window to facilitate the viewing and probing of 3-D data. The View Manager manages these graphics windows and the viewports within each window, keeping track of the view types and orientation for each window/viewport.

When the orientation or view of the graphics objects are modified (such as by a rotation, zoom or translation) the view manager will traverse the graphics database, determine what is visible and display it with the appropriate viewing transformation. The view manager can also determine what part of the graphics database needs to be redrawn when only a portion of a scene or window is modified.

Another important operation of the view manager is the support of animation, discussed in more detail in Chapter 7. Animation is important in the investigation of transient phenomena, such as unsteady fluid flow. Often the time taken by the visualization system to execute a set of visualization modules with data for a new time step is too great to produce a smooth animation. This problem can be solved if the view manager stores the geometry in the graphics database when an update of the graphics window is performed. Each set of geometry is stored as a snapshot (called a frame) of the graphics database, and, therefore, the analysis results, at a given time. After all of the frames have been computed, they can be replayed in real-time, if the graphics platform is powerful enough. Since the geometry has been stored, the user can perform rotate, translate and scale operations on the geometry as it is animating.

If the graphics platform is too slow to display the frames smoothly in real-time the frames may be rendered and stored as pixel images. The images can be replayed in a flip-book type animation. The disadvantage of this proceedure is the storage required for each image (between two and six megabytes for a 512×512 image) and the loss of the ability to interact with the animation as it progresses.

The production of videos has become increasingly popular as a medium used to convey information to colleagues, management and customers. Support for the making of videos can be of several forms. Geometry files may be written in a format readable by a commercial animation package, such as those offered by Wavefront (Santa Barbara, CA) and Alias (Toronto, Canada). Another strategy is to support the writing of images directly to the video medium. When each frame is complete a signal can be sent to the video equipment to record the frame on tape. The difficulty with this approach is the plethora of video equipment, and writing the software to interface to them. A solution would be to provide user defined functions which would allow the custom writing of video drivers by the user.

8.5.3 User Interface

The User Interface of the Graphics System provides the mechanisms for the user to edit and manipulate graphics objects stored in the graphics database. Depending on how the interface is implemented, editing can allow the user to interactively change items such as the color of an object, its rendering style (line, flat shaded, Gouraud shaded, etc.), its surface properties (shininess, transparency, etc.) and its visibility. Selecting objects for editing can be done either by picking them directly from the computer screen or selecting them by name from a list. The selected object should be highlighted or separately displayed in a small window.

There are several ways to manipulate an object's orientation (rotation). Two on-screen methods are *virtual sliders* and the *virtual track-ball*. The virtual slider method maps horizontal mouse motions to a rotation about the x-axis and vertical motions to a rotation about the y-axis. A right or up motion performs a positive rotation; a left or down motion performs a negative rotation. A rotation about the z-axis is performed by pressing a mouse button and moving the mouse in a horizontal motion.

Another method is the virtual sphere, described by Chen et al. [5]. The mouse is used to manipulate a virtual 3-D sphere (simulating a physical trackball enclosing the object to rotate) to produce rotations about any arbitrary axis. As the sphere is rolled the object rotates with it. For more exact rotations, dials or sliders and angle type-in can be provided even though these widgets take up quite a bit of screen space. Manipulation is such an important aspect of the interface that several methods should be supported to provide for different user preferences.

8.5.4 Graphics Applications Programming Interface

The Applications Programming Interface (API) provides an interface to the Graphics System via a library of graphics functions. This library should provide a device-independent layer for the visualization system so that the system can run transparently on various platforms. Functionality provided in hardware on some graphics platforms, like Gouraud shading, must be implemented in software on those platforms that do not provide it in hardware, like X terminals.

Underneath the Graphics API sits the device-dependent graphics library which interfaces to a particular platform. Since supporting different platforms is very time consuming and resource intensive, it may be beneficial to port the API to a graphics library which is supported on a variety of platforms so the API need only be ported to one library. There are several such libraries available now or in the near future: Open GL (Silicon Graphics), PEX (Phigs Extension to X), DORE (Intelligent Light) and HOOPS (Ithaca Software).

An important consideration for a graphics strategy concerns the duplication of data. For instance, the data structures used by a visualization module to store geometric primitives may not be compatible with those for the graphics library. Even if the data structures may be compatible, data still may be copied in the graphics library, depending on the graphics architecture.

8.6
INTERACTIVE DATA EXPLORATION

When the numerical analysis has completed the results must be interpreted by the engineer to determine the validity of the solution and to characterize and understand the mechanisms dominating the problem being solved. This requires the exploration of the results in a flexible and interactive mode. Some of the issues and techniques related to the interactive exploration of data are discussed below.

8.6.1 Probes

One of the most powerful tools for interactive visualization are probes. We will define a probe to be a geometric object defined in the 3-D space of the model that is used to investigate its interior. The probe can be interactively manipulated (rotated, scaled, translated) directly by the user employing the methods discused above in 8.5.3. The position and orientation of the probe is used to extract information from the model. The simplest example of a probe is a 3-D cursor, such as a cross. The cross can be moved within the 3-D space of the model. The location of the cursor is used to query the value of results at that location. For example, the value of stress at the cursor can be displayed as the cursor is moved.

Another example of a probe is a slice extractor. The slice extractor is displayed in the graphics window as a rectangle in 3-D space which can be rotated and translated by the user. The geometry of the slice extractor can be used to determine the equation of the 3-D plane in which the slice extractor is embedded. The intersection of this plane with the Finite Element Mesh can be computed and results data interpolated to produce a contour of the results data on the slice extractor. An example of two slice extractors can be seen at the top and bottom of the volume in Figure 8.9. A series of stacked slice extractors can be used to effectively characterize the interior behavior of a quantity.

A probe can also be used to discretely sample the volume of a model. Once

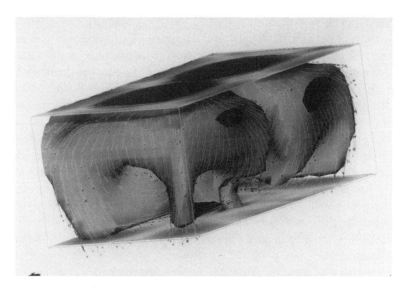

Figure 8.9. Air flow patterns in a multiphysics simulation of a room air conditioner can be studied through visualizations showing temperature isosurfaces, airflow velocities, and temperature contours. (See color section plate 8.9)

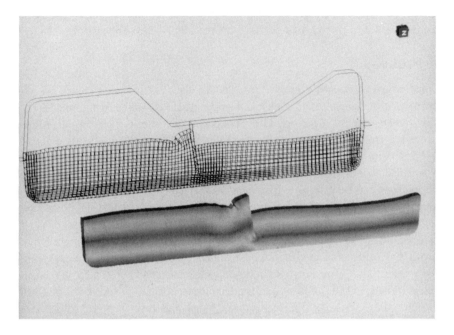

Figure 8.10. The sloshing behavior of a fluid with a free surface in a fuel tank and its complex interaction with a flexible baffle and tank roof can be simulated and characterized through visualization of mesh deformation and hydrostatic pressure contours. (See color section plate 8.10)

again we define the probe as a rectangle in 3-D space. The rectangle can be sampled at a fixed resolution (controlled by the user) to produce a set of points in 3-D. The points can then be used to query the values of results for those locations. Such a probe can be used to explore a vector field (such as an arrow displayed at each sample point) or a tensor field (such as an ellipsoid displayed at each sample point).

Manipulating a probe in 3-D can be very difficult. Multiple viewports can help in positioning the probe, but still require a steady hand. A better solution is to use constraints to define or fix the orientation or position of the probe. For example, if we have set the probe's orientation, its position can be set by selecting a point through which the probe will pass. The orientation of the probe can also be specified further by selecting three points to define the plane through which the probe will pass. The selected points can be any points in space, or can be clamped to an actual node on the model.

A visual representation of the data at a probe may not be the best way to understand the behavior there. Certain features of data, such as periodicity or some other pattern, can be better recognized by sound; the data is transformed with date sonification methods, and the audio hardware supplied with many workstations. Sound can be used to represent an extra dimension of the data (such as time in the case of a periodic fluctuation of data) or a particular feature of the data; for example, if a stress is compressive a rising sound can be produced.

8.6.2 Calculators

Insight into the behavior of a problem often can be gained by computing secondary variables from the primary variables (the variables that are actually solved for, such as displacement or pressure). Since the usefulness of such variables may not be known beforehand, the ability to compute such variables interactively should be supported by supplying a calculator. A calculator provides the mechanisms to compute new data from algebraic expressions containing terms representing existing data. The user selects the names of data and operators to form the algebraic expression and then executes it, creating the new data. A calculator also provides functions such as integration and differentiation. For example, the user could select an area of the mesh and compute the total flux across it.

8.6.3 Graphing

As unglamorous as they may seem, graphing visualization techniques are extremely important. Engineers rely on having stress/strain and time history plots to understand the behavior of a problem. The ability to interactively create such plots by selecting nodes and results data makes graphing visualization techniques more useful.

Another useful visualization technique is a graph probe. In this case the probe is a line sampled at a specified number of points (resolution). A graph is created by plotting the distance along the line against the interpolated values for the results data at the sampled points.

Haimes has combined a slice extractor with graphing to produce a visualization technique which allows the user to interactively graph the variation of data on a slice extracted from a finite element mesh. The extracted slice is displayed in a 2-D graphics window. The user interactively draws a rubber band line on the slice. The variation of the data along the line is then displayed as a graph in another window.

8.6.4 Color Manipulation

Color manipulation is a very useful technique used to enhance and highlight data. One way to do this is by direct manipulation of a *color map*. A color map is an array of color values that are used to map data values into colors for display. For example, the values of pressure for a face of an element can be mapped into colors and then used to produce a contour of pressure using Gouraud shading. By manipulating the color map we can change the colors of the contour. For instance, if we set all of the colors in a certain range to be blue and the rest to be red then we can easily see the regions of the mesh that have data within those ranges.

An interesting feature of the results data may be hidden by the way data is mapped to colors. Normally, a data value is mapped to a color using the linear function:

color_index = (num_colors − 1) × (data_value − min_value) / (max_value − min_value) + 1

where:

max_value = maximum value of the data
min_value = minimum value of the data
num_colors = number of colors in the color map
data_value = the data value to map to a color
color_index = index into an array of colors in a color map.

If something interesting is going on within a small sub-range of max_value and min_value then it will not be discernible because the mapping will obscure it. As an example, set min_value = 1, max_value = 64 and num_colors = 64. If the sub-range of interest is between 35 and 40, there are only five colors to represent the fluctuations within this sub-range.

A simple method to enhance data features is to interactively set the way colors are mapped by manipulating the ranges in the mapping of data we are visualizing. If the previous equation is replaced by:

color_index = (num_colors − 1) × (data_value − map_min_value) / (map_max_value − map_min_value) + 1
if (color_index < 1) color_index = 1
if (color_index > num_colors) color_index = num_colors

where:

map_max_value = a user defined maximum range
map_min_value = a user defined minimum range

then the color mapping can be clamped to a specified range within the actual ranges of the data. If the mapping ranges are set as map_max_value = 35 and map_min_value = 40, then there are 64 colors to represent the fluctuations of data within the sub-range between 35 and 40.

8.6.5 Quantification of Phenomena

When an engineer is exploring the results of a numerical simulation he or she is looking for a specific phenomenon (such as regions of high stress). Two ways to quantify a phenomenon is to determine where it occurs and how it develops. Operations used to quantify a phenomenon can be related to the examination of data, such as automatically displaying and highlighting the extrema of a data set. For example, the regions of high stress can be shown in red with the geometry of the mesh transformed so that the view is centered on this region. If the high stress is within the volume of the mesh then geometry can be cut away to reveal the areas of interest. Other interesting features, such as critical points, of a data set can be highlighted as well.

High-level characterization of a data set can be accomplished in an automatic way by using multiple techniques. For example, the user may ask the visualization system to characterize the flow around an airfoil. Several visualization techniques, such as slice planes and streaklines, will be positioned and released at relevant locations. The system would have to 'know' what is interesting about airfoils (e.g., boundary layers) and select the appropriate visualization techniques to display the interesting features. Specific knowledge for different physical scenarios could be implemented using expert system concepts.

8.7
PARALLEL AND DISTRIBUTED VISUALIZATION

The size of analysis problems being solved today can produce very large data sets. Visualizing these large data sets (created and stored on supercomputers) on a graphics workstation can sometimes be difficult if not impossible due to the lack and power of storage, memory or compute resources of the workstation. To alleviate such difficulties the visualization system can support parallel and distributed computation.

8.7.1 Parallel Computation

We will refer to parallel computation as the use of a collection of processing elements (CPU's, vector units, etc.) which cooperate to solve a computational task. There are two main models of parallel computation: Single Instruction Multiple Data (SIMD) and Multiple Instruction and Multiple Data (MIMD).

In the SIMD model of computation each processing element performs the same operation (e.g., addition or multiplication) on multiple data. For example, if we wanted to add two arrays, A and B, of 64 numbers each to get a third array, each processing element (say there are 64 of them) gets two data items (one from array A and B), adds them together and stores the results into C. Because the execution is done in parallel the computation is completed much faster than it would have been if performed sequentially. The cost of implementing true SIMD in hardware is expensive so the processors are implemented using special registers and pipelined hardware built into a serial processor. Such processors are called *vector* or *array processors* and are used on machines such as the CRAY and CONVEX.

The key to writing programs for a SIMD model is to perform as much computation as possible using arrays and simple looping constructs. An operation performed on an array within a loop can be compiled (vectorized) into instructions which can then be executed on a vector processor. Although much progress has been made with C vector compilers, the FORTRAN compilers are usually more robust and produce better machine code. One problem with vectorizing C programs is that some compilers will not vectorize the code if pointers rather than arrays are used to access data.

In the MIMD model of computation each processor has its own program that operates on its own data. For example, say we want to compute a complicated function for an array A of values and there is a subroutine FUNC that does this. In the case where we have 64 processors, we can divide up the array into 64 parts and execute in parallel the function on each MIMD processor with its part of the data. Even though it is possible for each processor to execute its own program it is usually the case that each processor executes the same program.

Programming for a MIMD model is very difficult because of the communication and synchronization mechanisms needed to coordinate the different processors. This is not performed by the compiler but by the programmer, who must explicitly write code to perform these tasks. In the past each vendor of a MIMD system supplied custom tools and language constructs to support program development, making programs non-portable. Lately, PVM (Oak Ridge National Laboratory) has been gaining acceptance as a machine-independent library of subroutines which can be used to perform MIMD tasking.

Even though MIMD is attractive because it performs well in a variety of applications, programming with a SIMD model, based on arrays, makes designing and implementing parallel programs much easier. This being the case, a workable strategy would be to use the MIMD model at a high level to interconnect a number of SIMD program blocks. The complicated (perhaps machine dependent) constructs used for MIMD tasking can be limited to a few areas while most of the parallel code is implemented using SIMD, making the workings of the program easier to understand. Even on a workstation, using a SIMD model can be of benefit because the ideas of data locality inherent to SIMD work well with the current generation of super-scalar pipelined processors.

8.7.2 Distributed Computation

We will refer to distributed computation as the use of the resources of a collection of separate computers operating autonomously. The computers are connected via a computer network. There are several typical computer environments with which we will be concerned. One is where we have a cluster of workstations with similar memory and processing power; the other is where we have a central compute server (e.g., supercomputer) attached to a cluster of workstations. We will only discuss the latter case since it has proven to be most beneficial to visualization.

Let the compute server be a supercomputer with a lots of mass storage and memory and powerful processor(s). The analysis is performed and stored on the supercomputer's mass storage, but we wish to visualize the results on a graphics workstation (much less mass storage, memory and compute power). The first problem to solve is gaining access to the data. If the database is not readable by the workstation, we must translate and transfer it to the workstation. We may not be able to transfer the entire results because the workstation may not have enough mass storage.

A solution to this problem is for the visualization system, as it is running on the workstation, to request and access data from the supercomputer's mass storage as it is needed. To facilitate this type of functionality the visualizer would need to communicate with a process running on the supercomputer. The visualizer would send a request (perhaps using the methods discussed in Section 8.2.2) to the process for data. The process would read the data from the supercomputer's mass storage and then send it to the visualizer.

Even if we can transfer the data to the workstation it still may not have enough memory to hold the data or enough compute power to perform the visualization computation in a reasonable amount of time. Once again, we can use a process running on the supercomputer to perform the desired visualization computation for us. The visualizer sends a request with all of the necessary parameters; (i.e., the name of the data) to instruct the process how to perform the desired visualization computation. When the computation is complete the resulting data, such as geometry (for example, a set of polygons representing an isosurface), is sent back to the visualizer for display.

The communication software needed for this type of distributed processing can be quite complex. However, there are some tools that can be used to simplify the implementation of such functionality. One is the External Data Representation (XDR) library that provides functions for the machine independent transmission of data for remote procedure calls. Another is PVM (Oak Ridge National Laboratory), mentioned earlier, that provides a machine independent library of subroutines that can be used to perform message passing.

8.8
VISUALIZATION SYSTEMS

In this section we will identify and briefly discuss some of the visualization systems available for engineering analysis. We will divide the systems into three categories: libraries, turnkey systems and application builders.

In order to select an appropriate visualization system for a particular application the requirements for that application must be well understood. Some applicable requirements are:

- *Functionality:* Does the system have the visualization techniques needed for my problem (techniques for fluids, solids or both)? Does it support the element types (higher order) I need?
- *Problem size:* Will the system execute efficiently for my size of problem on the platforms available to me?
- *Extensibility:* Do I need to write my own visualization modules? If so, do I have the resources to do this?
- *Ease-of-use:* Is the system easy to learn and use?
- *Integration:* Can the system be integrated with other software systems? Can I control the look and feel of the system?
- *Computation:* Can the system execute on a parallel computer or in a distributed environment?

8.8.1 Libraries

A library provides an API for the developer of a visualization system. The developer can create a custom visualization system around the library which will be used for the core visualization functionality, such as contouring and isosurface extraction. Three such libraries are: Visual3, CardinalVision and FOCUS.

Visual3 (Department of Aeronautics and Astronautics, MIT) provides sub-routines written in FORTRAN which can be called from a user's program. The functions perform all visualization (contouring, isosurface extraction, probes, etc.) and graphics (window management, hardcopy, rendering, etc.) functions for CFD. It supports both steady and unsteady flow.

CardinalVision (Wilsonville, OR) provides a library of objects written in C++ to perform visualization functions on the scalar, vector and tensor fields associated with finite element meshes. The library is machine-independent and can be used as the basis for visualization system development.

FOCUS (Visual Kinematics, Mountain View, CA) provides development libraries for data management, user interface, graphics and visualization techniques for both fluids and solids problems.

8.8.2 Turnkey Systems

A turnkey visualization system provides the interface and modules which allows the user to perform visualizations without any programming. Three such systems are: FieldView, Data Visualizer and SSV.

FieldView (Intelligent Light, Fair Lawn, NJ) provides a visualization environment for unsteady CFD. It supports cutting planes, isosurfaces and particle traces visualization techniques and has animation and video output.

The Data Visualizer (Wavefront Technologies, Inc., Santa Barbara, CA) provides a visualization environment for general finite element data. The user can work with multiple visualization techniques at once. It supports the writing of custom data readers.

SSV (Sterling Software, Palo Alto, CA) provides a broad range of visualization products (such as FAST) and services (animation production and recording) for CFD visualization.

8.8.3 Application Builders

An application builder visualization system provides the user with a set of tools to interactively construct a visualization application. A set of basic visualization modules is supplied as well to support the writing of custom modules.

Most application builders available today basically provide the same functionality, although some may be easier to use than others. Available systems include AVS (Advanced Visual Systems, Waltham, MA), Data Explorer (IBM, Hawthorne, NY) and IRIS Explorer (Silicon Graphics, Mountain View, CA).

8.9
REFERENCES

[1]. Bancroft, G.V., et al., "FAST: A Multi-Processed Environment for Visualization of Computational Fluid Dynamics," Proceedings of Visualization '90, IEEE Computer Society Press, October 1990, pp. 14–27.
[2]. Brittain, D.L., et al., "Design of an End-User Data Visualization System," Proceedings of Visualization '90, IEEE Computer Society Press, October 1990, pp. 323–328.

[3]. Buning, P., et al., "Flow Visualization of CFD Using Graphics Workstations," AIAA 87–1180, Proc. 8th Computational Fluid Dynamics, Conf., June 1987.

[4]. Cattell, R., "Object Data Management: Object-Oriented and Extended Relational Database Systems," Addison-Wesley, 1991.

[5]. Chen, M., et al., "A Study in Interactive 3-D Rotation Using 2-D Control Devices," Proceedings of SIGGRAPH '88 (Atlanta, Georgia, August 1–5, 1988). In Computer Graphics 22, 4 (August 1988). pp 121–129.

[6]. Dyer, D. S., "A Data Flow Toolkit for Visualization," IEEE Computer Graphics and Applications, Vol. 10, No. 4, July 1990, pp. 60–69.

[7]. Globus, A., "A Software Model for Visualization Of Time Dependent 3-D Computational Fluid Dynamics Results," NASA Ames Research Center, NAS Systems Division, Applied Technical Branch technical report RNR-92–031, November 1992.

[8]. Haeberli, P., "ConMan: A Visual Programming Language for Interactive Graphics," SIGGRAPH Proceedings, Vol. 22, Number 4, ACM SIGGRAPH August 1988.

[9]. Haimes, R., Giles, M., "Advanced Interactive Visualization for CFD," Computing Systems in Engineering, Vol. 1, No. 1, pp. 51–62. 1990.

[10]. Hultquist, J., Raible, E., "SuperGlue: A Programming Environment for Scientific Visualization," NASA Ames Research Center, NAS Systems Division, Applied Technical Branch technical report RNR-92-014, April 1992.

[11]. Legensky, S.M, "Interactive Investigation of Fluid Mechanics Data Sets," Proceedings of Visualization '90, IEEE Computer Society Press, October 1990, pp. 435–439.

[12]. Stevens, W.R., Unix Network Programming, Prentice-Hall 1990.

[13]. Upson C., et al., "The Application Visualization System: A Computational Environment for Scientific Visualization," IEEE Computer Graphics and Applications, Vol. 9, No. 4, July 1989, pp. 30–42.

Applications of Engineering Visualization to Analysis and Design

LARRY G. RICHARDS

VISUALIZATION AFFECTS THE process of analysis and design in a number of ways. Applying visualization concepts to issues such as computer aided design, geometric modeling, display of results behavior and simulation gives engineers a greater ability to comprehend their work, and the process of engineering itself. At the same time, the use of visualization must be guided by an engineer's own judgement.

This chapter discusses some of the major applications of visualization in engineering design and analysis, and also explores the issue of visualization in engineering education—both as a tool for learning, and a means for a better understanding of engineering subject matter. It looks at the state of a growing field as it is currently applied to the teaching and practice of engineering.

9.1
INTRODUCTION

One might think that visualization in science and engineering is a recent innovation. It was only in 1987 that an NSF Committee issued a major report identifying scientific visualization as an area worthy of study and support [25]. However, engineers, scientists, and artists have used visual cues to convey information for hundreds of years. Tufte shows exhibits from past centuries in which multidimensional data were effectively presented visually [39]. Shepard reviews the role of visual imagery in major scientific discoveries in a variety of fields [35]. Ferguson demonstrates the pervasive role of visualization in engineering [13].

In many fields, there have been major debates about the role and importance of visualization in scientific thinking—especially in mathematics and physics. Some scientists claim that visual representations are unnecessary, and may even obscure thinking. In this view, only pure symbolic reasoning is acceptable; pictures are crutches for those who cannot handle equations and numbers. There is often a tension between those who naturally use visual representation and those who "don't need it." Such disputes almost certainly reflect the cognitive styles of the people involved. Some people have highly developed visualization skills; others are unable to create an image "in the mind's eye" [34]. Each year in Engineering Graphics we have a few students who have difficulty visualizing and mentally manipulating objects and assemblies, but modern computer tools enable even those who don't naturally visualize to create and manipulate visual images.

The current emphasis on scientific visualization is driven by the role of the computer in producing visual representations and analyzing the information in images. Interactive computer graphics (ICG) is a fairly recent innovation, dating only from 1959 and Ivan Sutherland's Sketchpad. Over the next three decades, this field grew rapidly, with major developments in industry, applications, and theory. Requicha and Voelcker trace four sets of parallel activities which converged to define solids modeling by the early 1980s [32]. The early applications of computer graphics were in the automotive and aerospace industries [29, 31]. The defining textbook for the field of computer graphics was Newman and Sproull [28], followed nearly a decade later by Foley and Van Dam, now updated and completely rewritten [16]. Chasen brought together the mathematics of the field [5]. Now, visualization has been crystallized as a separate discipline by the NSF report and recent books by Friedhoff and Benzou and Kaufmann and Smarr [17, 21].

Our ability to create realistic, detailed two-dimensional images has progressed to an amazing level over the past three decades. Creating and rendering three-dimensional models is somewhat more difficult, but this capability is now widely available even on personal computers. Recently, research and development activities have focused on user interface design, interactive techniques, and rapid prototyping.

As a field, scientific visualization makes new tools available. It also enhances the utility of existing ones. Thus, computer aided design (CAD), finite element analysis (FEA), simulation, computational fluid dynamics (CFD), and data analysis have all benefitted from recent software enhancements. What has changed is the ease of doing visualization, and the scope and flexibility of the tools available for doing it. In the process, visualization has become a tool for understanding and communicating the meaning of data.

The NSF Report identified scientific visualization as a unifying set of concepts and techniques underlying a number of disparate disciplines: computer graphics, computer aided design, computer vision, image processing, signal processing, and user interface design [25]. This new field was defined by two kinds of problems: creating images (image generation or production); and understanding images (image processing and interpretation). The first set of problems develops images from information stored in computer memory; the second approach starts with an image and seeks to extract information from it. Presumably, similar methods, concepts and algorithms could be applied in both domains and the findings of each would enrich the other. Also, the definition of this area of study, and attempts to organize and formalize it, would lead to new research topics and to productive interaction between researchers from different disciplines.

In this chapter, several applications of visualization to engineering analysis will be described. Two main ideas underlie our approach: (1) emphasizing the importance of geometric modeling in the analysis process; and (2) a broad view of the concept of analysis. The educational implications of visualization techniques will also be discussed.

9.2
GEOMETRIC MODELING AS THE CORE
OF COMPUTER AIDED ENGINEERING

The process of generating an image on a computer display screen may result from one of two general approaches. In the first, the primary concern is with making pictures; in the second, with modeling objects and then viewing them. Is the image the reality we are trying to achieve, or is it the model? Are we merely trying to create the illusion of reality, or develop an accurate representation of reality? The second approach, in which the model is the fundamental concern, is the basis for modern computer aided engineering (CAE).

In CAE, we are primarily interested in models of three-dimensional solid objects and assemblies. Rendering these models raises a different set of problems from those involved in just creating pictures [36]. It requires projecting a three-dimensional geometric representation onto one or more two-dimensional display windows. The model is distinct from the pictures we use to represent it. Separating the model from its views is a fundamental conceptual step for students learning to use a CAD system. Given the model, we may choose how we want to view it, and then define the parameters necessary to achieve particular views (see Figure 9.1). Multiple views can be displayed simultaneously and we can discard or alter views at will. Changing the views does not alter the model. Once created, the model exists independently of any views of it. Further, we can manipulate the views to help us understand the model.

Geometric modeling is a fundamental step in the product realization process. The model provides the basis for analysis, optimization, and eventual fabrication of the product. Creating a model is an act of abstraction, representation, and visual thinking. A key aspect of visualization is the means to see the results of your modeling, and understand what is going on. One purpose of visualization is to provide information to the analyst so he or she may accurately perceive a model or a set of data.

Table 9.1 summarizes the levels of representation which can be achieved in either rendering or modeling. The rendering techniques are useful for viewing the results of modeling, but only the modeling approaches create sufficient information for analysis and fabrication.

Requicha and Voelcker identified six representational schemes for complete solid models: constructive solid geometry (CSG), boundary representation (b-rep),

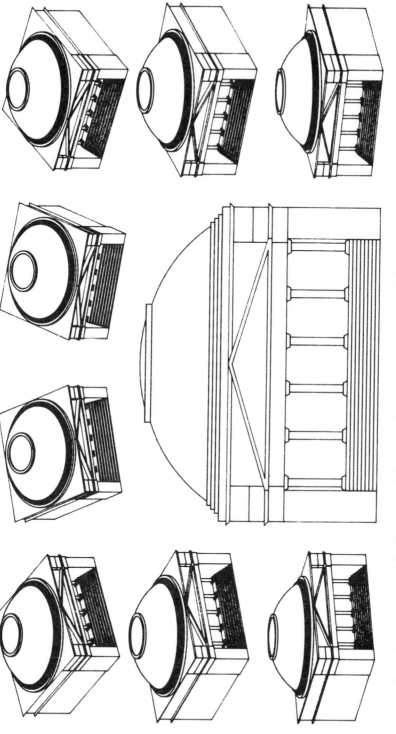

Figure 9.1. Nine views of the Rotunda. The model was create by Elizabeth A. Byrne at the A. H. Small Center for Computer Aided Engineering at the University of Virginia.

**TABLE 9.1. A Taxonomy of Approaches for
Rendering or Modeling Solid Objects**

Rendering

1. 2-D pictures of 3-D objects (wireframes)

2. Realistic images (with depth cues, hidden lines removed, highlighting, light and shadows, color and shading)

3. Motion; dynamics and animation provided by a sequence of views.

4. 3-D Images; to create the illusion of reality
    Holographic
    Stereographic
    Virtual reality

5. Volumetric rendering (looking inside the object)

Modeling

Computer models:

1. Geometric Modeling
    wire frame
    surface models
    solid models

2. Assemblies; collections of parts

3. Object-based virtual reality

Physical models produced from a computer data base:

4. Parts produced by N.C. machine tools

5. Rapid prototyping
    stereolithography
    ballistic particle manufacturing
    fused deposition modeling
    laminated object manufacturing
    selective laser sintering
    solid ground curing

6. Net shape manufacturing

cell decomposition (analytic solid modeling), spatial enumeration (octrees and quadtrees), primitive instancing, and sweeping [33]. B-rep and CSG have been the dominant representation techniques for solids in geometric modeling. ASM is commercially available in the PATRAN software. However, recent approaches have developed around volume-based representations (spatial enumeration) and primitive instancing (modern feature-based CAE systems). Volume visualization techniques from medical imaging are now available to engineers in finite element packages. Several CAD programs now incorporate standard families of parts (based on prototypes) and include sets of features which may be added to (or deleted from) the parts. Features are important constructs because they reflect the correspondence of design decisions to manufacturing operations and processes.

Creating models of assemblies and complex mechanisms requires generating a collection of parts and specifying their spatial relationships. Conceptually, this is a difficult task because the designer must work with multiple coordinate systems. Individual parts may be readily created in their own coordinate systems, but then must all be brought together in single coordinate system for the final model. Visual representation is necessary for most engineers to successfully design an assembly.

Virtual Reality (VR) is a level of simulation whose goal is to immerse the user in the display. This requires isolating the user from the real world, and providing interfaces with the computer which are intuitive and permit easy and fast interaction. Ideally, the frame rate and response time of the system will give the user the same quality of experience we enjoy in daily life. The visual component of VR is usually provided by computer-generated displays mounted in front of both eyes to produce stereoscopic images. VR may be either image based or model based. Often the goal is merely to provide a realistic sequence of images and create the illusion of reality. In model-based VR, physical constraints are introduced, and realistic relations between objects are maintained. The scene must not only look right, it must be right. For example, one would not be able to walk through walls or fly through the ceiling. Further, sight, reach, and mobility should all be constrained by accurate models of the environment. Practical applications of VR include the Virtual Windtunnel at NASA Ames Research Center, the Virtual Cockpit at Wright Patterson Air Force Base, and the molecular modeling project at the University of North Carolina. For complex systems and environments, virtual prototyping may provide the only reasonable design assessment before actual construction. It can also provide a preview of planned layouts, analysis of specific features of the design, and even a vehicle for training workers or potential inhabitants to function in special environments (such as the space station).

VR can be a model for other types of visualization systems, and a testbed for display and interactive techniques. The technology necessary to achieve convincing experiences in VR will greatly enhance the effectiveness of scientific visualization. For example, the level of direct manipulation and rapid response time needed to mirror everyday experience would also permit engineers to steer the computations of a simulation.

Actual physical models may be produced from the geometry data base. Indeed, this is the fundamental goal of integrated computer aided design and manufacturing. The earliest realization of this idea was the ability to generate NC tapes from a CAD data base. Techniques for rapid prototyping are now widely available. Six major approaches to fabricating designs directly from a CAD data base are, or soon will be, available as commercial products. Some of these technologies will be capable of producing actual final parts (in terms of material and finish) rather than just prototypes. At a recent Siggraph conference, these techniques were collectively referred to as "real virtuality": objects can be made real which have only existed as computer models.

All of the rendering approaches seek to facilitate the perception of the intended object. High quality photorealistic images are now standard in the entertainment and advertizing industries. Often in science and engineering we do not need photorealistic images. They contain too much information and may distract us from the phenomena of interest. In the real world, there is so much realism we often miss what is significant. Simple displays often reveal all we need to know. Abstract representation can often communicate more information than realistic images. We need to provide enough information, but not too much. We want to highlight what is important and eliminate distracting, irrelevant, or extraneous information.

A key skill of engineering drawing is to capture the essential features of a product as simply as possible—to eliminate distractions. In modeling, one must learn to identify the defining features of an object, and provide only the minimum information necessary to create the model. Redundant or irrelevant information may confuse the modeling software.

9.3
THE ROLE OF VISUAL THINKING IN THE DESIGN AND ANALYSIS PROCESS

Visual images can support the engineer at all stages of the design process (see Figure 9.2). During conceptual design, a CAE system permits the designer to capture ideas in preliminary form, to play with them and refine them, and eventually to produce an initial model of the concept. This model can be manipulated, experimented with, analyzed, and optimized. The designer should be able to model rapidly and easily, and to revise the model quickly. Later, during detailed design, it should be easy to edit the model, provide precise numerical information, and annotate the display.

Ease of modeling enables the design engineer to generate multiple designs—either many versions of a particular concept or realizations of multiple concepts. The ability to explore alternative design concepts, and to improve a concept through several iterations on a design, is enhanced by CAE systems.

Since much of engineering design is redesign, the engineer should be able to recall and review previous designs, and modify them to meet new applications, constraints or regulations. CAE systems are now being developed to reflect both the language of design and the recurrence of common design problems. Such systems emphasize design by features, parametric and constraint-based design, and variational geometry. This requires integrating CAD with group technology.

Many practical design problems are extremely complex. Modern CAE systems help manage design complexity. Mechanical systems can be decomposed into a series of subassemblies, components, and parts. Many design details can be embedded in the subunits. Models of all these subunits can be stored and accessed as needed. Libraries of such models may be developed to reduce redesign and re-inventing of existing components. Decomposition of a design problem allows the engineer to vary, and thus control, the level of abstraction on which she or he is focused. It also allows different members of a design team to focus on different components or problems.

In finite element modeling and analysis, the value of visualization has long been

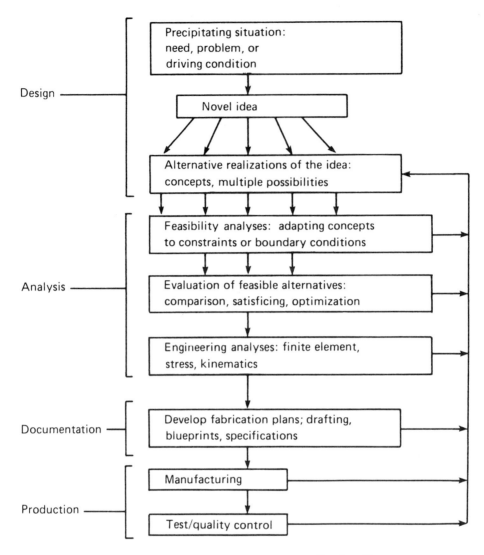

Figure 9.2. Elements (stages) of the Engineering Design Process.

apparent. Designing and conducting the analysis is heavily dependent on the analyst's ability to correctly specify the geometry of the model. When the results are returned by the program, the amount of numerical information is prohibitive. Visual techniques have made it manageable. Graphic interfaces are available for all the major FEA programs. Color coding reflects the magnitude of the measure (quantity) of interest; these colors are then mapped onto the model and the analyst can literally "see" the results of the analysis. Associating color with the structure of the model reveals patterns in the data which would be difficult to discern from a listing of the results or a table of numbers.

The analysis of a product or system numerically can provide insight to the person trained to interpret the numbers. It is possible to learn to see patterns in tables of data. Experts know how to organize and search large sets of data, but even they can miss important details. Visualization is valuable even for the expert; it can help in understanding results and seeing patterns in data which may be obscured in a "sea of numbers."

Visual images are important aids in communication. They help the designer convey his or her ideas to others. For example, a colored shaded image of a solid model is useful in showing the product to managers, customers, vendors (suppliers), and to manufacturing engineers. Seeing a rendered model of the product conveys much more information than seeing engineering drawings of it. This is especially true when working with non-engineers. However, there is evidence that even skilled draftsmen and machinists benefit from well rendered images accompanying the engineering drawings. The pictures alleviate uncertainty and facilitate accurate interpretation of the drawings. Thus, a 3-D CAD model can facilitate all downstream phases in the product's life cycle (analysis, planning, production, documentation, quality assurance, marketing and sales, etc.). Both design and analysis may be viewed as phases or stages in the overall product realization process. They occur early in the sequence, but their success determines all subsequent activities required to actually manufacture the product.

9.4
APPLICATIONS OF VISUALIZATION IN ENGINEERING ANALYSIS

In this section, we will review several applications of visualization in engineering analysis, and raise issues and concerns about how to best represent the information in models and displays.

9.4.1. Data Analysis and Display

Engineering data can be real (generated by experiments or measurements on objects or events) or simulated (produced by one or more models). In either case, current problems in engineering and science typically result in large data sets. Visual representations are necessary to make the data comprehensible to us. A table of numbers must be scanned (read) sequentially—one row or column at a time. Thus it is difficult to see what is going on in a large set of data, especially when we need to compare values from several sections of a table. We cannot easily see patterns or apprehend the totality of the data. A well constructed graph, diagram, or map can instantly convey a large amount of information. Our visual systems allow us to take in an array of information simultaneously if that information is appropriately represented. Visualization techniques are designed to allow us to comprehend the meaning of large amounts of data. "Scientific visualization, or any form of visualization, is a way of coupling the eye-brain system to increase the flow of information to the human being from the computer" [10, p. 39].

In any field, we face the question of how to effectively display information. Finding ways to best represent data requires the collaboration of scientists and engineers, computer scientists, mathematicians, artists, human factors experts, and cognitive and perceptual psychologists. Cox established the role of an artist on research teams using scientific visualization [10]. Haber and Wilkinson, reviewing different visual modalities, observed that "few graphic designers have used the procedures of experimental psychophysics to assess their effect on perceiving, comprehending, retaining, or retrieving information from displays" [19—pg. 30]. Psychologists and human factors engineers are often needed to assess the effectiveness of the visualization techniques. Does the message come through as intended? Do people correctly interpret the display? How much (if any) and what kinds of training and instruction are necessary to understand the visual output from an analysis?

Of particular interest to us is how information can be presented to the design engineer so that the implications of design decisions are apparent (obvious, visible), so he or she may "see" the results of design decisions. What does the engineer need to see to comprehend the downstream impact of his or her design decisions? Several types of information may be necessary, reflecting different stages in the overall product realization process: the magnitudes of variables in finite element analysis; paths and trajectories in computational fluid dynamics; movements and interferences in mechanism analysis; machine processing capabilities, material handling times, and product flow during production; measurements and uncertainties during inspection.

How can we design displays for accurate perception? Principles for the effective graphic presentation of data have been developed in two books by Tufte [39, 40]. He has tried to develop principles and techniques for creating displays that are simple, informative, and easily understandable. Wainer and Thissen reviewed empirical studies on the graphic display of information, and describe an impressive array of techniques [41]. Cleveland and Chambers et. al. organized many existing techniques and tried to develop the first principles of a theory of graphical perception [7, 9]. Haber and Wilkinson reviewed some principles of perceptual psychology relevant to designing computer graphics displays [19]. Gnanadesikan listed desirable criteria for data display techniques; they included: (a) descriptive capacity, (b) versatility, (c) data orientation, (d) potential for internal comparisons, (e) aid in focusing attention, (f) degree to which they are self critical of assumptions, and (g) adaptability to large volumes of data [41—page 196].

Numerousity or magnitude can be represented in many ways. Bachi has developed a scale of graphic rational patterns (GRP) for representing numerousity [1]. Others have used scales of grey (light to dark) and patterns of shading to reflect magnitudes. Representing the error or uncertainty associated with observations is more difficult. Typically, confidence intervals are displayed with lines or tick marks. Shading and intensity may also be used. Haber and Wilkinson describe a variation on the histogram (a Fuzzygram) in which the density of parallel line segments reflects the uncertainty associated with each category [19]. A related set of problems are concerned with how to represent tolerances in geometric models. No good solution has yet been found.

Color can be very effective when properly used. In theory, it can convey information about the levels of several variables simultaneously. Color can be varied in hue, saturation and value, and different mixes of color can reflect the influence of several variables. However, there is no inherent correspondence between hue and magnitude; colors have different meanings in different cultures; and visual illusions may be produced by certain patterns of colors. Some color schemes are highly effective in transmitting information. But the choice of colors and values is critical, and small differences can have major impacts on the effectiveness of the display. Simple uses of color are relatively safe, but its use in complex displays must be carefully designed and evaluated [41]. Sometimes the joint use of color in multivariate displays produces unexpected results.

Pickover designed a simple graphic representation based on color that permits the user to assess the quality of a random number generator [30]. Given the central role of random number generators in simulation, this technique is an important tool for the analyst. Colored balls are used to represent the data generated; these balls are mapped into positions in a spherical coordinate system. Triplets of random numbers are converted to coordinate positions (r, θ, ϕ) for individual balls. The colors of individual balls are also a function of the three parameters (r, θ, ϕ). The entire cluster of colored balls is a "noise-sphere." Patterns which appear in the noise-sphere reveal correlations in the data and thus may be used to detect a bad random number generator. Correlations may be evident as tendrils, strands of similarly colored balls.

Visualization allows us to explore our data in different ways and at different levels of abstraction (to find the right level of detail). Data visualization provides new tools for exploratory data analysis. Such techniques are most useful if they are highly interactive, permit direct manipulation, and include rapid response time. The analyst must be able to navigate the data, change its grain (resolution), and alter its representation (change symbols, colors, etc.). Graphic display of objects may use color differentiation (identity, type, attributes) or special symbols (glyphs, stars, boids). The user can experiment with the image to find "the correct representation." The goal is to represent data so that its meaning (significance) is apparent, and we can see patterns or relations in data.

In simulation experiments, data analysis, and display design, we want to incorporate the investigator into the process to guide and steer computations, to evaluate output and make decisions, and to control the simulation "on the fly." This requires representations that are intuitive and easily interpretable so their significance may be grasped quickly. The display must contain information at the correct level of detail (for the task) and ideally focus attention on key information. Human perception, cognition, and response time will be the key limitations of "person-in-the-loop" computation and simulation.

Visualization is essential for understanding the concept of multidimensional space. Clearly, the use of graphics has enhanced our appreciation of 3-D space and enabled us to understand how 3-D objects map into 2-D views. Banchoff has explored graphic techniques for representing geometric phenomena in four (or more) dimensions [3]. Shepard studied how people can construct meaningful representations of higher dimensional space [35]. Just as first year engineering students come to interpret multiple 2-D views and construct a mental image of a 3-D object, one can construct a 4-D model from a sequence of 2-D and 3-D images.

Special problems arise when we try to visualize multiple dependent variables.

A variety of special symbols have been invented to convey simultaneous variation on several measures taken on the same object [41]. In two-way displays, these include Chernoff's faces, glyphs, stars, and color mapping. Figure 9.3 shows a star display applied to quality of life measures for various states [41 p. 228] Such displays may be readily used with engineering data, and may even be incorporated into dynamic displays (creating "twinkling stars"!). The spokes could be color coded to identify the variables. Three dimensional extensions of these schemes are possible but the resulting objects are usually still mapped onto a 2-D screen.

A final problem concerns the display of variation over time. Multiple static representations can be used, but accurate representation of dynamic behavior requires animation. Two solutions are discussed below in the section on CFD: traveling icons (such as Kerlick's boids) and responsive icons (such as Haber's tensor glyph). The former go with the flow, while the latter respond to the wave as it passes.

9.4.2. Finite Element Modeling and Analysis and Computational Fluid Dynamics

Both of these approaches are concerned with the spatial distribution of values of one or more variables over, within, or around an object. They simulate the behavior of the object or system under specified conditions or environments, or trace the effects of the object on the surrounding environment. It can be argued that computer graphics is what made finite element analysis usable and comprehensible for most engineers. Until there were post-processors which allowed the results of the analyses to be presented graphically, few engineers were capable of interpreting the results of finite element analysis.

Finite Element Analysis (FEA) is an area in which visualization techniques developed in other domains have been readily adopted. Since analysts are interested in the behavior within the object, volume visualization methods are appropriate. Techniques from medical imaging, such as volume slicing, isosurfaces, and translucent displays, are now common in FEA research, and are even available in commercial FEA software (ANSYS 5.0). The application of these new techniques to FEA is a direct result of the kind of crossfertilization the NSF visualization report was designed to encourage.

Some applications of 3-D visualization techniques to analysis and modeling were given in Gallagher and Selker [18]. Figures 9.4 and 9.5 show traditional contour and isosurface displays of a rocket seal. Clearly the isosurface representation in Figure 9.5 gives a clearer picture of the 3-D variation in the model's interior. In Figure 9.6, the interior thermal distribution of a hair dryer model is revealed using shading and translucency. Volume slicing is used to show the state of stress in the interior of a model in Figure 9.7. These three examples are courtesy of Swanson Analysis Systems, Inc.

Visualization sometimes helps detect errors in the model, code, or procedures. Not all results are what we expect. An anomalous result is a puzzle. Are surprises "real" or artifacts? It is often difficult to tell. Da Rosa conducted an aerodynamic study of a test vehicle using the FLOTRAN CFD software [11]. The vehicle was an automobile bluff-body specified by Cray Research as a test problem

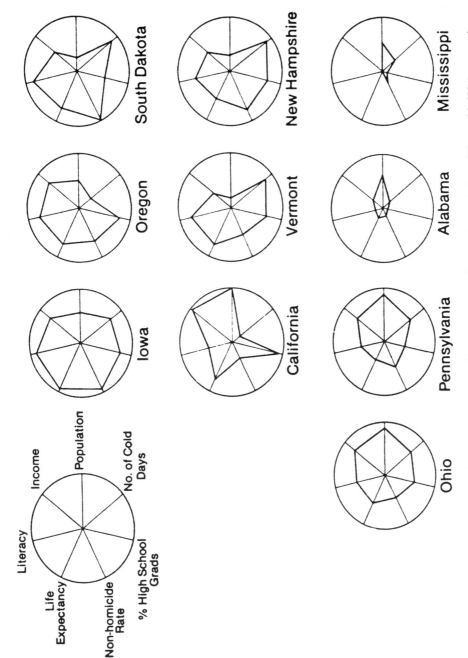

Figure 9.3. A Star display for data on seven quality measures for various states. (From H. Wainer and D. Thissen, "Graphical Data Analysis." (Reproduced with permission from the *Annual Review of Psychology*, Volume 32. Copyright 1981 by Annual Reviews, Inc.)

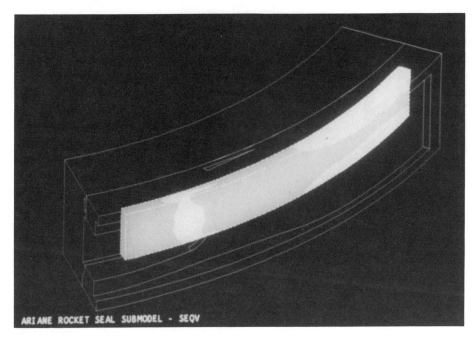

Figure 9.4. Contour plot display of a rocket seal. Ansys 5.0. (Courtesy Dedo Sistemi–Italcae SRL, Italy.)

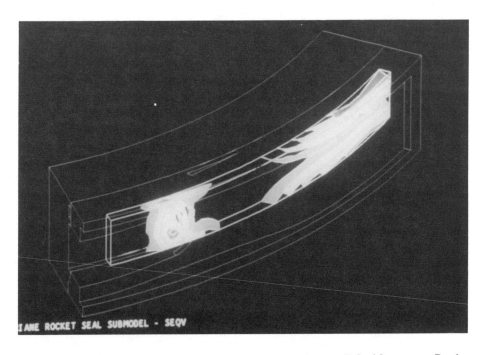

Figure 9.5. Isosurface display of a rocket seal. Ansys 5.0. (Courtesy Dedo Sistemi–Italcae SRL, Italy.)

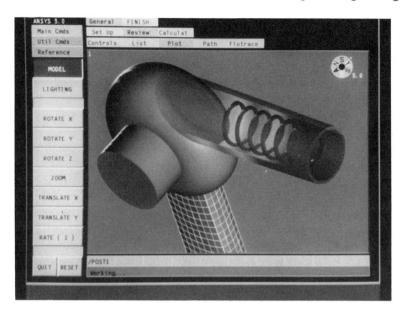

Figure 9.6. Interior thermal distribution for a hair dryer model. Ansys 5.0, Source: Swanson Analysis, Inc. (See color section plate 9.6)

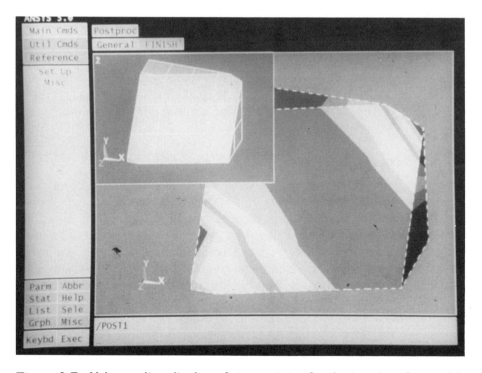

Figure 9.7. Volume slice display of stress states for the interior of a model. ansys 5.0, Source: Swanson Analysis, Inc.

for evaluating CFD software. Two distinct models were analyzed: a 17,000 node coarse model, and a 114,000 node refined model. The final solution from the coarse model provided the basis for creating the refined model. The details of the analysis and results need not concern us here. In this project the visualization results revealed a problem with the model vectors in the Ramp region as shown in Figure 9.8 (a) and (b). In the coarse model, the flow behaves as expected, but in the refined model, the flow pattern violates our intuitive expectations. Unfortunately, it also fails to match the results of windtunnel experiments. These anomalous results were readily apparent from the visualization. Of course, anomalous behavior in any part of the display causes us to question the overall results. With purely numeric displays, this problem would have been more difficult to detect.

There is a critical distinction between expertise as an analyst versus competence as an engineer. The analyst can tell if an analysis was done correctly, the engineer must know if the results are correct. Of course, with any model, its accuracy must eventually be verified by empirical results.

Computational fluid dynamics (CFD), by definition, involves patterns of change over time and space. To understand even simple phenomena often requires several types of representation. Truly informative displays must be dynamic. Through animation, we can watch icons move and change over time. Techniques for the display of flows include vectors, streamlines, streaklines, and particle paths [4]. Kerlick also discussed flow ribbons and boids (including sphere, arrow and dart boids) [23]. Boids are bird-like icons in that they travel with the flow. They change shape in flight in response to field variables. These icons are designed to represent multiple properties of the flow simultaneously and indicate directionality. The star technique could also be used in this context.

One of the most compelling demonstrations of the utility of many of these techniques is the simulation of the evolution of a severe thunderstorm developed at the National Center for Supercomputing Applications at the University of Illinois. This simulation is described in Kaufman and Smarr and is available on videotape from ACM Siggraph [21].

9.4.3. Mechanical Dynamics

Several programs allow us to animate assemblies, mechanisms, machines, vehicles, and structures (ADAMS, IMP, DADS), so we may study their behavior over time and visualize the interactions of their parts. These dynamic visualizations often reveal operational characteristics of the assembly that do not fit our expectations or intentions. They allow us to analyze multibody contact; mating/fit; interference; range of motion. Using these programs, we can follow changes of state or spatial location over time. Thus we can model the activity in a production cell complete with robots, machine tools, and material transport systems, evaluate its performance, and redesign it as necessary.

9.4.4. Ergonomic Modeling

In one sense, modeling humans is a special case of "Mechanical Dynamics." Anthropometric models are used to test the fit, reach, and motions of people in

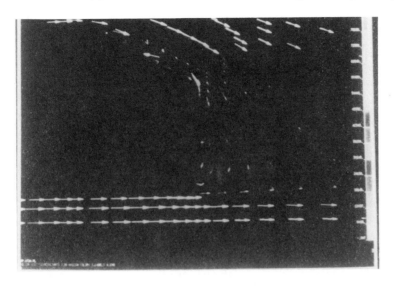

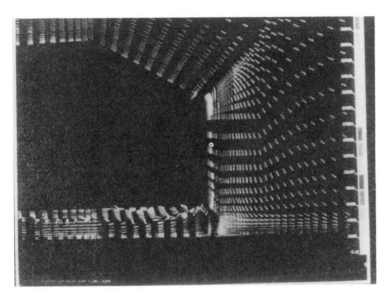

Figure 9.8. Flow fields around an automobile like bluff body. Using Flotran (a) Coarse model vectors in ramp regions, (b) refined model vectors in ramp region. (From Da Rosa, 1989)

vehicles and environments. They incorporate restrictions on limb and joint movements, and may be scaled for different body types and sizes. They also permit assessment of movement patterns of individuals and groups of people. Some programs include the ability to determine the visual field for the model. Ergonomic models have been developed for a variety of purposes and vary greatly in the type and amount of information they contain. Such models have been developed for automobile companies, aircraft manufacturers, and the space program. They have been used for cockpit design, aircraft crew cabin layout and instrumentation evaluation, aircraft maintainability studies, automobile seat and passenger comfort studies, and space station construction planning.

One early program SAMMIE (System for Aiding Man-Machine Interaction Evaluation) was developed at the University of Nottingham and used by British Leyland to assess the fit of drivers and passengers in their vehicles. It included variation in gender and somatotype: one could specify whether the model was male or female; heavy, average, or slight in build. SAMMIE was used primarily for vehicle design and the interior design and layout of rooms and office spaces. With such programs, we can assess how people fit into, and function in, their environments before the design is finalized and the space actually built. Other early anthropometric modeling programs were reviewed by Dooley [12].

At the University of Pennsylvania, Badler and his colleagues have developed human modeling at a much higher level of sophistication [2]. Their program JACK incorporates the major features of the earlier programs (reach and visibility analysis), but has a more complete representation of the human body. In addition to 88 articulated joints in the body model, JACK has a 17 segment flexible torso, a hand model with automatic grip, and strength guided motion. It also has a variety of features useful for animation and film (facial models, walking, etc.). Models of the human body have been used in a range of studies from simulated crash test dummies to the electronic cadaver for training surgeons or previewing an operation.

Usually visualization is helpful in the design process but sometimes too much detail or too literal a representation may interfere with problem solving. Finding the right visualization may involve discarding some of the information or freeing oneself from a model which is too compelling. Paul Chia and the author analyzed the ergonomic design of a work area in a furniture factory [8]. A hot press machine was systematically loaded by two workers and unloaded by a second pair. By mapping the motions and movements of the workers we hoped to duplicate their tasks with one or more robots. We found we could, in fact, replace these workers with machines which could repeat the same work patterns, but it would be expensive, and there were serious questions about the reliable operation of robots in this environment. Forced by reality to reconsider our solution, we found that a total redesign of the process and work area would eliminate the need for either humans or robots. Focusing on the concrete details of the task as currently done prevented us (initially) from finding a simpler more abstract solution. Visualization still guided our search for a solution, but it was more abstract and schematic.

9.4.5 Factory Simulation

Discrete event simulation and continuous process simulation represent an alternative type of modeling and analysis from those described so far. Here the goal is to predict the behavior of a system under various conditions and constraints. These models involve probabilistic mechanisms. For example, in the discrete event simulation of manufacturing systems, programs such as SIMAN/ Cinema allow us to model and visualize the effects of different factory layouts, machine cells, material movement patterns, and inventory buildup. With animation, we can control the pace and resolution of the model, and can explore what happens as we change features of the system. An investigator can actually watch the behavior of the system evolve over time.

CAD programs can be used to develop design alternatives (such as factory layouts or machine cells). Simulation can then be used to evaluate the proposed designs to see if they achieve their intended benefits. Keathley simulated production at a sheet metal production facility, identified operational problems, created part families using group technology, and then proposed, modeled, and evaluated redesigns of the layout [22]. Simulation can provide a means of assessing the manufacturability of proposed designs and thus will be an essential component of future DFM (design for manufacturability) programs. The designer could send his or her concept to a "design critic" which would assess ease of production and flag problems. The design critic would be based on a model of the production facility as it exists at the particular company.

Simulation can be a design tool—we can explore the behavior of systems that do not yet exist. Animation and graphics are essential to understanding and communicating the results of a simulation. Visual representations and especially animation can convey what is happening in a complex system, so that even those unskilled in the methods of simulation can understand the results. Such applications of visualization are fairly straightforward, but developing meaningful icons is important. Visualization is essential to convey the probabilistic nature of simulation. It reveals the significance of material handling, queues, inventory accumulation, and bottlenecks. Simulation can be extremely valuable for uncovering problems and assessing their probable causes, and then for assessing the adequacy of our proposed solutions.

9.5
EDUCATING ENGINEERS IN DESIGN AND ANALYSIS

9.5.1. Using Visualization to Improve Design Education

At the University of Virginia we have developed a unique approach to CAE education which emphasizes 3-D thinking, modeling, and visualization. Our approach emphasizes the central role of geometric modeling. Our students learn to do solids modeling from the start of their CAD experience. They use the CAD system to create 3-D representations of objects and assemblies. In our approach, the students learn to describe and represent objects in the simplest and most informative ways. They learn how to model, not just how to make pictures. To us, CAD means "Computer Aided Design," not drafting.

We start with simple 3-D models: extrusions and volumes of revolution. Students learn how to sweep profiles through space to define objects by linear translation. The basic ideas of modeling are introduced: the distinction between profile lines and information lines; the functions used to define solids, holes and depth points; and the difference between models and views (pictures of the model). Then, they learn about volumes of revolution: how to construct the profile, place center lines, and inform the system about the functions necessary to generate the model. With these two basic modeling techniques, students are able to generate a surprising range of simple models. They can also model several objects on the same display and relate these models to each other.

When they have mastered both types of models, they are introduced to Boolean Operations, and learn how to make complex parts from simple operations. This greatly expands the domain of possible models they can create. They can also start to appreciate the concept of feature-based design and the relation of design features to production operations. Other modeling techniques (slides, ruled surfaces, pipe and wire line models, and surface networks) are also covered.

After mastering all these various modeling techniques, our students learn how to control views of the model. This reinforces the idea that views (pictures) are distinct from the model. The model can be viewed from any direction or perspective we choose, and we may generate as many views of the model as we wish.

The final topic in modeling is assemblies—creating submodels (parts) which can be stored independently and then be brought together into a final product. By this time, the students are used to thinking about individual models. They must now solve the problem of linking separate coordinate systems—the parts (components) with the assembly sheet. After mastering these concepts with simple problems, the students are given a major project. They must select an assembly of 8 to 10 distinct parts and model it. The assembly should be inherently interesting to the student, and may involve a novel concept or design.

After creating a model for the geometry of a solid object, mechanism, assembly, or structure, most students proceed to analyze their model using either finite element methods or mechanical dynamics. There is a natural transition from creating a solid model to specifying the properties of the object represented by that geometry. The students lead us to advanced topics. When they want to assign material properties to their model and study its behavior, we introduce them to FEA. A design for a mechanism or vehicle leads to animation and mechanical dynamics programs. If they want to fabricate their object, they learn about manufacturing processes, operations, and strategies, and simulation software. Self-directed learning is the most efficient kind: when students are ready and motivated they quickly learn the material and retain it well. The visualization capabilities of all these software products facilitate ease of use and ease of learning, and are highly motivational.

9.5.2 Education for Visualization

A major potential benefit of visualization is its more general use in education. Developing expertise requires having experiences: doing things, seeing things, developing correct intuitions. With visualization, we can provide controlled experience, replicate situations, highlight selected aspects of a problem, control event timing, control grain (detail or resolution), control focus of attention, and isolate features of special interest. All of the applications discussed in this book are potential teaching aids as well as analysis tools.

The use of visualization in design and analysis, and the educational uses of visualization to teach a variety of subjects, are now well established. Even in our first year Engineering Concepts course, we teach our students to model and to visualize. They learn to sketch and draw. This helps them learn to see: they come to understand those features and aspects of the world which artists capture in pictures. They also study the psychology of visual perception. When we introduce CAD, they learn to model (create 3-D representations of objects) using the Silverscreen software package. The emphasis on 3-D modeling and visualization captures their interest and increases their understanding of both engineering design and the artifacts they are designing.

Students can develop a sensitivity to visualization through systematic exposure to it. Greater emphasis on visual representation in our courses can only enhance our student's ability to visualize and extract information from visual displays. Students must also learn to be critics of visual displays. Visualization can be effectively used to misrepresent information, as well as to accurately convey it. "How to lie with visualization" is now a popular topic at professional meetings. Graphics packages and visualization software allow one to generate really terrible displays as easily as producing good ones. Thus we must educate our students about how to display data, and how to avoid common mistakes and artifacts.

How do we teach visualization itself? Scientific visualization does not fit neatly into existing academic curricula or departments. The necessary skills and knowledge are found in various domains: art, psychology, statistics, and the subject matters of particular scientific and engineering disciplines. Currently, each domain teaches those concepts and procedures of visualization relevant to its own problems and concerns. But this approach fails to provide students an appreciation of the full range of techniques available. The collaborative research teams found at NCSA [10] may be the model for future teaching teams who will develop and teach the courses and curricula on visualization methods. Such crossfertilization has already yielded results for CAE research and commercial software development.

9.6
REFERENCES

[1]. Bachi, R., Graphical Statistical Methodology in the Automation Era. Graphic Presentation of Stat. Inf.: Presented at 136th Ann. Meet. Am. Stat. Assoc., Soc. Stat. Sect. Sess. Graphical Meth. Stat. Data, Boston, 1976, Tech. Rep. 43, Washington, DC: Census Bureau, 1978.

[2]. Badler, Norman I., "Human Modeling in Visualization" Chapter 15 in Thalman, N.D. and Thalman, D. (eds), cited below, pp. 210–228.

[3]. Banchoff, Thomas F., "Visualizing Two-Dimensional Phenomena in Four-Dimensional Space: A Computer Graphics Approach" in Wegman, E.J. and DePriest, D.J. (eds.) Statistical Image Processing and Graphics, New York: Marcel Dekker, Inc., 1986.

[4]. Bryson, S. and Levit, C., "The Virtual Windtunnel; an Environment for the Exploration of Three-Dimensional Unsteady Flows" reprinted in Introduction to Scientific Visualization Tools and Techniques, Course 02, Siggraph '93, Anaheim, CA, 1993.

[5]. Chasen, S.H., Geometric Principles and Procedures for Computer Graphics Applications, Englewood Cliffs, N.J., Prentice-Hall, 1978.

[6]. Chasen, S.H., "Historical Highlights of Interactive Computer Graphics," Mechanical Engineering, Nov. 1981, pp. 32–41.

[7]. Chambers, J. M., Cleveland, W. S., Kleiner, B., and Tukey, P. A., Graphical Methods for Data Analysis, Belmont, CA, Wadsworth International Group, 1983.

[8]. Chia, Moon-Hsiang, Robot Selection and Design Based on Ergonomic Modeling, M.S. Thesis, University of Virginia, Department of Mechanical and Aerospace Engineering, January, 1991.

[9]. Cleveland, W., The Elements of Graphing Data, Pacific Grove, CA, Wadsworth & Brooks/Cole, 1985.

[10]. Cox, Donna J., "Scientific Visualization: Collaborating to Predict the Future" EDUCOM Review, Winter, 1990, 38–42.

[11]. Da Rosa, W.A., Simulation of Aerodynamic Flow Over Automobile-Like Bluff Bodies Using Flotran Software, Senior Thesis, Aerospace Engineering, University of Virginia, April, 1991.

[12]. Dooley, M., "Anthropometric Modeling Programs—A Survey," IEEE Computer Graphics and Applications, 2, November, 1982, pp. 17–25.

[13]. Ferguson, Eugene S., Engineering and the Mind's Eye. Cambridge, Massachusetts, The MIT Press, 1992.

[14]. Earnshaw, R.A., "The Mathematics of Computer Graphics," The Visual Computer, 3, 1987, 115–124.

[15]. Fetter, W.A., Computer Graphics in Communication, New York: McGraw-Hill Book Company, 1965.

[16]. Foley, J.D. and Van Dam, A., Fundamentals of Interactive Computer Graphics, Reading, Mass., Addison-Wesley Publishing Company, 1982, second edition, 1990.

[17]. Friedhoff, Richard Mark and Benzon, William, The Second Computer Revolution: Visualization. New York; Harry N. Abrams, Inc., 1989.

[18]. Gallagher, R.S. and Selker, P.J., "Three-Dimensional Volume Visualization In FE Analysis," Mechanical Engineering, May 1992, pp. 54–57.

[19]. Haber, R.N. and Wilkinson, L. "Perceptual Components of Computer Displays" IEEE Computer Graphics and Applications, 2, May, 1982, pp. 23–35.

[20]. Hosmer, Trina and Edwards, Robert, "Imaging: a Tool for Data Reduction" The American Statistician, 38, 1984, pp. 322–327.

[21]. Kaufmann III, William J. and Smarr, Larry L. Supercomputing and the Transformation of Science, New York: Scientific American Library, 1993.

[22]. Keathley, Eric J., Group Technology and Simulation Applied to Manufacturing Cell Formation, M.S. Thesis, Department of Mechanical Engineering, University of Virginia, 1991.

[23]. Kerlick, G.D., "Moving Iconic Objects in Scientific Visualization," reprinted in Introduction to Scientific Visualization Tools and Techniques, Course 02, SIGGRAPH '93, Anaheim, CA, 1993.

[24]. Machover, C., "A Brief, Personal History of Computer Graphics," Computer, Nov., 1978, pp. 21–28.

[25]. McCormick, B.H., DeFanti, T.A., and Brown, M.D, "Visualization in Scientific Computing" Computer Graphics, 21, Nov. 1987.

[26]. McCormick, Bruce H. "Advanced Visualization Environments: Knowledge Based Image Modeling" in Mendez, R.H. (ed), pp. 135–149.

[27]. Mendez, Raul H. (ed) Visualization in Supercomputing, New York: Springer-Verlag, 1990.

[28]. Newman, W.M. and Sproull, R.F., Principles of Interactive Computer Graphics, New York: McGraw-Hill Book Company, 1973 (first edition), 1979 (second edition).

[29]. Parslow, R.D., Prowse, R.W. and Green, R.E., Computer Graphics: Techniques and Applications, London, Plenum Press, 1969.

[30]. Pickover, C. A., Picturing Randomness on a Supercomputer, IBM Journal of Research and Development, Vol. 35, No. 212, January/March 1991, pp. 227–239

[31]. Prince, M.D., Interactive Graphics for Computer Aided Design, Reading, Mass., Addison-Wesley Publishing Company, 1971.

[32]. Requicha, A.A.G. and Voelcker, H.B., "Solid Modeling: A Historical Summary and Contemporary Assessment" IEEE Computer Graphics and Applications, 2, March, 1982, pp. 9–24.

[33]. Requicha, A.A.G. and Voelcker, H.B., "Solid Modeling: Current Status and Research Directions" IEEE Computer Graphics and Applications, 3, October, 1983, pp. 25–37.

[34]. Richards, M.M. and Richards, L.G., "The Development of Language and Imagery as Symbolic Processes," Chapter 3 in Schiefelbusch, R.L. and Lloyd, L.L. (eds.), Language Perspectives: Acquisition, Retardation, and Intervention, Second Edition, Austin, Texas: Pro. Ed, 1988, pp.35–67.

[35]. Shepard, Roger N., "Externalization of Mental Images and the Act of Creation." In B. S. Randhawa and W.E. Coffman (eds), Visual Learning, Thinking, and Communication. Academic Press, NY, 1978.

[36]. Smith, Alvy Ray "Geometry vs. Imaging: Extended Abstract" in Mendez, R.H. (ed), pp. 151–156.

[37]. Taylor, D.L., Computer Aided Design, Reading, Mass., Addison-Wesley Publishing Company, 1992.

[38]. Thalmann, Nadia M. and Daniel (Eds), New Trends in Animation and Visualization. Chichester, West Sussex England: John Wiley and Sons, Ltd., 1991.

[39]. Tufte, Edward R., The Visual Display of Quantitative Information. Cheshire, CT: Graphics Press, 1983.

[40]. Tufte, Edward R., Envisioning Information. Cheshire, CT: Graphics Press, 1990.

[41]. Wainer, Howard and Thissen, David, "Graphical Data Analysis" in Annual Review of Psychology, 1981, 32, pp. 191–241.

[42]. Zhang, Z. and Rice, S.L., "Conceptual Design: Perceiving the Pattern," Mechanical Engineering, July, 1989, pp. 58–60.

Future Trends in Scientific Visualization

RICHARD S. GALLAGHER

THIS CHAPTER LOOKS at some of the issues affecting how scientific visualization will evolve in the future. These include trends in computing hardware and software architecture, visualization techniques, interactivity and virtual reality, and a growing synthesis between interactive analysis and visualization. Above all, visualization plays a role in changing the design and analysis process itself, towards a more interactive and intuitive environment.

10.1
INTRODUCTION

Visualization remains a very young field, whose origins as a unified discipline date to the late 1980s. Many challenging problems await solution, and much basic research remains to be done. Since visualization is defined as the visual study of behavior, future visualization research will seek to provide a deeper understanding of this behavior. In analysis, particularly, we need a greater ability to ask the question "What if?" For example, "What if I make this part half as thin?" or "What if I increase the flow rate through this chamber?". Scientists and engineers have always wanted computers to mirror the rest of their working environment, where one can experiment with ideas just as intuitively as in the physical world. New developments in visualization not only approach this ideal, but are poised to take the field much further. In the physical world, one can build an object and observe how it behaves when in use. With the right visualization tools, one can explore states of behavior which would never be apparent to the naked eye. Moreover, the relationships between cause and effect can be seen more rapidly than those examined in physical experimentation, as well as can the interplay between aspects of behavior.

0-8493-9050-8/95/$0.00+$.50

This chapter explores some of the new directions we can expect scientific visualization to take from this point in the mid-1990s. In a new and rapidly evolving field, one can only see clearly into the near future, but, at the same time, trends are apparent today in visualization techniques, computing hardware and the role of engineering itself that give a reasonable picture of where this field is heading.

10.2
THE MARRIAGE OF INTERACTIVE ANALYSIS AND VISUALIZATION

Analysis exists to simulate how something behaves, and the limiting case of such simulation is the ability to build, test and modify a model as one observes its behavior. Analysis and visualization began as separate capabilities, and even today are often viewed as separate processes.

In the early days of digital numerical analysis, analysis software functioned as a "black box" which received input instructions, and output numerical data. As interactive computer graphics and early visualization techniques became popular, separate software packages were developed specifically to perform graphics pre- and post-processing of this numerical data, often by separate vendors.

While it remains possible to purchase individual, stand-alone components for analysis and graphics, the commercial trends over the past two decades have been towards integrated packages with full modeling, analysis and graphics functionality. Figure 10.1 displays an overview of the growth in interactive capabilities over

1970—Batch analysis program with numerical result output

↓

mid 1970s—Batch/interactive program with graphical plotting output

↓

mid 1980s—Full geometric modeling and color graphics added

↓

1988—Interactive user interface menu added

↓

1992—Image-based volume visualization and animation added

Figure 10.1. The evolution of interactive capabilities for ANSYS, a typical commercial finite element analysis system.

time for the ANSYS commercial finite element system, as one example of a very common trend.

A similar situation exists today with newer 3-D visualization techniques for engineering. Real-time, 3-D visualization of behavior is now most commonly available through separate programs designed to interface with analysis software. At the same time, analysis software environments themselves continue to evolve as a result of visualization and interactivity issues.

This state of affairs is rapidly evolving, and current research points to a much more integrated, interactive environment for analysis and visualization. Specialists, such as Winget and Parker, have long proposed the ability to *track* and *steer* an analysis through the use of visualization [3]. Here, the traditional sequential process of modeling, analysis, and result display is replaced by an environment where one sees the behavior of a model as it is interactively modified or subjected to changing conditions. One of the main demands in creating this environment is raw computational processing power. The more quickly one can observe phenomena, the more data points there are in forming an observation. Within visualization, speed has two aspects: first, it increases the linear productivity of observing behavior itself; second, with increased computational and display speeds, dimensions of time, motion and complexity can be added to increase the depth of understanding itself.

The speed of computational throughput, particularly in the numerical analysis itself, remains the limiting factor that keeps visualization and analysis as separate processes in most production software today. At the same time, research in more productive analysis techniques and in interactive environments shows promise for a more interactive analysis environment in the near future. Problems being studied at this point include faster methods of analysis such as boundary element, wavelet and polynomial techniques, faster generation of element meshes, and direct volume visualization methods for analysis datasets. Given adequate computational resources for interactive analysis and visualization, advances in user interfaces, interaction techniques and even basic algorithm and database design will create a true interactive analysis environment.

As one example, assume you are designing a complex cylindrical component. Using 3-D analysis visualization, you see that the part is overdesigned, and want to reduce its radius and wall thickness. If its model geometry has a purely numerical representation, modifying every piece of geometry in the component can be onerous. On the other hand, if the analysis database uses a *parametric* approach defining this geometry relative to parameters such as the radius or thickness, rapid design studies become much more possible.

This integrated approach affects not only feedback for human-driven changes, but also feedback from machine-driven changes. There is now a growing use of automated *design optimization,* where design variables such as this radius and thickness are optimized iteratively by the software to suit constraints such as strength or deformation. An integrated analysis and visualization environment allows the engineer to observe the decisions of the computer, and override or change them as needed. Figure 10.2 shows an example of an automated, parametric optimization of a part using an integrated CAD and analysis environment.

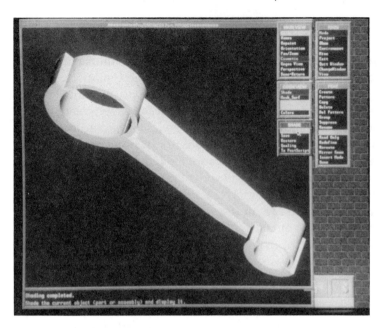

Figure 10.2. Superimposed images of a part before and after automated design optimization. The analysis software adjusted key model dimensions, parametrically, until an optimal solution meeting the design constraints was computed. (Courtesy Swanson Analysis Systems, Inc.)

This trend towards integration is clearly driven by the desire to increase analysis productivity, but, more importantly, it is helping scientists and engineers to work in an environment that is more like the physical world to which we are all accustomed. With such an approach, we try things, test them, and then revise their designs based on what we observe. In such an environment, visualization techniques increasingly become part of the overall process of design and analysis, rather than standalone capabilities unto themselves.

10.2.3 Interactivity and Virtual Reality

In recent years, *virtual reality* has become a fashionable term to describe a computer-generated environment one can move around in and interact with. In the minds of the general public, virtual reality often connotes three-dimensional video games, flight simulation and robots. At the same time, practical applications of virtual reality today revolve around a few key computing concepts which have become refined to the point of commercial popularity. These include *high-speed computer graphics, ergonomic interaction devices,* and *feedback.*

The latter two issues, in particular, distinguish virtual reality from the more general case of interactive computing. In the latter case, one might simulate a factory task by clicking a mouse and observing the results on the screen; with virtual reality, one is more likely to use devices such as a specially-designed glove which senses your hand position, and resists you when you "push" a virtual object.

[Commercial applications of virtual reality in visualization still remain largely in the domain of research. At the same time, the concepts behind virtual reality have the potential to improve some of the basic needs of visualization: interaction in a three dimensional space, navigation, and feedback of information.]

One example of a concept from virtual reality field that is finding its way into commercial visualization software is the Spaceball, a device specifically designed for 3-D interaction with a computer system shown in Figure 10.3. Its interactions are based on a stiff knob-like device which can be moved like a joystick, rotated like a trackball, or twisted circumferentially. The resulting outputs can then be interpreted by an applications program for tasks such as dynamically positioning a model or moving a 3-D probe through it.

There are numerous interactivity possibilities beyond geometric positioning as well, including the ability to switch to multiple views of an object, to change and compare different sets of results data rapidly, and to change the form of the model or results imagery. New and better interaction hardware and software techniques may provide a more intuitive use of these items, which remain largely in the domain of commands or menu picks today.

Beyond its obvious entertainment potential, true virtual reality applications in the future will be most needed where simulation of human interaction is

Figure 10.3. The Spaceball, a 3D tracking and positioning device for use with interactive computer systems. (Courtesy Spaceball Technologies, Inc.) (See color section plate 10.3)

295

important—examples might include remotely piloting robots into hazardous environments, or training people to use sophisticated equipment. In scientific visualization, concepts which evolve from virtual reality will help improve the interactive relationship between users and the data they observe.

10.3
TRENDS IN COMPUTING HARDWARE

The field of 3-D scientific visualization exists largely as a result of increasing computing and graphics display performance. While many of its capabilities such as isosurface generation and volume rendering began with the development of algorithms, such research generally followed the development of computing hardware for which these algorithms could be put to productive use.

Until now, the main issues in visualization-capable hardware have involved both processing speed itself, and increasing capabilities for 3-D graphics and animation. From this point, two of the key trends in hardware for visualization include expanding capabilities for 3-D real-time graphics, and a move towards massively parallel computer archtectures.

10.3.1 Increasing Real-time 3-D Graphics Capabilities

Commercial workstations continue to move closer towards offering real-time, 3-D graphics display as a standard capability. In an area which changes dramatically from year to year, such capabilities have broken the price barrier normally reserved for personal computer systems. This trend has a major impact on the visualization of scientific and engineering problems. Traditionally, most computer graphics applications have revolved around the production of one single image at a time. Although tools to generate interactive 3-D graphics imagery have existed for many years, their relative scarcity and lack of standards have made it difficult for software developers to create product architectures based on 3-D visual computing, but given current hardware trends, such real-time interactive processing is likely to become the norm in the near future.

One can measure the interactive, 3-D display capabilities of computing hardware in terms of the number of vectors or polygons which can be displayed per second. Since humans will perceive, as smooth motion, images re-drawn at the rate of 10–30 times per second, every 100,000 polygons per second in display speed represents the theoretical ability to animate an additional 10,000 polygons in real time. Over the past five years alone, peak graphics performance has improved by nearly an order of magnitude to over one and a half million shaded polygons per second as of the mid 1990s. This trend continues not only to grow, but to accelerate—as a result, visualization applications continue to support increasingly larger problems and higher throughput.

10.3.2 Parallel and Massively Parallel Computing Hardware

While the most obvious way to improve computing performance is to use a faster computer system, using multiple processors to perform operations in parallel often represents a more cost-effective boost in performance. Parallel processing once required special purpose algorithms, designed for independent processing and coordination of the parallel components. Today, software tools such as advanced compilers help automate the task of creating parallel applications. In addition, parallel hardware architectures have become more common in the market, ranging from multi-processor versions of popular workstations all the way to massively parallel supercomputers with hundreds of processors. One can also use a network of individual systems as an aggregate resource for parallel computing.

Perhaps the most promising application of parallel processing for scientific visualization is in the analysis itself, as analysis and visualization become more closely coupled. For the display of results, parallel approaches may be most useful in the increased use of continuum volume visualization.

Many of the data structures used in volume visualization lend themselves well to use with multiple processors. For example, one recent approach by Giertsen and Petersen [5] performed volume rendering across multiple systems by processing volume datasets as independent slices extended from the screen coordinate system. In today's computing environment, parallel computation can often represent the only means to interactively display large continuum images, where even low-resolution volume datasets can be on the order of hundreds of megabytes of data.

10.4
ANIMATION, VIDEO AND MULTIMEDIA

One of the most popular analysis visualization features in recent years has been the ability to animate imagery, as discussed in detail in Chapter 7 of this book. Much as graphics imagery has eased the perceptual bottleneck of evaluating numerical results, animated imagery has served a similar function with behavior that moves in space or changes over time. More importantly, the ability to animate increases human comprehension of more complex behavior, as motion shows trends which are not apparent from still images.

In addition to animation, growth in the general area of multimedia may have a major impact on the way we communicate and understand behavior. The ability to treat audio, video and other forms of information as digital data—and the ability to incorporate them into databases—expands the level at which engineers can share information.

As of the writing of this book, animation and multimedia are in a transitional phase, with at least basic levels of capability becoming more widely available. From here, the trends are clearly towards increased use of these technologies. Some of the developmenta which are driving these capabilities include:

The Growth of Software-Based Animation. Animation has typically required expensive, special-purpose hardware for the capture of individual frames of visualization. More recently, efforts such as Digital's Software Motion Pictures (SMP) capability are starting to allow the capture and playback of imagery in software, through image compression techniques [9]. Combined with video output, these software approaches allow animation to be stored digitally, or captured using common equipment such as videocassette recorders.

Better Standards for Communication. As audio, video and animation become more of a digital medium, computing networks and databases have become more of a home for multimedia information. It is not uncommon nowadays to send multimedia information as part of electronic mail, document annotation or applications software. As a result, it is quickly becoming another standard form of data.

Increasing Audio/Video Input and Output in Computing. Media such as CD-ROM have quickly become a standard for computing hardware, and function both as a distribution medium for software and data, and a means of supporting multimedia. In addition, capabilities for input and output between analog audio/video and digital data are becoming more common within computing platforms.

It is clear from such trends that visualization users can expect to find animation and multimedia as increasingly standard capabilities. As a result, simulations of behavior can be more easily understood, presented to others, and integrated with analog data from the real world.

10.5
DISTRIBUTED NETWORK VISUALIZATION

At the 1989 ACM Siggraph conference in Boston, a group led by Professor Robert Haber of the University of Illinois presented a live, interactive demonstration of visualization from a remote supercomputer [6]. User interactions from a workstation on stage in Boston were used to control a visualization session running in Illinois on a CRAY-2S supercomputer and a visualization server system, with the results displayed as video imagery in Boston.

This presentation was accomplished by using 9600 bits-per-second telephone lines for data transfer between the workstation in Boston and the remote supercomputing system, with computer graphics imagery and live videoconferencing between the researchers transmitted via an AT&T Telstar 302 satellite. Figure 10.4 shows a video image of Illinois researcher Bob Wilhelmson during the demonstration, while Figure 10.5 shows a video image from the visualization session.

A more recent research project lead by Haber involves a formal system for run-time visualization and interactive steering of high performance computing applications. The VASE system provides tools which allow the development of remote visualization functions for applications distributed across a network [7].

These and other research efforts such as these reflect how computing environments themselves have changed. Some years ago, many people accessed mainframe computers through dedicated terminals, but the user of the 1990s is as likely to have access to multiple system resources on a network; more often than not, it is controlled simultaneously through a desktop windowing system. Network-based visualization tools and architectures help harness resources from a system of computers, representing a key step beyond sequential processes on individual computer platforms.

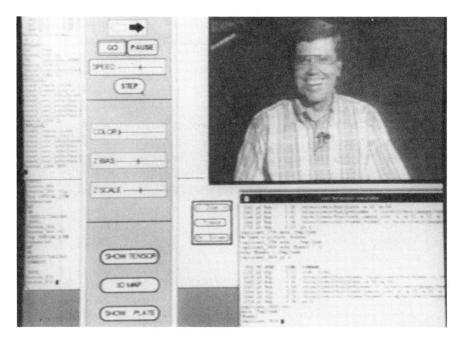

Figure 10.4. University of Illinois researcher Bob Wilhelmson takes part in a live interactive teleconference and visualization session between a supercomputing center in Illinois and a remote workstation. (From Haber et al, reference 6. Reprinted from *The International Journal of Supercomputer Applications* by permission of the MIT Press, Cambridge, Massachusetts. Copyright 1990 Massachusetts Institute of Technology.) (See color section plate 10.4)

10.6
SOFTWARE TRENDS IN VISUALIZATION

While computing hardware forms the basis for visualization capabilities, software issues may have the greatest impact on how this field evolves in the future. Some of the most active areas of research and development include a trend towards more modular software architectures, a unification of graphics standards in software, the growth of raster and volume graphics methods, and better algorithms for visualization itself.

10.6.1 Software Modularity and Configuration

Visualization systems of ten years ago were explicitly coded by computer programmers, a labor-intensive process whose result could not be changed by the end user. Today, many visualization and analysis systems use modular, reusable software components whose inputs, outputs and interrelationships can be modified by developers and users alike. While making applications more flexible, they also increase the rate at which new visualization applications and techniques can be

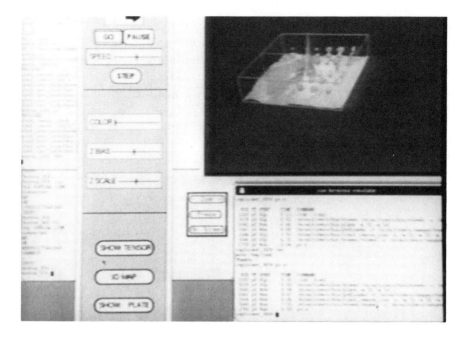

Figure 10.5. Interactive visualization imagery, displayed by satelite video imagery from Illinois under the control of the remote workstation in Boston. (From Haber et al., reference 6. Reprinted from *The International Journal of Supercomputer Applications* by permission of the MIT Press, Cambridge, Massachusetts. Copyright 1990 Massachusetts Institute of Technology.) (See color section plate 10.5)

introduced. In particular, many commercial systems for visualization use an approach of *function networks,* where capabilities for input data processing, image display and user interactions are assembled visually on the screen. In such a system, a user may define an on-screen dial, and have it represent the rotation of the model; and, perhaps later, might change this dial to represent the stress level of an isosurface. Other systems make use of configurable menus and higher-level languages that allow the user to customize the look, feel and behavior of an application.

These capabilities are part of a larger trend in the software industry as a whole, aimed towards making software development a more rapid and cost-effective process. In the process, configurable software applications put greater control and flexibility in the hands of users of visualization.

10.6.2 Unification of Graphics Standards

People may speak of computer graphics and visualization in the same context, but the requirements of these fields vary greatly. One area where the two specialties differ sharply is in their graphics display hardware and software needs. Computer graphics use languages to represent objects which are to be displayed on a screen. In the early days of computer graphics, most manufacturers of computer graphics display equipment designed and developed their own languages, specific to that hardware. Companies who produced computer graphics applications software have to this day been responsible for "porting" these applications to run with these different languages. This issue was recognized early on in the 1980s as an impediment to software productivity, and efforts were launched to develop common standard graphics languages. Some of these earlier efforts included the CORE standard produced by an ACM Siggraph committee, the European GKS (Graphics Kernal System) standard, and the CGM (Computer Graphics Metafile) approach. Later approaches included the object-oriented PHIGS (Programmers Hierarchical Interface to Graphics Systems) standard.

One problem with early standards is that computer graphics hardware evolved rapidly and at a pace which often outstripped the standards themselves. CORE, for example, was an object-oriented standard which presumed that imagery was downloaded to a display device and manipulated locally. Today, there is often a much tighter integration between display and computational hardware. Similarly, GKS emphasized "move" and "draw" operations, as seen in pen plotters and early vector graphics hardware, as graphics hardware evolved towards direct manipulation of entities in raster space.

Today, there is a much greater commonality among graphics languages, although a unified approach across all platforms remains a goal for the future. Graphics standards today can largely be grouped by type of platform, and tend more to be part of a system's network environment and graphical user interface (GUI) as these issues gain importance. Under Unix workstations and supercomputers, currently the most common environment for scientific visualization, the X-Windows network protocol is the standard for image-based graphics and interaction. In these environments, 3-D real-time graphics protocols are currently split between the proposed PeX (PHIGS extension to X-Windows) standard and OpenGL, an independent standard based on successful GL commercial language developed by hardware vendor Silicon Graphics.

An analagous situation exists on current personal computers, with languages for graphics existing as part of windowing protocols such as MS Windows and Apple's Macintosh interface. Over time, the differences between personal computers and workstations is becoming less distinct as time progresses, and personal computers in fact maintain a lead role in newer areas such as animation and multimedia.

10.6.3 Raster and Volume Graphics

The debate over graphics standards inherently presumes the need for a language to display higher-level graphics entities such as lines, polygons and surfaces. Another alternative is to compute the actual dots making up the image in software and, therefore, only requires a hardware-dependent language for the lowest-level step of displaying the dots themselves.

Years ago, the processing speed and memory requirements of computing dot values themselves in software made this technique prohibitive. Today, such *software z-buffering* has become popular in both applications software, and in the systems software for a number of newer computer graphics platforms. In general, the speed of software rendering is starting to allow individual frames to be computed and displayed fast enough to support real-time 3-D graphics, and visualization, from software [4].

A group headed by Professor Arie Kaufmann takes this concept one step further, proposing the use of voxel space as a means of representing geometry, and performing operations ranging from geometric modeling to graphics image generation as operations on the voxel space [8]. Kaufmann points out the historical progression in graphics data representation from surface-based data to raster space, and beyond to voxel representation. This concept of *volume graphics* is, much like software z-buffering, predicated on the need to allocate and manipulate large amounts of memory in exchange for greatly enhanced performance in areas such as both geometric and display operations. In particular, the speed of generating an image from a voxel field depends less on image complexity, which may allow this technique to serve as a unified basis for real-time volume visualization in the future.

10.6.4 Improvements in Visualization Techniques

The popularity of visualization has risen as computing capabilities have made their use practical. At the same time, visualization algorithms and techniques themselves are the reason this field began, and continues to exist. This book summarizes many of the methods used to display and visualize behavior. However, looking at how these techniques have developed over time, a few trends are clear for the future:

A Move from Imagery to Interactivity. Early work in both computer graphics and visualization almost exclusively involved techniques to generate individual images. This work still continues, but many newer visualization techniques today involve interactive operations on a field; for example, selecting a stress level in real time from a potentiometer, or moving a slicing plane interactively to reveal interior result values.

A Progression from Scalar to Multivarate Result Display. One of the key issues in visualization is the comprehensible display of a multivariate state of behavior. Numerous approaches have been proposed for looking at simultaneous multiple result values, with recent work centering around techniques such as the stream polygon and related methods for tensor field and flow visualization, concepts discussed elsewhere in this book [1, 2, 10]. With growing acceptance of core multivariate display techniques by the technical community, the means are becoming available for scientists and engineers to comprehend greater complexity and interrelationships as part of the visualization process.

Better Navigation in 3-D Space. One of the more subtle changes in visualization applications over time has been the move towards interacting with locations within a 3-D volume model. The use of techniques such as *data probes,* which change size, shape and color to show variables at locations within a field, has given rise to a number of innovative techniques to navigate within 3-D fields. Today, users are offered better hardware solutions for 3-D navigation within a field. In addition, software constructs such as potentiometers, positional feedback and better view manipulation now help 3-D exploration of behavior to be a more accurate and interactive process.

10.7
SUMMARY

Most of the issues discussed here are technical ones, but the future of scientific visualization involves both technology and social changes in the practice of design and analysis. Computing techniques for the simulation of how things behave provide a virtual "laboratory" whose capabilities are rapidly surpassing what can be observed in any real world. As a result, scientists and engineers are accomplishing more than ever before, and are changing their roles in the process.

Most of these changes are good ones. The automation of processes such as modeling, analysis and results visualization allows scientists and engineers to focus more on what they are best at—exercising the human design judgement which can never be automated. These computing tools have also moved much of the task of initial analysis from the specialist to generalist, a trend which must be approached with both promise and the proper amount of caution.

Above all, the growth of scientific visualization has afforded all parties in the design process a greater understanding of how things behave. This has made a tangible impact in both engineering productivity, and the sophistication of what can be achieved in design. Most importantly, visualization techniques continue to help technology become an increasingly visual, intuitive process leading to better designs in the real world.

10.8
REFERENCES

[1]. Delmarcelle, T. and L. Hesselink, "Visualization of second order tensor fields and matrix data," Proceedings of IEEE Visualization '92, IEEE Computer Society Press, October 1992, pp. 316–323.

[2]. Dickenson, R., "Interactive Analysis of Stress Field Data," in Computer Graphics and Database Management 1991, PVP Vol. 209, ASME Press, 1991, pp. 11–20.

[3]. Gallagher, R.S. et al, "Applying 3D Visualization Techniques to Finite Element Analysis," panel summary in Proceedings of IEEE Visualization '91, IEEE Computer Society Press, October 1991, pp.330–335.

[4]. Gallagher, R.S., "Why Graphics Standards Don't Matter Anymore," Computer Graphics World, September 1993.

[5]. Giertsen, C. and J. Petersen, "Parallel Volume Rendering on a Network of Workstations," IEEE Computer Graphics and Applications, November 1993, pp. 16–23.

[6]. Haber, R.B., McNabb, D.A. and R.A. Ellis, "Eliminating Distance in Scientific Computing: An Experiment in Televisualization," International Journal of Supercomputer Applications, Vol. 4, No. 4, Winter 1990, pp. 71–89.

[7]. Haber, R.B. et. al., "A Distributed Environment for Run-time Visualization and Applications Steering in Computational Mechanics," Computer Systems in Engineering, Vol. 3, Nos. 1–4, 1992.

[8]. Kaufman, A., Cohen, D. and R. Yagel, "Volume Graphics," IEEE Computer, July 1993, pp. 51–64.

[9]. Neidecker-Lutz, B.K. and R. Ulichney, "Software Motion Pictures," Digital Technical Journal, Vol. 5, No. 2, Spring 1993, pp. 19–27.

[10]. Schroeder, W.J., Volpe, C.R., and W.E. Lorensen, "The Stream Polygon: A Technique for 3-D Vector Field Visualization," Proceedings of IEEE Visualization '91, IEEE Computer Society Press, October 1991, pp. 126–132.

Contributor Profiles

JOHN BUCHANAN is an assistant professor of computer science at the University of Alberta. He is receiving his PhD in computer science from the University of British Columbia. His research interests include volume rendering, 3-D texture mapping, and non-realistic rendering.

THIERRY DELMARCELLE is a research assistant in the Fourier Optics and Optical Diagnostics Laboratory at Stanford, where he is completing work on a PhD in applied physics. His dissertation is on the representation of tensor fields, and his other research interests include multivariate data visualization, flow visualization, computer graphics, and color perception. Delmarcelle received a degree in physics engineering from the Faculté des Sciences appliquées of the Université Libre de Bruxelles (Brussels, Belgium) in 1988 and a MS in applied physics from Stanford in 1991. Delmarcelle can be reached at the Department of Applied Physics, Stanford University, Stanford, CA. 94305-4090.

ALAIN FOURNIER is a professor of computer science at The University of British Columbia, and co-director of its computer graphics laboratory. He received a PhD in mathematical sciences from the University of Texas, and is a member of the ACM. His research interests include ray tracing, texture mapping and the modeling of natural phenomena.

RICHARD S. GALLAGHER is head of computer graphics for Swanson Analysis Systems, Inc., developers of the ANSYS system. Rich has been involved in the development of numerous research and commercial systems for the visualization of engineering analysis behavior since the late 1970's. He has authored over 20 publications on graphics and visualization in engineering, including an early ACM SIGGRAPH paper on the 3-D volume visualization of finite element behavior in 1989. Rich has chaired numerous conference sessions and short courses on computer graphics visualization techniques, including a World Bank teaching appointment to China. He has served on the National Science Foundation's advisory committee on design automation, and is a member of the ASME.

LAMBERTUS HESSELINK holds a joint appointment as Professor in the electrical engineering and aeronautics and astronautics departments at Stanford University. He has served on several scientific advisory committees for industry and the U.S. Government, most recently on the advisory committee for the Hubble Space Telescope. His research interests include nonlinear optics, optical phase conjugation, optical signal processing, optical computing, optical diagnostics, and 3-D image processing. Hesselink received a BS in applied mechanics and a separate BS in applied physics from the Twente Institute of Technology in the Netherlands. He received his MS and PhD from the California Institute of Technology. He is a fellow of the Optical Society of America.

ARIE E. KAUFMAN is a Professor of Computer Science and the director of the Cube project for volume visualization at the State University of New York at Stony Brook. Kaufman is currently the chair of the IEEE Computer Society Technical Committee on Computer Graphics. He has conducted research, taught, and consulted in computer graphics for more than 20 years specializing in volume visualization, graphics architectures, user interfaces, and multimedia. Kaufman received his PhD in Computer Science from Ben-Gurion University, Israel, in 1977.

DAVID PARKER, of Centric, Inc. in Palo Alto, CA, is developing 3-D visualization software for a startup finite element software firm founded by a group headed by Stanford's Professor T.J.R. Hughes. Dave was previously with Stardent Computer, where he was responsible for the finite element visualization capabilities of AVS, a major commercial system for scientific visualization.

ERIC PEPKE recieved his Bachelor of Arts in Mathematics with a concentration on Computer Science from Florida State University in 1983. Since 1985 he has been doing scientific visualization and animation for the Supercomputer Computations Research Institute at Florida State University. He has collaborated on animations for many fields, including aerodynamic engineering, meteorology, quantum chemistry, and chaos studies. Since 1990, he has been leading the team to develop SciAn, a general-purpose scientific visualization and animation software package.

LARRY G. RICHARDS is director of the A. H. Small Center for Computer Aided Engineering and the Master's Program in Manufacturing Systems Engineering at the University of Virginia. He was one of the earliest proponents of incorporating computer graphics, CAD/CAM, and 3-D modeling and visualization into engineering education. He currently teaches solids modeling and visualization techniques to first-year engineering students, invention and design to third-year students, and mechanical computer-aided engineering to graduate students. Larry has published extensively on CAE/CAD/CAM, engineering design, innovation, and creativity. He is an associate editor of the Journal of Engineering Design and is writing a book on computer aided engineering.

WILLIAM J. SCHROEDER is currently principal visualization scientist in the Computer Graphics and Systems Program at the General Electric Corporate R&D Center in Schenectady, NY. He has developed the VISAGE visualization system that is in widespread use throughout GE and elected partners throughout the world, as well as numerous visualization algorithms including decimation—the simplification of polygonal meshes and the stream polygon—a 3-D vector/tensor field visualization technique. Previously, as part of his doctoral research, he developed the combined Octree/Delaunay automatic mesh generation system for finite element analysis. He holds a PhD in mathematics from Rensselaer Polytechnic Institute.

MARK S. SHEPHARD is the Samuel A. and Elisabeth C. Johnson, Jr. Professor of Engineering at Renssalear Polytechnic Institute. At RPI Dr. Shephard holds joint appointments in the departments of Civil & Environmental Engineering, and Mechanical Engineering, Aeronautical Engineering & Mechanics. He is also the director of RPI's Scientific Computation Research Center. Dr. Shephard has published over 150 papers, most of which are focused on the areas of automatic mesh generation and automated adaptive finite element techniques. He is the current Secretary of the US Association for Computational Mechanics, an Associate Fellow of AIAA, and a member of ASME, ASEE, ASCE and the American Academy of Mechanics. Dr. Shephard received his PhD from Cornell University working under the guidance of R.H. Gallagher. In 1985 he was awarded a Visiting Research Fellowship from GE to spend a sabbatical year at their Corporate Research and Development Center.

LISA SOBIERAJSKI is a PhD student at the State University of New York at Stony Brook. Her research interests include global illumination models and rendering algorithms for voxel-based data, animation, and visualization systems. She is currently working on a visualization system which incorporates several data types into a single, consistent global illumination model. She received her BS Cum Laude (1989) and MS (1990) from the Department of Computer Science at the State University of New York at Stony Brook.

Index